COLLECTED PLAYS OF
MAHESH ELKUNCHWAR

Mahesh Elkunchwar has written and produced some of the
most influential and progressive plays of post-Independence
India, and is part of the trinity, with Vijay Tendulkar and
Satish Alekar, who have shaped modern Marathi theatre.
His plays, with their wide-ranging themes, are staged to
critical and public acclaim.

This volume includes six of his acclaimed plays translated by
Shanta Gokhale, Supantha Bhattacharya, and the playwright
himself. Accompanied by production histories of each play,
the playwright's notes on his intense experience with Indian
theatre, and photographs of staging of these plays, this volume
introduced by noted theatre critic Samik Bandyopadhyay will
be indispensable for students and researchers of modern
Indian theatre, Indian literature in translation, and cultural
studies, as well as theatre lovers across the world.

Mahesh Elkunchwar, a leading figure in shaping modern
Marathi theatre, is today one of the most translated and
performed playwrights in India.

COLLECTED PLAYS OF
MAHESH ELKUNCHWAR

Garbo
Desire in the Rocks
Old Stone Mansion
Reflection
Sonata
An Actor Exits

with an Introduction by
Samik Bandyopadhyay

OXFORD
UNIVERSITY PRESS

OXFORD
UNIVERSITY PRESS

Oxford University Press is a department of the University of Oxford.
It furthers the University's objective of excellence in research, scholarship,
and education by publishing worldwide. Oxford is a registered trademark of
Oxford University Press in the UK and in certain other countries

Published in India by
Oxford University Press
22 workspace, 2nd Floor, 1/22 Asaf Ali Road, New Delhi 110002

Garbo first published in *Enact* 1974
Desire in the Rocks first published as *A Breath of Scandal* in *Enact* 1974
This version of *Old Stone Mansion* first published by Seagull Books 2004
Reflection first published by Seagull Books 1989
Sonata first published in *Theatre India* 2001

The moral rights of the authors have been asserted

First Edition published in 2009
Oxford India Paperbacks 2010
Third impression 2015

No performance or reading of any of these plays may be given unless a license
has been obtained in advance from:
Mahesh Elkunchwar, 4, Dandige Lay Out, Shankar Nagar, Nagpur 440 010,
Maharashtra OR maheshelkunchwar@gmail.com
and no copy of the play or any part thereof may be reproduced for any purpose
whatsoever by any method without written permission from the publishers

ISBN 13: 978-0-19-806992-8
ISBN 10: 0-19-806992-8

Typeset in Minion 10.5/14
by Eleven Arts, Keshav Puram, Delhi 110 035
Printed in India by Repro India Limited

For Nick, Leanne, and Holly India

Contents

Acknowledgements

I think of my late friend Rajinder Paul as this volume gets published. He died too young and I feel sad that he is no more with us to see the movement he started in the seventies coming to fruition. He would have been happy to see this book. He and his vivacious wife Sunita have done much more for the translations of plays from various Indian languages into English than anybody else. They got the translations done and published them steadily in *Enact* in the seventies. They were, in fact, instrumental in bridging the regional languages and their theatres. It would be appropriate to acknowledge their contribution. I remember them with gratitude and love. Shanta Gokhale, who has translated many of my texts over a period of thirty-five years, has been a tremendous help. She has done an enormous lot for the Marathi theatre by translating many Marathi play texts into English, all just for the love of it, a contribution vastly under-recognized. I express my gratitude to her. Supantha Bhattacharya, who has been my student and who also likes my work, has translated three of my texts, one of which is included in this collection. I thank him. Naveen Kishore of Seagull, Kolkata, magnanimously gave me permission to include *Old Stone Mansion* and *Reflection* (earlier published by him for Seagull Books) in this collection. I appreciate his kindness. Sudeshna Banerjee, a dear friend, offered to help put together the press copy of this collection and spent many days poring painstakingly over the texts. My thanks to her. My heartfelt thanks to Vivek Ranade, Harshavardhan Patil for making the photo prints, and Nemai Ghosh. I would like to specially thank the following people and institutions for providing photographs of the performance of the plays: Kalavaibhav, Mumbai for the Marathi production, Ensemble, Kolkata for the Bengali production, and National School of Drama, New Delhi for the Hindi production of *Old Stone Mansion/Wada Chirebandi*; Theatre Unit, Mumbai for the Marathi as well as Hindi productions of *Reflection/Pratibimb*; and Theatre and Television Associates, New Delhi for the English production and Samanway, Pune for the Marathi production of *Sonata*. My dear friend Sutinderpal Singh Arora was a generous help in many ways. I am grateful to him. My dearest nephew Advocate Subodh Dharmadhikari has always been a great and silent support to me in all my ventures all these years and although he would not like to be mentioned here, I must acknowledge his immense help I got while preparing a press copy for this collection. Although ferociously busy, he always drops everything to come to my succour. Thanks to him. My heartfelt thanks to friend and eminent critic Samik Bandyopadhyay for his erudite introduction.

Introduction

The six plays that constitute the present selection of Mahesh Elkunchwar's plays are drawn from three distinct phases of his work— *Garbo* (1973) and *Desire in the Rocks* (1974) from his first phase, when he felt that he 'was young, and wanted to assert my freedom in every possible manner, wanted to bring everything out in the open, protesting against a whole baggage of taboos and inhibitions';[1] *Old Stone Mansion* (1985) and *Reflection* (1987) registering his return to playwriting after a gap of seven or eight years spent in 'mental stocktaking';[2] and *Sonata* (2002/2007) and *An Actor Exits* (2005), his most recent works.

The six plays, torn out of a corpus of 22 plays, cover an intriguing trajectory, with the connections and continuities not always so obvious. Elkunchwar (b. 9 October 1939) has always taken pride in being based in Nagpur for just over fifty years now, away from Bombay or Pune, the traditional bastions of Marathi drama; that gives him a perspective on the metropolis and the hinterland alike, which is not always available to the metropolitan! It is his off-the-metropolis prospect that allows him to pick up the characters in *Garbo* and *Reflection*—Mumbaikars, but outsiders nonetheless, migrants to the metropolis, 'brought together by chance, rootless, with rootlessness as their only bond,' as he describes them now.[3]

When he wrote *Garbo* in the early 1970s, Elkunchwar had not read Badal Sircar's *Evam Indrajit*, which was already making the rounds in the country's theatrical circles, with productions in translations, in English, and several Indian languages. *Evam Indrajit* and *Garbo* were both about the class that Elkunchwar describes in retrospect as 'we young people'. As cities, Kolkata and Mumbai carried different histories, and hence different cultures, but the 'young people' in both places felt the same frustration of shattered political dreams, the diffusion of mediocrity, and the burden of inhibitions, as the post-Independence euphoria dissipated into thin air. If Sircar (b. 1925), from an earlier generation, could only lament the collapse of youthful aspirations, with a precarious reaching out to an Indrajit, who is different from the Amals, Bimals, and Kamals, lost in the mire of mediocrity, Elkunchwar's 'young people', a generation later, would rather break out into the defiance of living out their own lives with non-conformism for a credo; throwing up in the process a small minority culture, containing within itself its own seeds of destruction:

Suddenly the non-conformists among us had decided to shake off all this artificial baggage imposed on us by tradition. At the same time we had realized that we didn't know what to do with the freedom, and we almost abused it. Since we were not equipped to use this freedom creatively or constructively, we began to destroy ourselves in the process.[4]

As he engaged himself in the 'inner battles of these people', sexuality became his major concern.[5] For Intuc, the college professor, Pansy, the art school dropout, and Shrimant, maybe a small-time businessman, who gets a kick out of supporting the foursome, the only satisfaction, if it can be called satisfaction at all, lies in their sexual 'use' of Garbo, a dramatic construct who is at the same time a petty actress in B grade movies, fast losing her glamour, and a larger than life sex goddess for the three men cooped up in their 'sitting room'.

Of the foursome, Shrimant alone, the earthiest of them all, has a name for himself. The others carry their roles in their names. The play opens deceptively with a scene of cynical camaraderie on a Sunday morning, that soon breaks into 'bickerings', inevitably leading on to the theme of Garbo, whom all three of them invest with their particular desires and sexual fantasies. They are all 'involved with Garbo', whom Shrimant would like to treat as 'a sex-machine'; Intuc as 'a challenge', a living work of art, who 'grows older, but never stale ... even after fulfilling the needs of all three of us, a part of her still remains untouched'; and Pansy as a mother figure, a guardian deity. All the three hit out at one another and at Garbo too with bitter, offensive banter and bite, trying to hold on to their private images of Garbo, who, in her turn, hits back from time to time, often out of extreme self-contempt.

There is a short respite when they come together in a comic piece of play-acting in which they confront the neighbourhood moral brigade. But exhausted by the effort, they sink into a bout of self-pity, and once Garbo goes out for a while, a piece of information dropped by Garbo casually—that she is pregnant—suddenly occupies centrestage. A new battleground opens up at once. For the two older men, initially at least, it is a question of shirking responsibility; but faced with their own smallness and cowardice, they make a turnaround, seeking salvation in a collective fatherhood: 'We are doomed people. We have neither seen, nor experienced, nor created anything beyond filth. Let us grab this opportunity. It's our only hope. We will create something beautiful out of this filth. The world will know that there is a Life somewhere which is beautiful, pure, fearless, innocent ...' But even as Intuc spells it out, Garbo has her doubts: 'It's very beautiful and all that. To be the mother of a beautiful thing ... But do we have the guts to see the whole thing through? Suppose we suddenly get cold feet? And there are all the other difficulties. If we decide on this I'll lose nearly a year, and all my contracts will have to be cancelled one after another. What guarantee then of finding work again after the year's over? ... You have all gone mad ... Right now you're getting drunk on your own words. Suddenly one day you'll come to your senses and then there will be no escape.'

All the three men fall under the spell of their 'own words' and the dream they conjure up their 'only refuge', their 'only chance to create something beautiful'. The Act ends with an Adoration of the Dream, the characters elevated to a ritual plane.

The visionary spell hangs over Act Two for a while, with Intuc saying, 'I can understand now the joy those poor people felt when they saw the newborn Jesus in the manger ... I am weighed down by a feeling of deep respect.' But the spell slowly dissipates through the Act, as they realize that Garbo has lost the child while shooting a stunt scene. Garbo for a while makes a desperate effort to give it a touch of romance: 'The director was almost on the point of tears. Poor thing, he's such a kid. It was during a camel race. He said he would never have included the shot had he known about me. Poor chap felt terribly guilty. He kept insisting it was entirely his fault ... All that jogging up and down on the camel ... So unnecessary. They could have used my double. But I was so excited ... I'm playing the part of a Lamani girl. She's the second heroine ... She's terribly fiery, and terribly passionate. And terribly beautiful ...'

With the dream in a shambles, the fragile 'community' is on the edge of a break-up, with Pansy wanting to 'go home', and Intuc retreating to a cult of 'filth'—'Let's return to filth. The world we desired was not for us, could never have been. We were idiots, out to turn dreams into reality. Let us go back to our old world now. The world of filth. As a punishment. And as a sort of consolation too.'

But as the 'filth' proliferates, with a series of exposures and confessions, Pansy charging Shrimant with homosexual assault, Garbo taking responsibility for corrupting Pansy ('Initially I played around with him just for fun. Then it became a habit. An entertaining game ... I should have hardened my heart at least once. Pansy, you're still too young.'), Shrimant bringing his impotence out into the open, and Garbo giving the true story of her abortion, the illusions crash.

Elkunchwar's craft still keeps the denouement at bay, with an evocation of one of those long lost days that Intuc and Garbo had once shared, with poetry and rain 'like white flowers gently falling to the ground', hot black coffee, and sex. That fragment of memory, set to a different dramatic idiom altogether, seems to offer the ultimate measure against which all the strained gestures and pretences appear all the more inadequate, when they are repeated mechanically once again by all of them in a bizarre farce. The latter inevitably leads to near melodrama, with the animosities and tensions becoming sharper till they culminate in Shrimant stabbing Garbo to death. Melodrama is averted, with the last few lines virtually reconstructing in a minute the charade that looked as if it had been played out once and for all; with Shrimant again angling for Pansy, Intuc finding his rationale, 'The blood is real ... Garbo was false'; and Pansy screaming out for help only to face silence, and entrapment.

The drama in *Garbo* grows out of a claustrophobic real-life situation pushed to the limits of endurance, burgeoning into a surreal holy dream that is too unreal and brittle to stand the test. But what gives the fantasy its compelling magnetism is the sheer power of Intuc's words, coming in waves of cynicism, disgust, self-pity, lacerating introspection, flights of sacred vision. In a sense, it is he who builds Garbo up, and makes the others adore *his* Garbo, and Garbo has to destroy her false dream self to emancipate herself: 'You deceived yourself. You should never have expected so much out of me. I'm an ordinary woman of flesh and blood. You burdened me with all sorts of imaginary virtues. I carried on for as long as I could. But I couldn't keep up the pretence forever. That doesn't mean I have done any wrong. And anyway, who are you to make demands on me?'

One can see a natural extension from *Garbo* to *Desire in the Rocks*, in the same acknowledgement of raw passion gathering an all-encompassing force to overpower and control another being to the point of mutual self-destruction. If in *Garbo* the force was borne on words, in *Desire in the Rocks* it is held within the creative urge to carve a body in rock. If for Intuc it was Garbo's soul that he was hoping to master and elevate to the point where it would take the place of his lost and frustrated aspirations, for Hemakant it is Lalita's body that he would like to recast in stone so that it holds perpetually the passion that he draws out of her, with all the intensity of the forbidden and the defiance that is part of it.

Elkunchwar tells me:

Even before I started writing the play, I knew that this play had a white hot passion that should cut like a laser beam. There was no place for any other thing. I didn't want anything to pollute the purity of this expression.

When I wrote *Vasanakand* (*Desire in the Rocks*), I knew that the director would have to invent or find a different style—or space altogether—that was a demand.the text made.[6]

The shift from the cramped Bombay flat, more a temporary refuge to the *wada*, the ancestral mansion, with a history of its own, and the rugged terrain of rocks that leads to it, registers a shift to a more elemental space, where a heightened prose, verging on poetry, becomes a natural and necessary medium—Elkunchwar would not mind calling it 'a tool'. While the low locale of the former could end up in near melodrama, the richer ambience of the latter has all the potential of tragedy. But the theme—the unconscious as sexuality serving as resistance to both behaviour and expression frozen into fixed, institutionalized meaning, provoking the artist in his quest for creative fulfilment, would turn the woman into an embodiment of his desire, and destroy her in the process, even as he cuts himself free from her—surfacing in *Garbo* turns more complex in *Desire in the Rocks*. The burden of conventional morality, more amorphous in *Garbo*, has an architecture and a culture to sustain it in *Desire in the Rocks*, in the form of the mansion, with its 'rich, pedigreed, proud' carvings; and the community beyond that comes closer and closer to the fugitives as the play progresses; from the drumbeats in the distance assuming the body of the woman in trance, to the women in the temple who turn Lalita away, to the men who 'pick up stones, coldly vindictive ... drag Lalita away by the hair'. The slow growth and eventual outburst of violence in/from the community matches the course of the pitched battle between Hem and Lalita, though maybe at a different level. Primeval passions lie at the root of both the passages of violence; the passion that holds a conventional society together against inroads from outside, and the passion that will hurl itself at the constraints to break free. It is the violent confrontation of the two passions that charges the Hem–Lalita relationship with a corrosive, self-destructive force. The passion in the community and the passion shared by the lovers criss-cross and overlap as the sense of sin raises its head in the exchanges between Hem and Lalita. At the same time, for neither Hem nor Lalita is there any regret. They go the whole course of raw, naked passion, asserting their individuality in complete freedom, leaving Lalita at the end haunted by the question: where do you go next? They pay the price of self-annihilation—but only along with that of the wada that they burn and pull down with themselves—for their total submission to passion.

The difference between the two is evident right at the beginning, as both try to put the responsibility on the other. Lalita is terrorized at the prospect of loving in the dark. Hemakant says, 'You decide.' Lalita answers, 'You decide. Yes, you decide.' Hemakant says, 'I won't do anything against your will.' Lalita answers, 'My will? Where's the question of my will?' Her submission to Hemakant's will is complete: 'You decide. You planned everything ... after meeting you, I've no will of my own left.' Hemakant assumes the role of the master when he declares the situation as entirely his choice: 'It's a village of rocks. An invitation to a sculptor. His dream space.' Even as his ego has transformed his unconscious into an agenda, a creative urge repressed by familial/patriarchal authority turned into a defiance of taboo, and drawing energy from it, something that he thinks he can control and direct, he will be autocratic above all else. What Elkunchwar illustrates in Desire in the Rocks is the perverse and aberrant nature of the sexual forces that rise against the unjust, oppressive, repressive social norms internalized within the unconscious mind. The rebellious unconscious that ostensibly seeks a liberation in the making of art remains inherently authoritarian. 'My world is different from yours. It's a world that is mine alone ... I will pay any price to realize my dreams.' The artistic urge turns out to be the acquisition of a new authority against and beyond the bounds of ancestral-patriarchal authority, no less cruel and dominating than the latter. The woman remains the site of exploitation and domination in both cases. The fear from within the home that had been Lalita's fear earlier, now becomes fear from both within and without, and more multivalent than before as the fear from Hemakant, the deeper fear of sin, and the fear of social censure in the form of the growing threat from the local community. While Hemakant's return from exile after his father's death had brought to Lalita, his sister, a feeling of freedom, Elkunchwar takes care to underscore the fear that persisted: 'I was scared, but excited.' Even later, Lalita can read the power that looms over her, the power of artistic mastery, when Hemakant declares, 'I'm going to carve you in stone,' and she is driven to plead—the stage direction significantly is 'faintly'— 'Don't carve me in stone ... I'll be imprisoned in them forever.' The art of casting flesh into stone is more an atrophying of the flesh than a sublimation. An artistic endeavour that fights against the body will be destructive of the body both internally and externally. Fear becomes a tool in the process.

Obviously, the artist will not be content with a single image. To bring out several images from the same model, he will employ different devices, with every device conveying an attitude. He offers to put his hand on her head in a gesture of support as she cowers in a sense of insecurity, only to capture 'a sweet and good girl. Beautiful hair. How beautiful! Like a cascade of black silk. I will bring it alive for a second time. In my sculptures.' He will stand apart from her deliberately, even as she pleads for his touch, and in desperation breaks into a poetry of wild passion: 'Hem, I want to enter your eyes. Deep into them. I'll become a tiny drop of blood and travel through your body. Through your heart, brain, mind, soul. I'll talk to all your secrets. Discover all your dreams. Then I'll turn into a tiny pupil and live in your eyes. Will you let me?' Quite unaffected by the passion in the 'lovely things' she says, he can 'break her off' as she soon comes to complain, only to catch her in a 'bewitching' look, and concentrate on completing his sketch, which ends up as 'a picture of heavy, languorous, voluptuous youth. This moment and this mood will now be frozen in stone. She has no name. You're merely the excuse.' He can stretch the distance to its limits, drive her to desperation and then surrender abjectly to her wishes, and kiss her toes, her hands, her thumb, her fingers, her palms, making her cry. 'My breath can't take the weight of so much bliss.' But when she pleads, 'You've scattered live coals in my body. Quench them with your lips'—he moves apart, with the satisfaction of having conjured up yet another image, 'Wait. Stay as you are. You look like a self-willed palash tree flaming with red blossoms. This mood. One more mood. I'll catch it in my sculpture. You're trembling. How you tremble. The trembling will tremble again in my stones.'

If the games Hem plays are exercises to produce 'moods' for his sculptures, they draw out from Lalita passions that flow with a life of their own and often, if not always, draw Hem too along in their intensity; but there is something warped about a sexuality that will never accept itself on its own terms—is there even a suggestion of the curse that holds the wada in its spell?—but treat it only as a means to sculpting yet another form: 'The heady light of passion that surges and overflows through every pore of your body, will flow out of every pore of my sculptures. The sexual desire that palpitates in every sinew of yours will be seen breathing in my sculptures. This indestructible, eternal passion can be embedded only in another indestructible, eternal thing, Lali. In my sculptures. In art.' Lali rightly finds Hem's art impervious to the immediate ecstasy of the sexual experience itself: 'And what about the call of the sea that roars through my body in the moment of union? And the soothing melody of the flute that resonates in my blood? And the myriad tiny silver bells that ring in unison?' Hem acknowledges the void that yawns between the two when they come close to each other, when he can only answer 'No' to Lali asking 'Don't you feel any of these things ... the things I feel? Don't you feel them when you come down on my body?'

It is left to Lalita to probe this void, the difference/distance between the two, in a continuing argument, and to stretch the distance further in the process; though there are times when she falls to the spell of Hem's desire, and seems to vibe with it. But the violence implicit in this denial of her self leaves its scars behind, and the scars smart under Hem's contempt and indifference. As the argument turns on creativity, with Hem shutting her out of his world ('You have to be born an artist for that.'), she finds in her pregnancy a world of her own making, a space of creativity, which immediately provokes Hem: 'You've trapped me.' Lalita's thraldom cracks for the first time with her craving to bring her child into the world.

Spatially, the play too, as if with Lalita's yearning, spills over beyond the confines of the wada, to interface with the local community as it, in its turn, prepares for a childbirth; their songs growing out of the very processes of Nature/Nurture. The song of the women that wafts in at the close of Scene Three 'lingers on' to carry the play to Scene Four, where Lalita rises to the peak of the conflict, torn between her submission to Hem's obsessive, warped passion and her own desire to find fulfilment in the joy of giving birth, and collapses under the strain, but not before she has run out of the temple space of the community of women to the 'jungle of her sculptures'. The subsequent scenes move between the inside of the mansion and the space outside, the configurations too now take place on two levels simultaneously, between the couple and the community, and between the lovers. There is violence at both the levels, though perhaps more physical and collective in the former, and more verbal and mutually recriminatory in the latter. Even as the violence accumulates, and the stillborn child brings in its train a fresh sense of sin, Hem persists on his aesthetic distanciation: 'I stand apart. I observe life dispassionately.'

Lalita has to go away, seeking punishment for her sin, and to come back as a prostitute, leaving Hem by himself, for Hem to realize how he had made use of sexuality and not accepted it in its totality: 'I was going to use you without getting involved. I thought this was what being aloof meant. This was strength, to look at everything dispassionately.' The distanciation, he comes to realize, had distanced his artistic works too to a point where when the mob destroys his sculptures 'limb by limb', he feels no instinctive urge to come to their rescue: 'Not once did I feel that I should rush in to save them.' Even as he comes to recognize his self-alienation in his quest for an absolute art, he can now 'understand'—'for the first time, the very first time', Lalita underscores, 'overcome with emotion'—how Lalita 'must have felt when' she 'gave birth to a dead child'.

Having borne the burden of guilt, Lalita is in a position to accept the end without 'anger' or 'regret'. It is her 'involvement' in the act that gives her the capacity to take charge of the situation and sound the judgment on Hem: 'You are involved for the first time. You cannot stay aloof now in this moment of defeat ... there is an aching truth at the centre of every reality. You never laid your lips to it to absorb it. Hem, it doesn't help to deny life. You must accept it first, and then cut the strings. Otherwise it sits on your back forever .... You struggled to make sculptures of physical desire. But you didn't go to the source from where that desire surges. You did not discover the truth about desire. Perhaps you avoided it. That truth was here. In Lali's heart. In her mind. Not in her body alone. To reach there you would have had to suffer and endure everything that Lali did. Hemakant! All you did in life was to collect the empty shells of things.'

There is yet another confrontation—brutal and destructive—with the mob, which leaves both them and Lalita close to death. But it is Lalita, still master of the situation, who puts 'an end to it,' as she 'picks up a torch and sets fire to the whole mansion,' and 'the whole mansion bursts into flames.'

One wonders if the play has not had its due in the theatre, notwithstanding the sheer claustrophobic power of the original production by the Palekars, because of what Elkunchwar describes as 'this fear of poetry in theatre, fear of the beauty of words, absolutely elemental, fear of raw passion'.[7] At the same time, in *Desire in the Rocks*, Elkunchwar seems to have come to the limits of the dramatic potential of fervently charged, deliberately heightened poetry.

With *Raktapushp* (1980) Elkunchwar ended the first phase of his playwriting, and 'stopped writing for seven or eight years. I didn't write a single word because I was not happy with what I was doing. I thought what I was writing was sub-standard. There was another personal reason.

I had somehow lost the desire to talk to people, to anybody. I had a feeling that I had nothing to tell people, nothing to say. And when you have nothing to say, it is better to withdraw, to do your gardening, or read or listen to music, or go to college and teach, or simply sleep, look at the ceiling and spend your time, which I did for seven long years, and I think I was very happy .... Maybe I was gradually changing ... I think I am now a different person. After the seven long years, I again began feeling I could write. That is when I wrote *Wada Chirebandi* ... the first play in which I find myself going out of myself, looking at the world with sympathy.'[8]

Quite unashamedly, Elkunchwar describes Strindberg, Lorca, and Chekhov as his 'gods'. If Lorca and Strindberg had presided over *Garbo* and *Desire in the Rocks*, Chekhov holds sway over the *Old Stone Mansion*, where the slow process of history runs ineluctably through traditionally defined relations—cracking and disintegrating under the bitter strain of a desperate struggle for survival. The very setting of the old stone mansion, exposed/segmented in spaces marked for the different generations, situates the traditional family in its terrain.[9] The see-saw between historical time and the timelessness of hereditary memories is played out on this terrain, as four generations housed in the wada come to terms with a death in the family and the visit of two members of the family who have moved out of the ancestral home and relocated themselves in the metropolis. The real and the surreal jostle throughout the play. The play opens in 'dead silence', lasting till Dadi's voice breaks upon this silence, tearing it to pieces, calling on the departed Vyenkatesh, her son!—that amounts almost to an invocation of the dead, and a denial of the real: 'The wretched time does not pass.' While the play is very much about the passage of time, for Dadi, ensconced in her haunt in the past, time holds still. As cultures and temperaments clash, she becomes the still point of reference. At the end of Act One, Scene One, after Prabha, the only rebel in the play claiming her rights and her rightful place in an ideal dispensation more in tune with the changed times, has made her first protestation, and been snubbed, she can only look at Dadi, as 'dust falls' on her body; and the scene closes with Dadi still calling on the dead Vyenkatesh and sensing 'all the mice running about,' and 'Prabha goes on looking at Dadi. Then she is absorbed in thought.' In these situations, rich with suggestions, Elkunchwar explores a vein of dramatic poetry quite different from the impassioned surges, punctuated with terse, sparse, clipped snaps that marked *Desire in the Rocks*. The poetry here lies in silence—in the act, the look, or a happening allowed to hold attention. The clash of words that leaves Prabha even more frustrated changes to a moment of contemplation, as Prabha reads in Dadi's state her own fate—and the cruel history that determines it.

Elkunchwar uses the same mode of dramatic poetry—poetry as carrier of the burden of memory—as he passes within a few minutes from Aai's evocation of the emotional charge of the family jewellery—

The gold belonged to the women. Lakshmi was never hawked in the bazaar. Prabha, my dear, the gold is not just money. One generation passes it on to the next. They in turn give it to their children. That is the link we have with our ancestors. When one wore those ornaments one felt—how many hands have touched them? How many necks were adorned by them! I would feel the presence of all the Deshpande women standing around, admiring me when I put on those ornaments—

to Vahini actually putting them on and 'feeling' them as Aai had felt them—the same words come back—and recalling how Aai had once 'explained each piece' to her just as Aai's mother-in-law had 'explained' them to her; and Dadibai's 'radiance' is repeated/reflected in Vahini's new look: 'Now her personality seems completely changed. Glowing, splendid, grave, aloof, representing Woman whose inherent beauty has come down through the ages.' More than obvious narrative links, connections like these provide dramatic growth and continuity in Elkunchwar's new dramaturgy. A play that centres on traditions rooted in ancestry and caste, which are crumbling under the onslaught of changing values and the natural temptations from a distant metropolis, builds the myth of the family gold only to tear it apart with Ranju, representing the new generation, stealing it (and demolishing the tradition with one blow) to further her dreams of finding a place in the cinema in Bombay.

Speaking to me, Elkunchwar acknowledges:

Around the time I was writing *Party*, but more from *Old Stone Mansion* onwards, I became more aware of the responsibilities of a playwright. During *Old Stone Mansion*, watching Vijaya Mehta at work, I became conscious of the dynamics of space in theatre, the visual space as well as the acoustic space. You know how she works, with such a meticulous sense of detail.[10]

As one sees dramatic progression—or maybe the falling curve—in the narrative of the jewellery, from the build-up of its ancestral/traditional glory, moving from verbal evocation to the almost epic 'armouring', to the gross triviality of the stealing and the escape to Bombay, one can see yet another running/falling curve in old Dadi's recurrent appeals to the dead Vyenkatesh, as they gather into a text of despair, coming virtually upon Vahini taking off the jewellery and putting the pieces in the box (Bhaskar notices: 'You seem to be in a trance'). While she evokes a nightmare world of the mice running all over the house and digging up the whole mansion, and the dead laughing, Aai wonders how she, incapable of mobility, could have 'come here, near the tractor', and is herself haunted with a sense of the presence of the dead, with their 'desires not fulfilled'.

If old Dadi, hovering between life and death, time and timelessness, and driven by strange impulses and energies, creates an aura around herself, she remains a theatrical presence nonetheless, as tangible and concrete as the tractor which is not visible, but makes its presence felt by the slashes and wounds that it inflicts. The tractor, once acquired in a half-hearted urge to modernize, stands as a sign of the relentless process of decay that is endemic to the culture of the place: 'More than half of it is sunk in the ground where it stands ... a little more sunk every time I come here. The plates are so rotted they are falling apart.'

Old Dadi and the tractor are the icons that frame the battles within the family which comes to a precarious truce when Sudhir, the brother from the big city, who had sparked off a series of encounters with his arrival, takes it upon himself to find and bring back the runaway Ranju and restore the breach in the family's dignity.

When Elkunchwar closed *Old Stone Mansion* on a note of restoration, he was not thinking of the long trajectory that he would chart out later into a trilogy. But he had left the potent seeds in the text itself—in Chandu's acquiescence, and the silent withdrawal and defiance of Prabha and Prayag—and the falling dust that would eventually bury the village at the end of the trilogy.

The relentless realism of *Old Stone Mansion* contains glimpses of a visionary surreal—the conscious passing into the subconscious and returning to the real—that takes over in *Reflection*, with the protagonist's loss of reflection, his mirror image, bursting on the mundane which defines his existence as a paying guest in a one-room apartment. *Reflection* is surreal in the space it creates between the palpable and the impalpable. Elkunchwar avoids the use of the word 'surreal' and prefers 'poetry in theatre': 'A play written in excellent "literary" verse may fail to be poetic while a text unadorned by any literary flourishes may have situations that render a poetic glow to the play. *Waiting for Godot*, for instance. I wonder if an entire text can be poetic. It is only a few moments or scenes in any text that are poetic but they lend a poetic charge and luminescence to the whole text by their evocative power.'[11]

The conflict between the palpable and the impalpable, the conscious and the subconscious, comes into its own, in the opening of the play, in a comic game that ringing bells—from the clock, the telephone, and the door—play with the unnamed protagonist; with his waking-up turned into a piece of pure farce. The play of sounds continues for a while, setting the tune for his daily routine on which he embarks as he 'picks up his towel and goes to the bathroom'. It is left to the landlady-housecleaner to appear at this point and set down a code of norms which the protagonist has obviously defied to her annoyance, underscoring at once the disorientation that has marked the protagonist's movements and reactions all along. His scream from within followed by his reappearance in a state of frenetic panic is the consummation of a neat piece of black farce.

The 'discovery' of the loss of his reflection, a shock to the protagonist, appears merely 'funny' to the landlady, who would like to put it into the papers and turn her lodger into a celebrity. She cannot understand why he should resist the idea. In her ceaseless chatter, she builds up an elaborate logic to rationalize/legitimize the extraordinary phenomenon. From her cascade of words that leaves the protagonist unrelieved, she moves to suggest a game of entering each other's minds. The game played initially between the two is repeated with two visitors, viz. Flags and the protagonist's 'girl' colleague at the office, both of whom have lost their reflections; the game proving, in each case, the impossibility of the desire/dream. While the two other victims of loss of reflection come to terms with it, adjusting their personal desires to it, it is only the protagonist who 'realizes' the enormity of the loss and recalls/re-experiences it as a slow process that has been part of his life—'but I didn't notice'.

As he recognizes, 'So. Good. Now I don't have to worry about the future, the past, and the present. Because all time is dark in the same way. And there is no difference between optimism and pessimism'— 'He calmly walks to the window. Climbs up. Jumps out'; leaving the Woman, still entrenched in her formidable commonsense, utterly disappointed: 'Nothing wrong in killing oneself. But after falling five floors right into the middle of the road without so much as a sound, or a blood-stain or a traffic pile-up, something huge and black gushed out and spread on the road like sticky oil. What kind of death is that! Huh!' But there is something in that death, even as she tries to accommodate it as usual into her commonsensedom, and that is what strikes her into her climactic scream. And once again the 'normal' doorbell 'goes on ringing along with the scream'.

Elkunchwar uses an elaborate stock of trivialities to chart out the domain of the ordinary with the daily chores, the diversity of ringing bells calling for immediate response/action, and a cumbrous body of unquestioned, conventional ideas and ideologies picked up by rote;

with habit as the ultimate silencer—and upholder of the tyranny of Order, which, in spite of its illusion of authority and grandeur, is fragile enough to crack whenever a simple individual begins to doubt, and the extraordinary takes over. The ordinary, working out of habit, denies the eruption of the extraordinary and tries to bring it into the confines of the mundane; but all that it manages at the end is to downscale the tragic and the heroic which, in its turn, nonetheless strikes at the acquiescent ordinary like a deadly virus.

The three single working women in *Sonata*—a journalist, a teacher of Sanskrit, and one employed 'in a big post in a multinational'—share a life with all the signs of solidarity and freedom. Aruna and Dolon have been sharing their flat for seventeen years. They are all 'fortyish', were in the same class in college, can afford to flaunt their temperamental and cultural differences, and can, once in a while, break out of their stance of self-sufficiency and address the audience together in a choric avowal:

'What awful women we are!
We're alright. We're self-sufficient. We earn, spend.
Self-centred. Do nothing for society.
Without any commitment. Without any aim.
No ideology.
We're not even feminists.
We blow money, smoke, drink.
And my affairs.
Sheeeee! What kind of people are we!
Decadent. But happy. We're happy.
Unabashedly happy.
Abominably happy.
Obscenely.
Nirlajjam sada sukhi.'

Elkunchwar gives them a physical/stage site, which seems to float among the heights of the Mumbai skyscrapers with a sense of cocooned security that is threatened from within again and again; the lonesome intimacy itself provoking the barbs and charges that fly between them. Their entente is so precarious, fragile, and desperate that every lunge calls for a response that would contain it and blunt its edge. It is only rarely that the sallies strike, abrade, and leave wounds, but the resilience of the other is prodigious. Almost invariably, the attacks rise from hidden animosities and secrets lying beneath the slightly laboured fraternization. The secrets that surface are not necessarily contentious; in fact, more often than not, they appear to be the conditions of their bonding, the grudging recognition of qualities in the other, or occasions cherished with gratitude, which are not without a sting!

Aruna and Dolon, the central double, have Subhadra and her 'affairs', and the lonely typist neighbour as their measures of reference, for that little kick of privilege/superiority they need! Elkunchwar develops the drama from a supposed state of stability to the challenge of disorder that Subhadra brings to it with her appearance. Subhadra represents a spirit which the double cannot quite take, and yet they feel its tug, and the tension is palpable. There is the same mixed feeling on the part of Subhadra, who has to come back to the haven of the double, maybe temporarily—what Dolon mockingly calls 'a transit lounge'; hoping for a respite to which she cannot ultimately submit anyway. And yet it is Subhadra's entry that breaks up the uncertain truce between the double.

Elkunchwar shows perfect theatrical timing in bringing Subhadra in right at the ending of Dolon's song—a song that carries the sombre shades of gathering clouds darkening, a darkening evening as one waits for the other, 'alone beside the door' in dubious hope; followed by Elkunchwar's stage direction:

Dolon's voice gradually trails into a silence, long and heavy. The evening becomes deeper and heavier. Aruna is staring vacantly at the heap of papers. Dolon is shaking her empty wine glass listlessly and looking at the TV that is not on.

The soulful tone of Tagore's *tappa* set in Mishra Shahana charges the silence that follows; to be shattered by the accumulated violence of sounds, one growing upon the other—the rumble of the lift, the opening of the lift doors, then the slamming of the doors, culminating in the doorbell ringing non-stop, registering Subhadra's entrance.

Subhadra exudes an infectious violence culminating in the explosion of abuse that she directs at the caller on her mobile, who informs her that she has lost her job for moral turpitude. Although the defiance of social mores and decencies that she has made her position continues in the long tirade, it is already touched with a despair which Dolon and Aruna can read. Subhadra's vulnerability gives them the power to take the upper hand of benevolence and charity, which Subhadra finds unacceptable, more so as she 'gets tired so easily these days. Getting old, I guess.'

With Subhadra's exit, Aruna and Dolon lose their moment of triumph and glory. They can cling to their lost privilege, only by being judgemental. When even that fails to serve, Dolon drops all the niceties of their solidarity to attack Aruna directly and viciously. The fangs are bared for the first time. And what surfaces for the first time in the play, after the laborious and long-drawn holding back, is the spectre of sexuality, denied and repressed, out of fear. They hit out at each other, till Aruna calls for truce, and the precarious bonding of the two is restored, with Dolon's confession of a betrayal giving Aruna something to hold on to—against and for Dolon.

The vulnerability and delicacy of the relationship among the three is played out simultaneously in terms of the continuing shifts in position and the private obsessions that they cherish and project to hide their raw sores, for example, Dolon's bottles of perfume and Rabindrasangeet, Subhadra's adoration of the male à la Stanley Kowalski, and Aruna's intellectual-creative pretensions are obsessions that manifest themselves in intensely private spaces, often with a touch of poetry as when Dolon turns Aruna into a veiled beauty and 'adores' her, visualizing a secret, unspoken desire.

If in *Sonata* Elkunchwar had come a long way from his disturbing/ disturbed playscapes in the earlier phases, and achieved an almost perfectly orchestrated play of tones against tones rising to a height to crash to a quiet restoration of the disrupted quotidian, in the last play of this volume, *An Actor Exits*, he engages in a theatrical critique of theatre's engagement with life. An actor, or maybe *the* Actor, comes out of a lifetime of acting, a prolonged experience of putting masks on and off, cheating and denying real life in the process, and all in a perpetual state of discontent, chafing against the authority of the director; to face an array of challenging masks, from theatre and life alike, till life takes over, not so much as memories of loss or separation, which have their place in the scenario that breaks forth, but as the nostalgia of a lost childhood and a lost father charting out an escape into infinity.

Elkunchwar's development has covered a course from an almost uncontrolled outpouring of raw passion to a superbly controlled interplay of emotions barely emerging into view; but all through, he has been committed to extending the real just beyond its immediate contours, often reaching out to the surreal. His works have posed a challenge to directors who do not dare to cross the imaginary barriers between the real and the surreal. But those who have been able to defy those imaginary constructions have created remarkable pieces of theatre, which have gone beyond the frontiers of the Marathi theatre—particularly into Bengali, Hindi, and English.

SAMIK BANDYOPADHYAY

Notes

1. Mahesh Elkunchwar, speaking to Samik Bandyopadhyay, in an unpublished interview in Nagpur, recorded on 14 January 2008. Henceforth described as Elkunchwar, Nagpur interview.
2. 'A playwright in search of his own reality', *Hindustan Standard*, Calcutta, 17 February 1977.
3. Elkunchwar, Nagpur interview.
4. Ibid.
5. In my last interview in Nagpur, talking about this early phase, I asked Elkunchwar, 'Was sexuality one of your major concerns?' He answered, 'Very much so.'

6. Elkunchwar, Nagpur interview.
7. Ibid.
8. Transcribed from a recording of a talk given at the Natya Shodh Sansthan, Kolkata, on 24 February 1988.
9. Cf. Samik Bandyopadhyay, 'Introduction' to *Old Stone Mansion* (Calcutta: Seagull Books 1989): 'In its first draft, the play had begun in the morning, with Sudhir and Anjali approaching the *wada*. It was Vijaya Mehta, the director of the first Marathi production, who suggested that the play should open in the night. Elkunchwar asked her, "Why do you want this?" She said, "It would be visually beautiful. It's total darkness, the crickets chirping outside, and there are these three lanterns in the three corners of the stage, and everybody is waiting for the city boy to come down. It is late night, and there is this tension in the atmosphere." Elkunchwar said, "Fine, I like the idea. I can write it in no time."'
10. Unpublished note on 'Poetry in Theatre': 'hurriedly written and it is only for your use. You may quote from it.' Received some time in late January 2008.
11. Ibid.

Garbo

Translated by
Shanta Gokhale

Characters:

Shrimant

Pansy

Intuc

Garbo

Act One

A sitting-room furnished in a casually luxurious style. Intellectual relaxes, puffing on a cigarette. Pansy noisily twiddles the knobs of a radio. Some time lapses.

INTUC: Pansy.

(*Pansy isn't listening.*)

Pansy.

(*Pansy is still unconcerned.*)

I'll chuck that radio out Pansy.

(*Pansy still pays no attention.*)

Beats me what fun he gets out of that thing.

PANSY: Not a decent song anywhere.

INTUC: Then switch it off.

PANSY: You'll never understand this kind of joy.

INTUC: Oh really?

PANSY: Where the hell has Kuwait got to now?

INTUC: You'll find it on the map.

PANSY: Very funny. Sunday mornings Kuwait plays all the latest hits one after the other. Just can't get it today.

INTUC: What do you expect out of that old box? Chuck it out and let's have some peace. Damned noise begins at the crack of dawn.

PANSY: The cells are kaput. (*Pause.*) I told Shrimant yesterday ...

INTUC: Oh fine. Then you'll get new cells.

PANSY: Much use they'll be after the programme's over. He knows very well how crazy I am about Kuwait on Sunday mornings.

INTUC: You know something? You're alright in a way. There's always a hit song playing somewhere or the other. Just set the thing blaring and start dancing. Or there's always the record player. Killing time is no problem then. It's only poor bastards like me who have no fun.

PANSY: That's rot. If you like music, I mean if you like it a lot, I mean really like it a helluva lot, like it's part of your blood, then you should like these songs too.

INTUC: Well, well. This little bird has picked up some really big words.

PANSY: I'd just go crazy without music. I've got to have it every day.

INTUC: You want to grow up a bit. Then you'll know nobody ever goes crazy.

PANSY: D'you know what I used to do back home? There's no radio there. So I'd go and stand in front of the *pan* shop or the cafe. Or barge straight into the barber's. Listen to the songs for a while and then beat it, pretending there's too much of a rush. Of course in those days it was only Hindi songs for me. But English songs are the greatest. I'd never heard them before I came here, and now it's nothing but ...

INTUC: I don't seem to enjoy even classical music these days. (*Pause.*) Do you know Pansy, in the old days, just a single *taan* fluttering somewhere on the distant breeze was enough to give me goose flesh. And of course listening to the real thing would bring me to tears and all. (*Pause.*) Strange bloody experience.

PANSY: I feel like dancing. Haven't they opened a new place somewhere? Shrimant was saying something like that.

INTUC: If there's a new place anywhere and if he said so, then he's bound to take you there.

PANSY: Why don't you come along? You're a dead loss, Intuc. God knows what fun you get out of all that lalalala classical stuff.

INTUC: Who said I get any fun out of it?

PANSY: Why else would you go to all those stuffy concerts?

INTUC: My dear boy, that's a different thing altogether. You should see the crowds that come there. God knows where the bastards buy all that enthusiasm. The vocalist, male or female, sits under the arch of two tanpuras like some deity. They go crazy about their own marvellous voices, belching out with sublime ardour at all those sublime idiots sitting out front with their overdressed, simpering idiot wives. That's why I clap the longest and the loudest at the end of every song. Alone of course, and with this terrific solemn face. And people think, this chap's a great lover of music. It's a real laugh.

PANSY: But you do understand music, don't you? I mean, classical.

INTUC: It is assumed that I do. After all I'm a professor. I'm supposed to understand everything. Crap!Once you get yourself stamped 'professor', you can literally run amuck. I'll tell you about people. Once I was clapping the skin off my hands when a baldie next to me says, 'Wonderful Kaushi Kanada, wasn't it?' I made my face even more dreadfully solemn and said, 'It wasn't Kaushi Kanada. It was Nayaki Kanada.' So the chap turns to his dolled-up wife and says, 'Terrific Nayaki Kanada, wasn't it?' That's the way it is. So what's so damned fantastic about a concert?

PANSY: But this has nothing to do with the music itself. Surely you enjoy it within you, inside of you; you're not concerned with the people around you?

INTUC: Those days are gone, kiddo, when you could enjoy music as a private pleasure. Nowadays these musical conferences are an immense fraud perpetrated by the community upon the community. Everybody from the singers down to the listeners are under religious obligation to pretend to be intensely interested in art. They sing 'Mishra ragas', *sale*. *Bacchu*, try to sing simple, straightforward ragas first. But people are only too keen to pop-

clap them. What more do you want kid? You've got everything there except good music. You should come with me sometime.

PANSY: Thanks. I'd go mad with boredom.

INTUC: Mad? The whole world rushes to these concerts, and this twerp says he'll go mad. My dear chap, you'll see our illustrious ministers there. They sit in the front row on the VIP settee. The singer treats them to one helluva humble bow from the stage. Then there are some cultured ornaments strewn around, chaps who've been accepted as art-lovers by the world, who come scrounging there for free culture. They also sit in the front row like stuffed tigers wearing suitable expressions of appreciation. Then there are the social workers, male as well as female. The females are generally sexy as hell in their modish outfits. We've all seen their pictures in newspapers, donating blood and such-like—short-haired, plump, fair cows sprawled on a table, smiling false, timid smiles. And the doctor, waiting for their rotten blood, smiling stickily, as if a great honour were being bestowed on him. Crap! All he's pleased as a pig about is getting into the picture.

PANSY: Then why don't you arrange a private concert, just for yourself?

INTUC: And the money? Do you think Shrimant will shell out? He's another type. I once said to him, come on, cough up a thousand chips for some really good music. So he says, I hope she's going to be a female. So I said, 'Done. A female it shall be.' So the bastard says, 'What are her tits like?' That was the end of that little plan.

PANSY: You know, Intuc, if you've got music in your blood ...

INTUC: Where the hell have you picked up that phrase? Spare me the blood will you? This sort of bloody language only comes from being immature. Mr Pansy, there's nothing whatsoever in one's blood. If it was ever there, it's drained right away. Only the blood flows on. We endure this incessant flow and continue to exist. We attend musical conferences, and listen to speeches, and see films, and go out with good-looking chicks. On and on. That's the way it is. Now are you going to switch off that sound-box, or do you want me to chuck it out of the window?

PANSY (*switches off the radio*): Oh, alright. (*Long pause.*) Now talk.

INTUC: What?

PANSY: Say something or I'll go mad. Intuc, sometimes you go yap-yap-yap-yap seventeen to the dozen, and then you suddenly dam up. It's scary. (*Pause.*) If only Shrimant would come, time would pass pleasantly.

INTUC: Grammatical error. Time won't pass. Time never passes. It has to be spent.

PANSY: Wish we'd been as rich as Shrimant.

INTUC: You're not doing badly for yourself even now.

PANSY: You're just jealous of me. And of Shrimant.

INTUC (*contemptuously*): Jealous? Just because somebody has got a few paise more than I?

PANSY: What a life though! Get into a car when you please and drive around. (*Pause.*) Sundays are a bore, aren't they?

INTUC: Pansy! Seventeen years old and bored! Observe this youth. Bored at seventeen. What will you be when you get to my age?

PANSY: Exactly what you are.

INTUC: I? I'm managing to exist. But at seventeen I was fired by a raging fever. Libraries, lectures, music, poetry, love, the lot. I was bent on becoming great, don't you see?

PANSY: You are that. Out of the four of us, you and Garbo are the great people. Hey! You've dedicated your new collection of poems to Garbo, haven't you? I want to be great too. I must attend art school regularly now. Do you think I'll make it?

INTUC: Of course you will. No trouble at all. Anybody can achieve greatness in this country. Look at me. I wrote four stories and four poems and won instant fame. World famous! Of course the world is just Maharashtra. Soon people began spouting about how great I was. I let them spout.

PANSY: But don't you think you are great?

INTUC: I thought so at first. And then suddenly I felt disgusted. And this talk of fame is utter crap! People are fools. They call you great, but do you feel that way from within? Idiot. Think carefully before you answer. Pat came the reply, 'You are not great. Then what is all this about? These stories and poems.' 'They are a hoax,' came the second answer. 'Why are you doing it?' 'To become famous.' Well, there's nothing wrong with wanting to become famous. But what exactly is fame? What does it mean? What are you when you're famous? Fame is a sort of pleasant allegation foisted upon your name. And that's when you put a stop to writing and all that sort of nonsense. Forget about the whole thing and wallow happily in boredom. But is that the end? Certainly not. People are worse frauds than you think. They start singing another tune. 'Here's a writer who knows when to stop. His single-minded devotion to art—blah blah blah.' All they want is somebody's boots to lick. Pansy, you're not listening.

PANSY: Carry on.

INTUC: You're not paying attention.

PANSY: I'm bored, *yaar*. Not a single word has sunk into this skull.

INTUC: Tch, tch. Pansy. Your future is shrouded in gloom. If your interest in life continues to decline like unto the waning of the moon in the darker half of the month ...

PANSY: Oh shut up.

(*Suppresses a giggle.*)

INTUC: Don't dare shut me up, Pansy. Here's the world-famous man of letters from Maharashtra offering you his jewelled thoughts.

PANSY: Shut up, shut up. (*Laughing helplessly.*) Oh God, Intuc, is this how you talk *to* your students?

INTUC: I speak fairly good English in class and am solely responsible for corrupting the English of a hundred brats. They are a kind of wildlife sanctuary. If you want to keep them under control, you must pretend to possess the wisdom of sages, the chastity of saints, the ascetism and strict moral code of monks. Moreover ...

(*Shrimant enters noisily, Intuc pretends extreme annoyance at this interruption.*)

Shrimant.

SHRIMANT (*roaring*): Pansy.

INTUC: Shrimant, you ...

SHRIMANT: Shut up. Pansy, stand up. Intuc stand up.

INTUC: I am already standing Shrimant.

SHRIMANT: Shut up. I don't want any back-chatting from you. Stand on even if you are standing.

INTUC: Shrimant, I only wished to point out that your behaviour in thus rudely interrupting me in the very midst of a highly intellectual and committed discourse is not becoming of a gentleman.

SHRIMANT: Here you, cut out the fancy language, and how dare you call me a gentleman huh? I am stooding here ...

INTUC (*screaming*): English!

SHRIMANT: Shut up. I am stooding here ...

INTUC (*pretending to faint*): Pansy.

PANSY (*playing up suitably*): Help! Help! Get water somebody. Get an onion.

INTUC (*quickly opening his eyes*): No don't. Onions are forbidden during this holy month. We are Hindus, aren't we?

SHRIMANT: I said I'm stooding here ...

INTUC (*screaming*): Shrimant, your English. For God's sake use it correctly. Are you not aware that a leading litterateur of Maharashtra, an authority on language and literature, is standing before you at this moment?

SHRIMANT: And I am a police officer standing before you, so my English has to be bad. That is mandatory.

PANSY: Shrimant.

SHRIMANT: I am a police officer. Now stood up. Come on, come on. Mr Intellectual, you too. I've got a warrant for your arrest.

INTUC: From where?

SHRIMANT: From where? From society. As long as blaspheming, degenerate, mean worms like you are eating into society ... society ... society ...

INTUC: Don't worry If you can't remember the next bit, Inspector Sir. We've got your point.

SHRIMANT: Get going. To the police station. Come on, come on.

INTUC: Sir, you are the protector of law and order. We are prepared to go anywhere with you. But before we do, could we, humble creatures, beg to know the charges against us.

SHRIMANT: Charges! Listen. Charge number one. You are guilty of using impossibly clean language shorn of all obscenities, thus causing acute embarrassment to those who are in the habit of using abusive language. Charge number two. You are both guilty of expressing contempt and disgust towards drinking, meat-eating, smoking, opium, hemp, and LSD. Number three. Instead of having a bit of fun with good-looking chicks and letting them go, you soppily indulge in pure and sublime love, and, in your attempts to remain celibate, you either soil your underwear at nights, against which habit the entire race of dhobis is soon going to launch a protest in the form of a demonstration, or/and you lock yourselves in the toilet at odd hours of the day and night causing great inconvenience to others. There are many more such charges, but you'll hear them in court. Now come on. Come along.

(*The three of them walk round. Shrimant sits down on an elevated seat.*)

SHRIMANT (*in the role of Judge*): Order. Order. Accused number one and two. Do you plead guilty to the charges against you?

INTUC, PANSY: Yes, milord.

SHRIMANT: Do you wish to make a statement?

INTUC: Milord, we are decent, white-collar, middle-class intellectuals. However eloquent our speech outside the court may be, it is a sacred tradition with us, going back thousands of years and fully endorsed by society, that our lips shall remain sealed at the time of judgement.

PANSY: I second it.

INTUC: Shoo, You've not supposed to second any thing in court, you idiot. Forgive us milord.

SHRIMANT: Right. The court will now declare its verdict and pass sentence on you. Taking into consideration the serious nature of your crimes, the court has decided that gold medals shall be hung around your necks for each of the following charges: integrity, extensive scholarship, ardent selflessness, boundless philanthropy, humble service, burning patriotism, and an unblemished character. Accused will then he made to sit in a cushy, flower-bedecked Impala and driven all around the town to the accompaniment of a brass band. At every square pious *suhagans* wearing traditional pearl nose ornaments will give them a heroes' reception. Reports and photographs of the event will appear prominently in newspapers throughout the country.

(*He mimes the breaking of a pen-nib. Intuc mimes repressed sobs.*)

PANSY: Milord, milord.

INTUC (*throwing himself at Shrimant's feet*): Milord, it would be infinitely kinder to sentence this unfortunate creature to death by hanging.

PANSY (*also throwing himself down*): Milord I beg for the same punishment.

(*They begin to tug at Shrimant's legs.*)

SHRIMANT: Hey, cut it out. You can't pull the Judge's legs like that.

(*Shrimant comes crashing down. Pansy and Intuc pounce on him. All three wrestle for a while.*)

Get off my chest, you bastards. You can't sit on top of Justice itself. Phew! They really made me sweat.

INTUC: This is all fat. It's a wonder you can walk around with a paunch like that.

SHRIMANT: To hell with you. (*Stroking his stomach.*) This is the wealth I was born with. And now a sign of my extreme love of beer. Do you get me kiddos? Come on. Out with it Pansy. Where's the beer?

PANSY: It's finished.

SHRIMANT: What do you mean 'finished'? Get some.

PANSY: Today is Sunday. The liquor shops are closed.

SHRIMANT: Get it from somewhere else.

PANSY: Why didn't you get it yourself when you were driving all over town?

SHRIMANT: Shit! And there's still the whole day to get through. Whisky? Or is that finished too?

PANSY: This early in the morning?

SHRIMANT: Yeah. Why not? I'm bored without a drink.

(*No one stirs. All are silent, lifeless. After some time. In a tired voice.*)

Talk. Will somebody talk? (*Pause.*) For God's sake talk. (*Pause*)What's the matter with you, all of a sudden? Like bloody corpses, both of them.(*Pause.*) Pansy. (*Pansy doesn't answer. Shouts.*) Pansy! (*Pansy doesn't answer.*) Pansy!(*Furious, he begins to throw whatever comes to hand from where he is sitting.*) A whole morning wasted. Didn't meet a soul. Those girls need bringing down a peg or two. Shirin wasn't home. Babi said, 'I'm indisposed!' To hell with you.(*Pause.*) And there's still the entire day to get through. I hope at least Garbo turns up. (*Pause.*) Talk, damn you. (*Pause.*) Dropped in at the restaurant. Those joints look really frightening that early in the morning. The steward looked at me as if I was some kind of insect that he'd found crawling over him. It was dark as hell, and all those empty chairs, and me sitting there alone, eating chomp-chomp-chomp like a bloody idiot.(*Pause.*) Pansy. Come here. (*Pause.*)

PANSY (*suddenly angry*): Stop calling me Pansy.

SHRIMANT (*tired*): Now what's got into him?

INTUC (*sarcastically*): He can't get Radio Kuwait.

PANSY: Did you get the cells?

SHRIMANT: To hell with Radio Kuwait. Play some records.

INTUC: Did you get the cells for him?

SHRIMANT: Pansy.

INTUC: His cells.

SHRIMANT: Pansy, have you gone deaf?

(*Pansy is sulking. He kicks at the transistor.*)

There is gratitude for you. You spend your life pandering to their needs and the bastards turn round and kick you.

PANSY: Don't call me dirty names, Shrimant.

INTUC: Don't call me any names at all.

SHRIMANT: I don't have to take orders from you Intuc. This place belongs to me. You think you can sit on your bloody arse having a ball at my expense, and then lord it over me, you sons of bitches? Get out. Just get out.

INTUC (*in cold anger*): We'll do that. Come Pansy.

(*Begins to leave.*)

SHRIMANT: Pansy is not coming. Get lost alone wherever you want to.

PANSY: Shut up.

SHRIMANT: Say that again. This sissy stood blubbering like a girl on the railway platform one day and now he tells me to shut up. (*To Intuc.*) You've been teaching him these things.

PANSY: Shut up, shut up, shut up.

SHRIMANT: He hates me. Because of you.

INTUC: Look here Shrimant. I was quite ready to leave when you told me to leave. I only came to this house because you asked me to. There's no need to be offensive.

PANSY: I'll go with you. I won't stay with this man.

SHRIMANT: 'This man'! Listen to his bloody language. 'This man.' Where will you go with him? Just tell me that. And you? Where are you going?

INTUC: That's entirely my business.

SHRIMANT: Sure. Go fuck yourself. (*Noisily pulls open a drawer and takes out a small parcel. To Pansy.*) Here take this. Cufflinks.

(*Pansy is obviously tempted, but he makes an effort to overcome it.*)

Come on, take it. Once you're out of here, you're not likely to set eyes on such things again.

(*Pause.*)

PANSY (*pouting*): But why are you quarrelling?

INTUC: Pansy.

PANSY: Tch.

INTUC: So long, I'm off.

SHRIMANT: Where?

INTUC: None of your business.

SHRIMANT: I guess you're right. How am I concerned? Intuc, you make me feel cheap and guilty. I was wrong. I'm sorry. Pleases stay here, both of you. This is your home. I'm the intruder, the unwanted man.

INTUC: There is no need to become maudlin.

SHRIMANT: Damn it all—If I could have kept my cool the way you do, there'd have been no problems. But just tell me how I can keep calm when the people I've gathered for myself turn around and kick me? (*To himself.*) I'm disliked. I'm the most disliked person. Intuc, I'm sorry yaar.

(*Pansy has meanwhile donned the cufflinks and is busy admiring them.*)

INTUC: Oh forget it.

SHRIMANT: Forget it? Just listen to him. He sounds as if he is bestowing a goddamned favour on me. It's maddening.

INTUC: In that case, I'll be off.

SHRIMANT: Intuc, stop blackmailing me. You know I'll go stark staring mad if I have to live here alone.(*Pause.*) Do you mind if I have a drink?

PANSY: The house is yours. And so is the liquor. Who are we to interfere?

SHRIMANT (*hurt*): Pansy.

PANSY: Sorry.

SHRIMANT: Go on, torture me. There's happiness in it for you. And for me too. What other way is there of passing the time? (*Taking out a liquor bottle.*) Anyway. I'll drink. I'll drown myself in this glass.

INTUC: And sentimentality.

SHRIMANT: Yeah. And sentimentality. Am I forgiven?

INTUC: Sure. (*Pause.*) Shrimant.

SHRIMANT: Have a drink.

INTUC: It's too early.

SHRIMANT: Pansy.

PANSY: No thanks.

SHRIMANT: Well.

INTUC: Just a simple question. Why do you suddenly lose your shirt and get all worked up like this?

SHRIMANT: Do you know? I can't understand it myself. Perhaps, as Garbo said the other day, it's another side of my sentimentality.

PANSY: When did you meet Garbo?

SHRIMANT: God knows why people ridicule sentimentality. That's also become a bloody fashion.

INTUC: Ten years ago, the sentimentalists were a fashion. Stuffing their handkerchiefs and their sari ends in their mouths, and sobbing their bloody hearts out. On the stage one female would ask another female for pickles or some such nonsense, and out there in the auditorium, the entire lot of fancily dressed females would collapse in spasms of grief. What a laugh.

PANSY: But Garbo is very rational.

INTUC: I hope you're listening, Mr Shrimant.

SHRIMANT: Rational my foot. Why don't you try and tell me what exactly you mean by rational, kiddo?

PANSY: I mean, doesn't she think things over carefully? And she never seems to lose her emotional balance.

SHRIMANT: She did the other day.

PANSY: Did she talk about me?

SHRIMANT: Yeah. She said, send Pansy. I want to have my saris washed.

INTUC: I suppose you had sex.

SHRIMANT: You suppose! Why the bloody hell should I go visiting Garbo? She's is the only one who's available any time you go. And she is just great in bed.

PANSY: I know. (*Pause.*) But then, she is a great woman.

SHRIMANT: Oh no! I see the light of devotion in his eyes! Honestly Pansy, you really are the most terrifyingly deadly humorist around. In what way is Garbo great? Her only business in life has been jumping from bed to bed. She's nothing but a sex-machine.(*Pleased with the phrase.*) A sex-machine. Yeah boy! A sex-machine.

PANSY: Don't talk like that about Garbo.

SHRIMANT (*shrieking in glee*): A sex-machine. She's a sex-machine. That's a damn good idea. Just get on top of this machine, one machine on top of another, and presto! printing begins.

INTUC: Hold on Shrimant. You've made two statements in the last few seconds which are diametrically opposed to each other. Completely contradictory. First you said Garbo is great in bed. Then you said she is a sex-machine. Now, if she is a machine, she is devoid of emotions. And if she is devoid of emotions, she can't be great in bed.

PANSY (*claps*): Bravo!

SHRIMANT: Once a teacher, always a teacher. He is throwing philosophy at us now. Sir Intuc, kindly tell me where emotions enter the picture. Once you get going, there's nothing but the body. And then a peaceful smoke.

INTUC: Terrifying! First the body, then a cigarette.

SHRIMANT: Okay, okay. How has it been between you and Garbo then? I suppose you're brimful of emotions and all that. Not that you don't use your body. But it's a bit of a bloody obstacle.

PANSY: Stop it.

SHRIMANT: What's eating you?

PANSY: You're making the whole thing look so ugly.

SHRIMANT: Then what do you think it is, something sacred and sublime?

PANSY: It is. It is a rare and beautiful experience.

SHRIMANT: Intuc. This one is straight out of Intuc.

PANSY: Why? Don't you think I've brains of my own? Or experience?

SHRIMANT: Your're seventeen, lollipop. I suppose Garbo has to undo your fly-buttons every time?

PANSY (*furious*): Why do you talk about her as if she's is some common whore?

SHRIMANT: What, then, is she, may I ask?

PANSY: You're sickening.

SHRIMANT: There's gratitude for you. Observe him Intuc. This is how he shows his gratitude.

INTUC: Are we by any chance going to start another quarrel or something? If so, I'll leave. I'm tired of this kind of bickering day in and day out. I'm fed up.

I've just about had it.

SHRIMANT: Come off it, yaar. Who's bickering? Aren't we all involved with Garbo? I mean physically? I mean, I certainly am, only physically. If this is so, and is openly admitted to be so, and Garbo doesn't seem to mind, why the hell are we chucking weighty words at each other? Sheer hypocrisy. And we don't want that. Do we?

INTUC: Doesn't matter.

SHRIMANT: Doesn't matter! Just like you.

INTUC: Well, does it really make any difference whether we call Garbo this, or that? Names don't change things. Garbo will remain Garbo, while we will continue to search for the kind of Garbo we want. If we find her, well and good. If we don't we will suffer a bit. Or not even that, after a while.

SHRIMANT: I refuse to suffer. If I don't have you, I have someone else. If I don't have someone else ...

INTUC: Then why do we try to define her? Or any woman? Or anything in the world for that matter? I think we should just lay back. Let

Garbo be what she is. The important thing is to know what we are. If we do, that becomes a sound enough basis for our relationships with her.

SHRIMANT: Do you?

INTUC: No. But I know what I want from her. As far as I'm concerned, Garbo is a challenge. She grows older but never stale. What is it in her that gives her this quality? Maybe she is a great artist, and that helps her to preserve her infinite freshness.

SHRIMANT: Artist, my foot.

INTUC: But we don't have suitable roles for her. Her genius is completely wasted.

SHRIMANT: Not in bed. What rot you talk Intuc. She's not stale, she's fresh ... Do women ever go stale?

INTUC: Don't they? Sleep with a woman twice, and you know her inside out.

SHRIMANT (*laughs leeringly*): 'Inside out!'

(*Pansy giggles.*)

INTUC: Don't make foolish witticisms please. All this business about woman being an enigma and all that is a myth. A bit of literary stupidity to tell you the truth. Once you've understood a woman, you don't want to look at her again. Once you've explored her the thrill is gone. A woman should be able to satisfy you fully, and yet withhold a part of herself from you ...

(*Shrimant mimes a large, uninhibited yawn.*)

SHRIMANT: It's always like this with you. Once the tap of your mouth starts flowing freely, that's the end. Pansy, have you filled the bucket of your mind to the brim? If you haven't, say so. Here's a tap that's lost its washer. It keeps running day and night. Keep listening you bastards. What do you think, we cant talk literary like you?

PANSY: I'm not sure I understood everything. But I know Intuc was saying something terribly profound.

SHRIMANT: Would you mind giving me the whole thing in a nutshell Mr Professor? A sort of Guide to 'Garbo—Slut and Enigma'.

INTUC: To put it in a nutshell, Garbo never becomes common. Even after fulfilling the needs of all three of us, a part of her still remains untouched.

SHRIMANT: Three of us? Only the three of us? What kind of fool world are you living in? There's a queue, a regular queue outside her house. At the head stand film producers, then the directors, then the cameraman. The queen of whores receiving everybody into her enigmatic embrace. Wonderful!

PANSY: But she is a great artist isn't she, Intuc?

INTUC: Doesn't matter.

SHRIMANT: There he goes again. Doesn't matter. For as long as she's ready to hoist her sari at a word, nothing matters to dear old Intuc. What bastards some people are. They eat shit and wipe their mouths on silk handkerchief. Ugh. (*Pause.*) Anybody for whisky? (*Pause.*) Can't you answer? (*Pause.*) Oh, go to hell. (*Pause.*) Must have Garbo today dammit. (*Pause.*) Pansy, why don't you play some records? (*Very loudly.*) A hard day's night ... (*Silence. Shouts.*) Bastards. Doesn't this silence get you?

INTUC: Pansy, play some records.

PANSY: But you don't care for pop music. You're always shouting.

SHRIMANT: He doesn't like anything pop. He's a bloody highbrow. Or at least pretends to be.

INTUC: Even pop music is better than Shrimant shouting.

PANSY (*putting on a record*): I'm fed up with listening to the same songs again and again. (*Pause.*) I wish Garbo would come. Time would pass beautifully then.

(*The song begins. Pansy undulates in a slow dance. Sometime later.*)

SHRIMANT: He's got a girl's body.

INTUC: But this whole business is a bit frightening and all that. You go out there and dance and people sit staring at you.

SHRIMANT: You are an intellectual professor. You bastards spend your bloody lives being scared of people.

INTUC: The whole thing's ugly though. It's like, you know, having your bath out in the open with everybody gaping at you.

SHRIMANT: I suppose you do your dancing in the bathroom? Bolt the door nice and tight and then let yourself go, ding-dong-ding-dong. People are bloody funny I tell you.

(*Intuc is staring out.*)

INTUC: Garbo's coming.

PANSY: Garbo? Where?

SHRIMANT: That's right. Run.

PANSY (*at the window*): Garbo.

GARBO (*off*): Hi!

PANSY: Garbo is here.

SHRIMANT: Good. So now all of us may look forward to being pleasantly occupied for at least ten minutes each.

PANSY: Shut up Shrimant.

SHRIMANT: Let's welcome her.

PANSY: Good idea.

SHRIMANT: Alright?

PANSY: Right.

SHRIMANT: Pansy, beat on something good and loud when she comes in and I ... (*Garbo enters.*) Here she comes. The greatest sex-machine on earth.

GARBO: Shrimant!

SHRIMANT: Now three cheers for Garbo the sex-machine. Come on. Darling Garbo ...

PANSY, INTUC: Hip hip hurray!

(*They repeat this twice.*)

SHRIMANT, PANSY, INTUC: Heave ho!

(*They lift her up and put her in a chair centre-stage. She struggles.*)

GARBO: What nonsense is this?

SHRIMANT: It's the kind of welcome you deserve.

PANSY: We've been waiting for you for hours.

GARBO: But I hadn't said I'd come.

PANSY: Even then we were waiting.

GARBO: Why? Didn't you go to art school today?

PANSY: It's Sunday.

GARBO: I'm a real scatter-brain. I'd forgotten.

INTUC: Not that he goes to the school on other days.

GARBO: What do you mean? Has he given up?

SHRIMANT: Like Intuc, he finds everything a big bore these days. Everything is phony. Isn't that right?

GARBO: Is this true, Pansy?

PANSY: I used to get bored there. Maybe painting isn't my medium.

GARBO: God, what long words this child uses. 'Medium', he says. Silly child.

SHRIMANT: All this is the result of Intuc's terrible influence.

GARBO: Come here.

(*Pansy goes to her.*)

SHRIMANT: There she goes. Garbo, you ...

GARBO: Shut up.

SHRIMANT: You'll ruin him.

INTUC: At the age of seventeen I suppose everybody likes the idea of being ruined and all that. That's the only time there's some chance of any such fortune befalling you. Later, it's nothing but idiotic existence all the way.

GARBO: They torture you, don't they? I've decided to take you home with me, pet.

INTUC: Where we'll live happily ever after.

SHRIMANT: Perhaps madam needs a toy. Garbo, did you know that Pansy was once on the verge of committing suicide?

GARBO: Don't talk like a fool. Why don't you give me some beer instead.

SHRIMANT: Beer's finished. There's some whisky if you like.

PANSY: We've got beer.

(*He goes in.*)

SHRIMANT: Pansy!

GARBO: Why do you torture the child like that? Actually you should be looking after him, the two of you.

INTUC: You're taking him with you, aren't you? Look after him yourself. Give him motherly care. Shower him with love. Hell, Garbo.

GARBO: You shouldn't talk about things, like suicide, in front of him. The poor thing has run away from home as it is. And he's so sensitive.

SHRIMANT: That's true. You're never sure what he'll get up to. The other day I drove down to the art school to pick him up. He wasn't there. So I went to the station. There he was, sitting right at the end of the platform, staring vacantly at the rails. (*Pansy enters with beer.*) Actually, that beer is mine.

INTUC: Thus Pansy allowed a golden opportunity to slip through his fingers. Pansy this is the time. You're at the right age for a beautiful deed, like suicide. Later on a man becomes thick-skinned, and continues to cling to life shamelessly like a leech.

GARBO: Stop filling his head with this kind of nonsense. The crazy boy will honestly do something dreadful one of these days. Pansy, don't pay any attention to these chaps.

PANSY: I won't.

INTUC: I must say Pansy's doing well as the obedient son and all that.

SHRIMANT: Christ! That makes him a motherfucker.

GARBO: Button up your dirty mouth, will you? I'm not in the mood today for this kind of talk.

PANSY: Garbo, let's go to the flicks today.

GARBO (*promptly*): No. (*Pause.*) Oh dear, look at his face. Why are you so sensitive?

PANSY: I was only ... Because you said you weren't in the mood to ...

SHRIMANT: What solicitude!

GARBO: I don't want to see anything today. I'm fed up with films and plays, I spend my days dancing around in them. Can't bear the thought of spending my evenings watching them. Why don't you come and sit near me?

SHRIMANT: Sit!

INTUC: Garbo, what you are doing is fine by me. And it's none of my business. But then what is so terrifying about this chap being similarly seduced by the idea of suicide?

GARBO: You know, I'm beginning to feel quite worried.

INTUC: That's as it should be.

GARBO: Not about Pansy. About you. You're going on and on and on about suicide. Tell me boys, is Intuc growing more and more morbid everyday?

SHRIMANT: Perhaps that's the only escape left to him. I'll never go morbid like this. I'd rather become a pervert. What I mean is that, if I must commit suicide, I'll strip myself naked first.

GARBO: You'll look dreadful with that paunch of yours.

INTUC: And it won't be much use, because the police will cover you up in any case. Things must always be covered up. Do you think the police use their own sheets for this sort of thing?

SHRIMANT: But my dear chap, I will make a will to the effect that, if I am to be covered, it shall not be with a sheet, but with one of Garbo's saris. Don't you think that would be exquisitely perverted?

GARBO: The kind of gibberish you talk would make people go round the bend.

SHRIMANT (chuckling): Christ! It would really shock people.

INTUC: Oh yes. All the neighbours will turn up to see you. The Tatyasahebs, the Annasahebs, the Dadasahebs. They'll rub their hands gleefully at finding yet another example of how man is hurtling into a dark valley ... sorry, I mean into the very jaws of annihilation.

PANSY: Tatya from next-door came across today, mad as a coot.

SHRIMANT: What was he mad about?

PANSY: About my playing the radio too loudly and dancing.

SHRIMANT: So?

INTUC: Pansy is a bad reporter. Tatya's exact words were, 'Please remember that you live in a respectable neighbourhood. If you want to dance naked, shut your doors and windows first. We shall have no objections then.'

SHRIMANT: Christ! Why the hell should we close our doors and windows? If they don't like to see us dancing naked, let them shut their doors and windows. Mind you, if it was Garbo dancing naked, then they'd start complaining against our keeping our doors and windows shut.

GARBO: Just lay off me will you?

SHRIMANT: Honey, since when have you started objecting to our laying on you?

GARBO: You have a dirty mind.

INTUC: And a dirty body as well.

PANSY: You're disgusted, aren't you?

INTUC: Disgusted is the word since Garbo is basically a pure, chaste creature and all that.

GARBO: Of course I am.

INTUC: A chaste woman of chaste family livings in a chaste, tradition-bound society, once gave birth to another chaste woman ...

SHRIMANT: Garbo, I must say that photograph of yours in one of those Diwali magazines showing you with an *arati* was a real hit.

GARBO: Oh dear. I was flooded with letters after that. 'Dear sister, will you adopt me as your brother?' I said I would. Don't you remember? Even Pansy used to tell me in the old days that I was like an elder sister to him.

SHRIMANT: So that makes him a sister-fucker as well.

INTUC: Pansy, I suppose your mother's also a chaste type?

SHRIMANT: The poor woman will faint if she comes to know that Pansy leaves dirty stains in Garbo's bed.

INTUC: Do you know what she'll go round the town saying then? That's the admirable thing about these chaste types.

PANSY: Don't bring my mother into it.

INTUC: Why? Is she extra chaste? A sort of deluxe model of chastity. But whether they are extra chaste or just plain chaste, you must always remember one thing my boy. All women, however chaste, are liable to suffer from runny noses and rheumy eyes. Similarly, everyday they are obliged to ....

GARBO: I think I'll go.

SHRIMANT, INTUC, PANSY: Garbo!

GARBO: Don't shout. I am going.

PANSY: But why?

GARBO: Because of what's going on here.

INTUC: Whew? What?

GARBO: Are you going to continue talking like this?

INTUC: Like what?

GARBO: Intuc, I ... I ... Look. I don't feel too bright today. Just spare me.

SHRIMANT: But he's not saying a thing. What are words? Bubbles. Mere bubbles.

INTUC: You've got it boy-o. Bubbles. Woman, don't you know, there's an emptiness inside all of us which gives rise to bubbles. They keep coming up to the surface.

PANSY: Bood, bood, bood.

GARBO: Pansy.

INTUC: So we keep on going bood, bood, bood all the time because of this emptiness inside us.

SHRIMANT: Hell! That's a great idea. People look at each other and go bood, bood, bood ...

GARBO: There's no emptiness inside me.

INTUC: Of course. This one's a woman! I forgot.

SHRIMANT: I hope you don't forget at other time?

GARBO: Intuc, I'm going to become a mother,

SHRIMANT: Hoo hoo hoo hoo hoo hoo hoo.

INTUC: That's really great. So now you have no problem about filling up your emptiness. Of course this kind of solution is a bit of a physical impossibility for us.

PANSY: But you can have your sex changed these days.

INTUC (*sarcastically*): Which Shrimant is going to make you do one of these days.

SHRIMANT: Hee hee hee!

INTUC: So your emptiness has been filled up, has it?

GARBO: Intuc.

SHRIMANT: What superb dialogue you come out with at times, Garbo. Let's see. (*Touches her stomach.*) Hey, she's right. It's hard.

INTUC (*puts his ear to her stomach*): And no sound of bubbles.

SHRIMANT: Can you hear any squealing?

INTUC: No. But I can hear some choice language. Looks like this one's yours, Shrimant.

SHRIMANT: Let me see. (*Puts his ear to her stomach.*) What rot! I can hear an English lecture in progress. Intuc, there's one of yours in there too.

INTUC: And who's that singing pop song in there? Pansy, yours. Come and listen. (*Pause.*) Garbo, you will soon be the mother of three babes of good fortune They will be like Dattaguru incarnate. O Mahasati Anasooya.

(*Garbo's eyes fill with tears.*)

PANSY: Garbo's going to cry.

INTUC: Those are tears of joy.

SHRIMANT: Garbo, this is not like you. Why are you so sensitive today?

PANSY: Garbo, we are only fooling around as usual.

INTUC: Mind you, Mahasati Anasooya's part is damned difficult to play and all that. Moreover, it is an outdated part. A blatant insult to a woman who is used to acting in avant-garde plays.

SHRIMANT: Avant-garde my foot. In that last film of hers, all she did was to dance around bouncing her tits flip-flop, flip-flop.

INTUC: That is the commercial aspect of it.

GARBO (*losing her temper*): Yes, that's the way I danced, and that's the way I'll dance for the rest of my life. And you will watch. There's nobody else who'll entertain you like this.

PANSY: Garbo!

GARBO: Go away. Don't slobber over me like a dog. And don't call me Garbo again either. I don't want any of you to do that. Are you trying to merely flaunt my failure before me? I'm aware of my failure, perhaps better than you. And I'm trying to come to terms with it. I don't claw at people, draw blood, and then dance with demonic joy the way you do. (*Silence.*) I'm sorry. (*Makes for the door.*)

INTUC: Garbo.

PANSY (*throwing his arms around her*): Garbo, please don't go. We're sorry. We were wrong.

GARBO: Nobody was wrong. What am I after all? Just a cheap whore. Why should I take such violent offence? Please carry on with your game.

SHRIMANT: Garbo, you're being mawkish today.

INTUC: Why shouldn't she be? That is her escape. I have my morbidity, you have your perversity, and she, she has her sentimentality. Go my dear, drench yourself in sentimentality.

PANSY (*kissing her hand*): Please don't go Garbo. Be a sport. Please stay.

GARBO: I'll stay. Start the game.

SHRIMANT: We won't play without you. You must take part.

INTUC: Garbo looks rather done in.

GARBO: Look here. Don't come up with any more new ways of annoying me.

PANSY: Tch!

GARBO: What's 'tch' supposed to mean?

PANSY (*hurt*): Nothing.

GARBO: Look here. There's no going back now. Let's start the game. The Slut and Three Gentlemen.

INTUC: Now who is annoying whom?

SHRIMANT: Garbo you are ... Why do you torture yourself like this?

GARBO: I'm not torturing myself. Facing the truth about oneself isn't self-torture.

PANSY: Garbo, Garbo.

(*Goes to her.*)

GARBO (*pushing him away*): Go away from me. For God's sake learn to behave like a man.

SHRIMANT: Who? Pansy? Like a man?

GARBO (*pointedly to Shrimant*): I know more than you who is capable of behaving like a man.

SHRIMANT: But Pansy's scared stiff of sluts. Didn't you know? We went one day, all three of us, just for a lark.

PANSY: Ugh!

SHRIMANT: And Pansy actually broke into a dripping sweat.

GARBO (*eyes fixed on him*): Did you go in with him?

SHRIMANT: I asked her afterwards. She couldn't stop laughing for an hour after that.

GARBO: And you? What did you do in there? I'll tell you how.

SHRIMANT: Garbo!

GARBO: Intuc, why didn't you ask him how he made out? You should have. You'd have heard some very amusing details.

SHRIMANT: Garbo.

INTUC: I'm not interested in trivia. My aim was to get-out of there as quickly as possible.

GARBO: Come on. Start the game.

SHRIMANT: Shall I imitate Pansy for you?

INTUC: Brilliant idea. You can be Pansy. I'll be Shrimant. And Pansy, you can do me. This is going to be terrific. To be somebody else. It's a way of feeling alive for a little while at least.

PANSY: Is that why you became an actress?

GARBO: Who knows?

PANSY: But don't you live your roles?

GARBO: Why do you talk like a book? 'Live your roles.' Yes I do. (*Bitterly.*) All the way through.

SHRIMANT: Alright. That's enough. Aren't we going to play?

GARBO: Come. Let's start. (*Assuming the stance of a prostitute.*) Psst ... Mister. Come 'ere Mister.

SHRIMANT: How much?

INTUC: Shrimant, you're talking like yourself. You're supposed to be Pansy.

SHRIMANT: Hell, I forgot. (*Pansy chuckles.*) Pansy.

PANSY (*bursting with fun*): Call me Intuc. That's me. But I can't spout English like him!

INTUC: That's enough.

GARBO: Come 'ere Mister.

INTUC: How much?

GARBO: Why don't you come and have a look at the stuff first Mister?

PANSY (*trying to repress laugher*): Shrimant is ... is ... a ... a... sickening ...

INTUC: What?

SHRIMANT: I say, why don't w-we g-g-go home?

INTUC: Hell Intuc, I think he's scared.

GARBO: Look love, pipe down on the talk and come in will ya.

PANSY: A perfect ... a ... a ...

INTUC: What will you take?

GARBO: For all three of you? A tenner will do.

INTUC: It will, will it? Who do you think you are? Cleopatra?

SHRIMANT: L-let's go home ...

PANSY: Pansy shut up.

(*Mops his face.*)

GARBO: Look. Hurry up will ya. Don't waste my business time.

INTUC: I'll give you five.

GARBO: Five? (*Angry gestures.*) Over your rotten dead body. Who do you think I am? A cheap twenty-five paise piece?

INTUC: Oh no, you're sweet sixteen, Juliet herself. Come on.

GARBO: Shove off.

(*Pretends to spit vehemently on the ground.*)

PANSY: Terrific. Great. Garbo, you're a truly great actress.

SHRIMANT: Pansy, you're forgetting.

PANSY: Oh God! That one spat just like that. Garbo, how did you know?

SHRIMANT: Pansy's spoilt the whole game.

GARBO (*exhausted*): Are you satisfied?

PANSY: Tatya from next door should have been here to watch this game. Oh Christ. What a laugh that would have been. Ha ha ha ha.

INTUC: Wait. Listen. We'll play Tatya and Us now. (*Putting on a solemn face.*) *This* was a most disgusting performance blackening the fair name of our civilization.

SHRIMANT: Wrong.

INTUC: What's wrong?

SHRIMANT: You must first come in and stand glaring, with dilated nostrils, trying to shame us by a show of moral indignation. When you see we are not ashamed, you come on with the speech about Indian culture and heritage etc.

PANSY: Right ...

INTUC: Okay. (*Stands looking scandalized. After glaring for some time.*) Who is this girl? Who is she?

SHRIMANT: Tatya, surely you mean lady, and not girl.

GARBO: Don't take any notice of him Tatya. Call me a girl. I love it. After all, I am like a daughter to you, aren't I?

INTUC: Watch your tongue.

SHRIMANT: Your trap.

INTUC: Yes. Watch your trap. How dare you presume to call yourself the daughter of a man of spotless character like me? Of my nine daughters none bears a character as besmirched as yours. So what if they are ugly?

GARBO: Oh dear, are they? Then who would besmirch them?

INTUC: You are shameless. They are modest. Even today, they dare not lift their eyes to my face.

SHRIMANT: My God, Tatya. Isn't it terrible; that even your own daughters can't bear to look at you?

PANSY: Hee hee hee.

INTUC: I have lived with a blind wife for fifty years, but never have our feet strayed from the path of morality.

SHRIMANT: Nor have hers, she being blind. Dear people, listen. I bring good tidings. The key to an unblemished character has been found. Go blind, deaf, and dumb, and enjoy instant morality.

GARBO (*pretending to sob*): Don't, Shrimant. Don't harass this pious man. Tatya, Tatya, I was wrong. Forgive me. I would feel that the entire world had rejected me.

PANSY (*screaming*): Great, great, great, Garbo.

SHRIMANT: Shush!

GARBO: I had been alone. I'd have thrown myself under a train or some such thing, without a second thought. Or drowned myself. Or else I'd have hung myself from the end of your sacred shawl and forever disappeared from before your spectacles.

INTUC (*pretending to be deeply moved*): My daughter.

(*Begins to stroke her back.*)

GARBO: Tatya, why do you lavish such caresses on this miserable creature?

INTUC (*repressing a sob*): My dear, you are like a daughter to me.

GARBO: But Tatya, what you are stroking is not my back. It is one of this wretched creature's most defiled and erogenous part of body.

(*Pansy screams with laughter.*)

SHRIMANT: Tatya, shall I fetch you your glasses?

INTUC: My daughter, how could you have said such a thing, how could you?

GARBO: I was wrong. My mind is evil. How could I have doubted a saintly man like you? Please, please give me your shawl. I shall hang myself with it.

INTUC: Don't my dear. My shawl is brand new.

(*Pansy continues to laugh.*)

And you must think of the other life within you. What sin has that innocent, pure and unknowing little creature committed?

GARBO: Then where shall I go?

INTUC: Come to me, my daughter. Did Valmiki not give shelter to Sita? I shall travel to the four corners of the earth to bring your Rama to you.

SHRIMANT: But Tatya, she has too many Ramas.

INTUC: My daughter, I plead with you to give up the company of these libertines. Where is that professor? He is nothing but licentiousness incarnate.

GARBO: But Tatya, I wish you would give me some medicine instead. Why should I bring this young life into the world to face its cruelty?

INTUC: Don't say such things. Oh God, oh God. Infanticide is a sin, my daughter.

GARBO: But Tatya, wasn't it you who once brought some medicinal root for your Shaku to take?

INTUC: My dear, hers was a totally different case. She is the respectable daughter of a respectable family. Traditionally, she is not forbidden from committing infanticide.

GARBO: Oh well. Then shall I come to your house?

INTUC (*stroking her back*): Come, my deer, come. Since my wife was struck down by paralysis, I have suffered such terrible neglect. (*Pretends to blow his nose. Pansy runs all over the room screaming 'Great, great'.*) I'm not too happy about this poor boy. (*To Shrimant.*) Listen, you. I want to have a talk with that professor of yours one of these days. I shudder to think what he teaches those girls and boys at college. What kind of influence are dirt-grubbing worms like you on young minds? Eh? Tell me that. There's only one way of leading today's sex-obsessed generation back to the path of morality, and that is to impress upon them the supreme importance of strict celibacy ...

SHRIMANT: Tatya, what are those stains on your dhoti?

INTUC: None of your business. How dare you insult your elders. Come, my dear ...

SHRIMANT: But Tatya, I honestly don't think you should go out in that dhoti. Can't you imagine what people would say? I suggest you take it off here.

PANSY (*jumping up and down*): Off with it. Off with it.

SHRIMANT: I don't think he'll do it that easily. Pansy, you'd better hold him.

INTUC: No, no.

SHRIMANT: Catch him, catch him.

(*Together they catch him. A mock struggle. They pretend to take off Tatya's dhoti. Intuc, feigning embarrassment, stands hiding his 'nakedness' with his hands.*)

You may go now Tatya. To tell you the truth, you've got nothing that's worth hiding. Nor worth showing.

INTUC: No I can't. What will people say?

SHRIMANT: They'll say nothing. They are all like that Tatya. Now go. Off with you. Go.

INTUC: Come my dear.

GARBO (*suddenly losing her temper in real earnest*): You creep. What do you take me for? Get out. Get out.

SHRIMANT: Out, out, out.

(*Kicks Intuc out. Intuc is back the next moment. Everybody is in fits of laughter.*)

PANSY: Oh God, I'm going to pass out. Save me, I'm!

SHRIMANT: That was terrific.

INTUC: Garbo, you've got to hand it to me. I'm a bit of alright as an actor.

GARBO (*exhausted*): You're a big-head.

INTUC: Damn. This girl never gives the devil his due.

SHRIMANT: Anyway, we're almost through the morning. Garbo, why don't you stay here today?

GARBO: I'm tired.

SHRIMANT: I'll take you to a party tonight.

GARBO: No thanks. I refuse to go to any more of those pot-luck parties of yours.

PANSY: The morning's been great.

INTUC: Great. (*Silence.*) Great.

(*Very long pause. They are all tired. And then they become restless.*)

GARBO: We're terribly frivolous at times. (*Pause.*) Like filthy pigs.

INTUC: Socrates says, it's better to be a discontented man than a contented pig. We are pigs, and yet we are discontented. We have to be, or else we'd suffocate to death.

PANSY: Bood, bood, bood, bood. (*Garbo Is holding her head tight.*) Does your head ache?

GARBO: I'm feeling dizzy. I find everything revolting. Including myself. We are wallowing in filth, all of us.

SHRIMANT: You are becoming emotional again.

INTUC: You feel revolted. You think we are wallowing in filth. Fair enough. Can you show me a single place that is clean? Show me. There's none left. If we are wallowing in filth, there's no escape for us. We must continue to live in this same filth. And we will say this filth is beautiful. In order to render this filth endurable, we will have to make up new theories about beauty ... A sort of aesthetics of filth and depravity.

(*Silence. Garbo is about to retch. She staggers out of the room.*)

SHRIMANT: Garbo really looks upset today. She's never been like this before. This is a different Garbo.

INTUC: Do you think she's really pregnant?

SHRIMANT: I thought she was joking.

PANSY: Intuc, why did you have to be so morbid? She had just started to enjoy herself.

SHRIMANT: Pansy, see if she needs anything. (*Pansy goes in.*) She's been behaving very strangely today. But why should she let it upset her so much?

INTUC: And why the hell did she get into this messy situation when motherhood is the easiest thing to avoid these days? (*Pause.*) It can't be the first time it's happened to her. Why come here and tell us about it? (*Pause.*) Do you think she's going to plant this on one of us? Shrimant? Shrimant?

SHRIMANT: You make me sick.

INTUC: That's rich, coming from a model of morality like you.

SHRIMANT: At least I'm not busy saving my skin like you.

INTUC: Good God. He's turning into a philanthropist. Look here, I know Garbo's our friend and all that ...

SHRIMANT: Did I hear you say friend, you bastard?

INTUC: Stop abusing me.

SHRIMANT: What do I do then? You talk of friendship in one breath and in the next you get busy rejecting it.

INTUC: Oh button up. How do I know that this child is mine? And if it isn't, why should I feel responsible for it? This is commonsense. Would you accept such responsibility?

(*Garbo and Pansy enter.*)

PANSY: Would you like to drink some water? (*Garbo shakes her head.*) A little brandy?

GARBO: I don't want anything.

(*Silence.*)

INTUC: How do you feel now?

GARBO: Better.

SHRIMANT: It's true, isn't it?

GARBO: Yes.

SHRIMANT: We thought you were joking.

GARBO (*looking up*): Why should you think that?

SHRIMANT: Intuc's getting scared.

INTUC: Shrimant!

PANSY: Are you really going to be a mother?

GARBO: For God's sake don't be so melodramatic. It gets on my nerves. (*Silence.*)

INTUC: What have you decided?

GARBO (*guessing the reason behind the question*): Why are you looking so uncomfortable?

INTUC (*angry*): Garbo, you have no reason to doubt my motives.

GARBO: Then why are you getting so worked up? Have I accused you of anything? What I did say was that I'd look after myself. Why are you harrowing yourself with anxiety?

SHRIMANT: But who is the man?

(*Pause.*)

GARBO: I don't know.

INTUC (*to Shrimant*): I told you so.

GARBO: So, you've talked the whole thing over, have you? The minute I become pregnant I also become cheap. We'll allow ourselves to forget those days when you followed me around like dogs and couldn't do without me. Look here, I haven't come here to throw myself on your mercy. I don't want any help from you. I came here simply because I was feeling restless and uneasy. But today I've seen you in your true colour. Remember one thing though. I could implicate all three of you in this if I wanted to, so don't think you can shrug off responsibility.

PANSY: But Garbo, I haven't talked to you the way these two have. Why are you lumping me with them?

GARBO: Oh shut up. Idiot. (*To Shrimant and Intuc.*) I take it that you understand what I'm getting at?

SHRIMANT: Garbo, take a hold on yourself. Aren't we allowed to ask you who is the responsible man?

GARBO: I say to hell with who is responsible. You are my friends aren't you? Then accept the responsibility. What difference does it make? There's so much chalked up against us as it is. This shouldn't make much difference.

INTUC: What have you got in mind?

GARBO: To rid myself of this burden.

PANSY: Garbo ...

GARBO: Please send him out.

INTUC: Let him be. He'll get wise quicker this way. And how do you know he's not responsible?

(*Pause.*)

SHRIMANT: What shall we do then?

GARBO: Give me money.

SHRIMANT: How much?

GARBO: At least ten thousand.

SHRIMANT: Garbo!

GARBO: Why? You won't even miss it. You're rolling in the stuff.

INTUC: This is nothing less than blackmail.

GARBO: There's no other way. You'd have done the same if you were in my shoes.

INTUC: But why ten thousand?

GARBO: You miserable creature. How would you understand that? Do you want me to go to some back-alley quack to have my insides scraped out and die in the process? Anyhow, you're not giving me a rotten paisa out of your pocket so what's bothering you? You're nothing but a parasite sponging on him for a good time.

INTUC: I'll bash your face in Garbo.

GARBO: You're not capable of anything else. You are the world's prize coward. Isn't he the one who was talking about extracting beauty out of filth?

PANSY: Stop it! Stop it!

GARBO (*screams*): Go in!

(*Silence.*)

SHRIMANT: I'll give you the money. But will you answer one question?

GARBO: Yes?

SHRIMANT: Don't you also earn in thousands? Haven't you got anything saved up?

GARBO: No. Not a paisa. (*Shrilly.*) Don't you know that I'm not such a hot draw at the box-office anymore? (*Pause.*) I'm on the wrong side of thirty-five, and prepared to go to bed with anybody who'll give me a role.

PANSY: Garbo, you're a great actress.

GARBO: One of these days I'm going to throttle this boy. (*Pansy holds her hand tight. She pulls it free.*) You know, you're sickening. But pathetic as well. Why don't you go back to your parents? (*Pause.*) Great actress! I've lost my youth and beauty waiting for greatness to come. I act in stunt films now. (*Pause.*) I need ten thousand rupees. (*Pause. Shrimant begins writing out a cheque.*) Shrimant, I don't want money from you.

SHRIMANT: Does it matter who gives it? You need it. So take it.

GARBO: I will not take it from you.

SHRIMANT: It will wash away my sins.

GARBO: It's not yours, and you know it Shrimant.

SHRIMANT: Garbo!

GARBO: You are not involved in this. And there's nothing sinful about it.

INTUC (*interrupting*): Take the cheque Garbo.

GARBO (*cold anger*): Give. (*Intuc hands it over. She slaps it hard across his face.*) You son-of-a-bitch.

(*Silence. Begins to leave.*)

PANSY: Garbo!

SHRIMANT: Garbo, don't just walk out like that.

GARBO: I'm so tired Shrimant.

SHRIMANT: Sit down then.

INTUC: Forgive me Garbo. (*Garbo laughs dejectedly and shakes her head.*) Honestly, I mean it. I behaved like a cad.

GARBO: Forget it Intuc. Finally it is my own, personal problem.

PANSY: I am with you Garbo.

(*Pause.*)

SHRIMANT: Then what have you decided?

GARBO: I don't want it. I'll have to find a way out.

(*Pause.*)

INTUC (*suddenly*): I want that child.

SHRIMANT: Intuc, you ...

INTUC: I do want that child. Garbo, don't even think of destroying it.

GARBO: You don't have to feel that bad about the way you behaved. I was wrong too.

INTUC: No. That's not the reason. I want that child badly.

GARBO: You're really funny, the way you suddenly get intense about something. You're so temperamental. Now for the next hour, you'll eat your heart out with remorse.

SHRIMANT: And what are you going to do with that child?

INTUC: I'll look after it.

SHRIMANT: Excellent!

INTUC: Don't make fun of me Shrimant. Don't you see? Don't you understand me? Within a second Garbo has shown me up for what I am.

GARBO: So you've decided to look after this child as a form of penance, have you?

INTUC: No, but it's a chance to pull out of all this, and live bravely. To show some guts. (*Pause.*) I'll look after him. We'll look after him. He'll be our only hope, and our only refuge. He'll be pure, fearless, clear-eyed, and clean.

SHRIMANT: I don't understand this man at all.

PANSY: Will he be completely unlike us?

INTUC: Yes. And we will all humble ourselves before him. He will be our creation. And we will bow our heads before our own creation. A single smile from him will move us. (*Pleading.*) Garbo let us do this. We are doomed people, we have neither seen, nor experienced, nor created anything beyond filth. Let us grab this opportunity. It's our only hope, our only chance. We will create something beautiful out of this filth. The world will know that there is a life somewhere which is beautiful, pure, fearless, innocent .... And Garbo, we cannot achieve this without you. Do you know? Do you know what a tremendous role you have to play?

GARBO (*warily*): Here, don't you go loading me with new responsibilities.

INTUC: Don't you feel the immensity of this thing?

GARBO: Of course I do. It's very beautiful and all that. (*Dreamily.*) To be the mother of a beautiful thing!. (*Practical.*) But do we have the guts to see the whole thing through? Suppose we suddenly get cold feet? And there are all the other difficulties. If we decide on this I'll lose nearly a year, and all my contracts will have to be cancelled one after the other. What guarantee then of finding work again after the year's over? Not to mention the compensation I'll have to pay to all my producers. And even if I am offered roles later on, how do I know I'll be physically fit to accept them?

INTUC: You are not to work again.

GARBO: Intuc!

INTUC: Your job will be to love this child. Garbo, Garbo, we will all shower the child with love.

GARBO: And while we are doing this, what do we eat?

SHRIMANT: Garbo, if that your only worry, well, hell, what am I here for?

GARBO: Are you also falling under his spell?

SHRIMANT: Why not? It sounds so beautiful. And, if you like, I'll transfer a whole lot of money to his name right away.

GARBO: I'd better go.

INTUC: Garbo ...

PANSY: Please wait Garbo.

GARBO: You have all gone mad. What I intend doing isn't unheard of. It happens all the time. And please don't think you're to blame for this. Right now you're getting drunk on your own words. Suddenly one day you'll come to your senses and then there will be no escape.

PANSY: You don't have an iota of motherly love in you.

GARBO (*suddenly angry*): No. I haven't. This whole business of motherhood and fatherhood is crass hypocrisy. I am a woman. Just that. A woman who flits from one man to another. (*Breaks down.*) Why are you torturing me?

INTUC: Stay with us Garbo.

GARBO: What's the use of having this child? Doesn't he need a name? A father?

SHRIMANT: He'll be my son. (*Dreamy.*) People will say, do you see that sweet boy? He's Shrimant's son.

GARBO: I'm scared.

INTUC: We are with you Garbo.

GARBO: Suppose I die of taking some horrible drug to get rid of it? I can almost smell the warm odour of flowing blood. The thing taken out furtively then, and thrown away, like throwing away a rotten fruit.

PANSY (*softly muttering*): Garbo, Garbo.

GARBO: I want to love somebody one day. To lose myself in love. Is this possible? There's a heap of ashes within me. Will I find one live ember in it? I have no more strength left. Will I be able to live intensely again?

INTUC (*in a voice hurry with emotion*): Not just intensely, but beautifully Garbo. This is your chance. Your life will once again shine forth like the sun, and the child will bloom like a flower in the warmth of your light. Garbo, Garbo, Garbo, a new life is beckoning you. Don't reject it. It's our only chance. Garbo, this is our only refuge. Our only chance to create something beautiful. You are life itself. We will do anything for you. You only have to say the word. We'll do it. Come Garbo. Come. Come and stand here in the centre. You are Life. We bow our heads before you. Garbo, Garbo.

(*Pause.*)

GARBO (*deeply moved*): I'll have the child and rear him.

(*She is in the centre. The three others stand around her like humble devotees.*)

SHRIMANT, INTUC, PANSY:

> You are life
> and the root of all life.
> The spring of fearless-beauty,
> the source of all hope,
> the fulfillment of all promises
> are you. You are the beginning of belief.
> You are the everlasting.
> All future Suns are in your womb.
> Give us your light.
> Give us your sun.
> He will burn up darkness and destroy it.
> Retribution in the face of injustice,
> Compassion in the face of suffering,
> Sympathy in the face of calamity,
> Courage in the face of death.
> This he will be. He will be creation out of destruction.
> Mother!
> Mother!
> Mother!

Act Two

A month later. Preparations for the arrival of a baby are evident, with nursery stuff strewn around the place.

SHRIMANT: Pansy, put that monkey down. You'll break it. (*Pause.*) Pansy!

PANSY: Do you think I'm a kid?

SHRIMANT: So why the hell are you playing with that thing?

PANSY: I was just looking.

SHRIMANT: Put it down. (*Pause.*) Pansy.

PANSY: Oh all right. This Shrimant is a nuisance at times.

INTUC: Do you notice? Shrimant is positively reeking with father-love and that sort of crap.

SHRIMANT: Do me a favour will you? Just don't pull the cynic on me. I always knew your cynicism was phony. You're actually more sentimental than I am.

INTUC: Well, don't you feel there's something tremendous happening?

PANSY: Garbo's going to be really pleased to see all this.

INTUC: You can't tell about Garbo. She's unpredictable. I wonder if she even knows what a great thing it is to be a woman. (*Pause.*) I can understand now the joy those poor people felt when they saw the newborn Jesus in the manger. Garbo is not alone. We are all with her.

SHRIMANT: But where is Garbo? Here we've been going batty getting everything ready, as if there's some fantastic festival coming up, and she's been hiding the whole month as if she were in mourning.

INTUC: She'll come. She'll have to come.

PANSY: Pregnancy is supposed to make women temperamental.

SHRIMANT: We shouldn't have let her go that day.

PANSY: But she promised to come back within a month. It was exactly a month yesterday.

SHRIMANT: Mind you, she never breaks a promise.

INTUC: Promise or no promise, temperamental or not, it's all of no consequence. Nothing is in our hands, anymore. As long as she comes here. What an awesome thought, that we are the cause for the birth of something beautiful. Garbo, come. You are life about to give birth to another life. (*Pause.*) Surely every woman knows this intuitively? (*Pause.*) I wonder what the earth feels when a sapling takes root, grows, and blossoms. To give birth to a life, a living, breathing bit of blood and bones which grows ... (*Pause.*) We'll watch it grow. Garbo will give it birth. We will give it awareness. I wonder what he will be like. Strong? How strong? A messenger from the gods, who will wander around the world embracing its sorrows.

PANSY: What shall we call him?

SHRIMANT: Pansy talks like a bloody woman. What shall we call him, he says.

PANSY (*angry*): What's so womanish about that?

SHRIMANT: Suppose it's a girl?

INTUC: We'll call her Shakti. (*Pause.*) But why are you quarrelling? (*Silence.*)

SHRIMANT: I'm worried about Garbo. Where is she? There's no sign of her. (*Pause.*) He'll bear my name.

INTUC: Shrimant, why should he have a surname, and a father's name? Let him be without these frills.

SHRIMANT: He will bear my name.

INTUC (*laughing*): Oh all right. I understand how you feel. (*Pause.*) When Garbo comes we mustn't hurt her by a single word. (*Pause.*) I am weighed down by a feeling of deep respect.

(*Silence. Then Garbo comes warily, appraising the situation. Intuc stares, fixedly at her. For a moment their eyes meet. She avoids his eyes.*)

GARBO (*to Shrimant and Pansy*): Here I am.

(*Pansy and Shrimant are jubilant.*)

PANSY: Garbo, Garbo, my Garbo.

GARBO: Crazy kid.

PANSY: If you hadn't come today, we were thinking of going to Rajasthan in search of you.

GARBO: Charming. That would have been the end of my shooting. (*Mustering her courage, to Intuc.*) Aren't you happy I've come?

SHRIMANT: He? He's not with us these days. He floats about ten thousand feet above the ground.

GARBO: And what is all this?

SHRIMANT: What does it look like? It's all for the son and heir.

GARBO: What large toys you've bought.

PANSY (*putting the monkey to her ear*): Hup, hup, hup!

GARBO (*uncomfortable*): You've gone crazy, all of you. (*Pause.*) Intuc, aren't you going to speak to me? What's the matter with you? I suppose it's because I didn't write. Look, we were literally shooting round the clock. And in that terrible heat. By the time I got back to my tent, I was ready to collapse. Impossible even to think of writing letters. (*Turning.*) So what have you been upto in the last month?

SHRIMANT: Getting everything ready as you see.

GARBO (*to Pansy, playing with his earlobe*): I don't suppose you even thought of me.

PANSY: Did you think of us? What were you doing the whole month?

GARBO: Didn't I tell you? I was busy shooting. The sand below, the sun above. Look how tanned I am.

PANSY: You could have called us long-distance at least once.

GARBO: Oh dear. What a nuisance he is. Look, tell me. Where was I supposed to ring up from in that desert? And to tell you the truth, I had become so involved with my part. It's ages since I've done such a challenging role. There's so much I can do with it. Of course it's a great help having a young novice for a director. I've managed to get around him not to meddle but to let me play the part as I want to and see the result.

(*Intuc wordlessly begins to gather up all the toys.*)

SHRIMANT: What are you doing? Let them be.

GARBO (*ignoring them*): This director was acting terribly hoity-toity to begin with. He thought he was somebody great, a genius. You know how these callow young men are.He would keep on telling us to do this and to do that. Nothing but showing off. One night I took him to my tent. I said, 'Sweetheart, you're not much older than my Pansy. Don't keep on calling out orders. Come.' Well, that was that. I had him eating out of my hand. (*She laughs a false laugh alone.*) Have all three of you ... (*Doesn't have the courage to continue. Returns to her former tone.*) What sort of men are you? You're all the same wherever you are.

(*Intuc throws the toys he has gathered to the floor.*)

PANSY: They'll break.

GARBO: Were you entertaining yourselves with these toys the whole of last month? Give me a couple of them. I'd like to present them to my director. He starts drooling the minute he sees me these days.

INTUC (*in an angry, choked voice*): Stop it!

SHRIMANT: Garbo.

GARBO (*ignoring them*): God, it was too funny for words. To begin with he was shivering as if he was freezing, and then he literally wept.

INTUC (*shouting*): Stop it!

(*A tense silence.*)

SHRIMANT: Garbo, why are you talking frivolously again?

GARBO: Oh don't be such a stuffed shirt. Since when has frivolity begun to bother you?

SHRIMANT: Just don't talk like that. Understand?

PANSY: None of us feels like talking that way now. Intuc says he feels deep respect for you. I do too. That's why you mustn't talk like that, Garbo. (*Pause.*) Do you know what Intuc says? He says we are preparing for the coming of the new Christ.

(*Pause.*)

INTUC: Tell them.

GARBO: Intuc ...

INTUC: Tell them.

(*Pause.*)

SHRIMANT: What's the matter with you two?

PANSY: Intuc, didn't you say we mustn't hurt Garbo?

INTUC: Shut up. (*To Garbo.*) Do you see that? Do you see the enthusiasm of these insane people? Tell them. Tell them. (*Menacingly.*) Tell them, I said.

PANSY: Intuc!

INTUC (*shouting*): The child is no more. No more.

(*Silence.*)

SHRIMANT: How do you know?

INTUC: It's true, isn't it? Isn't it true?

GARBO: Don't shout.

SHRIMANT: Garbo, is this true?

INTUC: I guessed it the minute she came in. I knew she had come to us a beggar. She weighed up the situation for a moment and then started all that flippant talk. She thought we'd get taken in. (*Pause.*) We've been cheated. Completely deceived. And to hide it from us, she's deceiving us some more. You've deceived us Garbo.

PANSY: No, it's not true.

GARBO: Are you going to let me have a say or are you going to continue jabbering yourselves? (*Pause.*) Intuc isn't far wrong. I was helpless. (*They all turn away.*) And don't think I'm not as sorry as you are. Perhaps I'm sorrier. After all I was going to be the mother. (*Becomes one with the role she's playing.*) Do you know what agonies I suffered when it happened? It rent my heart just to think of you waiting, yearning. But there was nothing I could do.

(*Pause.*)

SHRIMANT: You shouldn't have gone on location at all.

GARBO: Then I'd have had to go to jail. I was under contract. To tell you the truth, I had no idea this sort of thing would happen.

PANSY: How did it happen?

GARBO: Pansy ...

PANSY: Who was with you Garbo?

GARBO: Oh dear! How he worries! There were many people with me. They did everything they could for me. Shooting was stopped for eight days. They were all eaten up with anxiety for me, poor things. The director was almost on the point of tears. Poor thing, he's such a kid. (*Pause.*) It was during a camel race. He said he would never have included the shot had he known about me. Poor chap felt terribly guilty. He kept insisting it was entirely his fault. (*Pause.*) But honestly, even I didn't think it would happen. All that jogging up and down on the camel .... So unnecessary. They could have used my double. But I was so excited ... (*Pause.*) I'm playing the role of a Lamani girl. She's the second heroine. It's a character role. She's terribly fiery, and terribly passionate, this Lamani girl. (*Pause.*) And terribly beautiful. (*Pause.*) They could have used my double, but I just didn't think ... (*Pleading.*) Why aren't you talking? Don't you believe me?

INTUC: Garbo! Garbo! Garbo!

GARBO: Please. I'm not lying. I was under oxygen for two days.

PANSY: Why didn't you let us know Garbo?

GARBO: How could I have done that? Nobody there knew you were my friends. When I regained consciousness, I wished I had died.

INTUC: Don't, Garbo.

GARBO: Forgive me.

INTUC: No, Garbo. Don't talk like that. It was an accident after all.

GARBO: Caused by my stupidity.

INTUC: Never mind, let's forget it.

GARBO (*putting her hand on his head*): There's so much I owe you, and yet I couldn't do this little thing for you.

INTUC (*suddenly catching hold of her hands*): Love me, love me, love me. (*Garbo is trembling.*) Don't leave me alone now Garbo. (*Pause.*) So it's over. All over.

SHRIMANT: Over?

INTUC: Shrimant, just pick up all these pieces and chuck them out.

SHRIMANT: What are we going to do now?

INTUC: Let's return to filth. The world we desired was not for us, could never have been. (*Laughs bitterly.*) We were idiots, out to turn dreams into reality. (*Pause.*) Let's go back to our old world now. The world of filth. As a punishment. And as a sort of consolation too.

SHRIMANT: But what about me? I was going to give him my name, (*Silence.*)

PANSY: I want to go home. (*Pause.*) I want to go home. (*Pause.*) Shrimant ...

SHRIMANT: No!

PANSY: I can't bear to remain here now.

SHRIMANT: Stop fussing and pampering yourself. What do you think you'd do at home? You ran away from there because you couldn't stand your parents.

PANSY: Garbo ...

GARBO: Let him go if he wants to.

PANSY: Or else I can come and stay with you.

GARBO: No. Go home.

SHRIMANT: No. He cannot leave us now. Once he has been with us, part of our world, he can't just get up and go, leaving us, high and dry. He cannot back out now. Pansy, you'll just suffocate in that poverty-stricken place of your parents. Walls blackened by smoke, and a harassed mother. Un-pressed clothes and meagre meals. That's all you'll get. You'd better stay here. Our life is more beautiful. Much more beautiful.

INTUC: Don't use that word again Shrimant. We are at war with it. With the very concept it represents. Where is beauty? Is there any? It's just a figment of the imagination. A sort of mirage. A trap. I'm tired of struggling within it. We're free now. Filth. That is the only truth. We are free now to choose it. Let's choose it, make it our own, and live with it. We're honest people.

GARBO (*to herself*): Are we honest?

INTUC: And strong.

PANSY: I want to go home.

SHRIMANT: I'll kill him.

INTUC: Pansy, there's nothing to fear now. All illusions have vanished. Melted away. We are free. We can drag ourselves now through life without experiencing any emotion.

SHRIMANT: Pansy, if you go ... I just don't know.

PANSY: Will you kill me? If I go away from here? I hate you, you know. It makes me sick just to hear your voice. Do you know that?

SHRIMANT: I was given only one chance. Just the one. And it's gone. And now Pansy says he wants to leave. Why? What harm have I done anybody?

(*Pause.*)

INTUC: Who are these invisible powers ranged against us? (*Pause.*) There's only one way to face them now, Garbo. Either we turn and fight those who wish to fight against us, or we gore ourselves bloody before they get a chance to inflict the first blow. We will choose the second way. You didn't believe what I said that day. But it is true. These powers desire to crush us and force us into filth. But before they can, let us throw ourselves headlong into it. Let us create our world in filth. And then, the very winds blowing over us will turn our enemies black and blue with their rotten, hate-filled breath. We cannot avoid these antagonists now. They are our eternal foes. We need to become very powerful. That is, more rotten. More perverse. Corroded with hatred.

GARBO: You talk too much.

INTUC: Because I must. I must talk incessantly. I'm scared of silence. If I don't bury myself under an avalanche of words, this silence will choke me. Garbo, what has happened? Why have we been destroyed like this?

GARBO: You talk too much.

PANSY: Please, please let me go.

INTUC: There's no escape for you, Pansy. Even if you leave this place you are not free. And where can you go?

PANSY: Home.

SHRIMANT: And what about me? I pampered you, pandered you, you funk. Take off that watch, that chain. Off with all those clothes. And everything else that I've given you. I'll kill you, you bastard. I'll strip you naked out in the open.

PANSY: I won't give back these thing. They are mine now.

SHRIMANT: Off with all these clothes.

PANSY: Garbo, Garbo. He's always getting at me like this. Let me come with you.

SHRIMANT: He's come into my bed a thousand time.

PANSY: That's a lie. A lie. He's the one who's always after me. He used to barge straight into the bathroom. So I began locking the door from inside. He took off the bolt and threw it away. He had all the hangers removed from the bathroom so I couldn't take my clothes in with me but had to come out to dress. He's always hanging around in my room when I'm changing. I'm sick of you, you dog's vomit.

(*Shrimant suddenly despairs.*)

SHRIMANT: Oh God.

GARBO: Shrimant ...

SHRIMANT: What will become of me Garbo?

GARBO: Shrimant ...

SHRIMANT: Don't keep saying Shrimant. If I make you sick, say so. Spit
    in my face. Maybe that's all I'm worth.

PANSY: You're right. I'll spit on your face.

SHRIMANT: Pansy!

PANSY (*flinging something at him*): My name is not Pansy.

SHRIMANT: Where can I go? If you leave me I'll kill myself. There's no
    other way. (*Pause.*) Garbo are you angry with me? But this is how it
    is. Why? Why? Tell them if you like. Tell them. (*Pause.*) What's the
    point of hiding anything now? I stand naked before you. Tell them
    everything. (*Silence. Shouts.*) I'm a flop in her bed these days. D'you
    know that? Flop, flop, utter flop. (*Pause.*) You know it now. Now
    let me have it. Your scorn. Your ridicule. Oh God.

GARBO: Don't excite yourself Shrimant.

SHRIMANT: You'll never understand it Garbo. It's a terrible thing. You're
    the only one who's never laughed at me. Babi laughed. Shirin
    actually spat. (*Raging.*) There was a time when I could tire these
    girls out night after night and still had more to give.

GARBO: This ... this may be temporary.

SHRIMANT: It's not. The doctor says so. I'm over-drugged. I used to
    take drugs to bring myself on. Injections! Now even they don't
    help. I'm lost. I have so much money. But what's the use?

GARBO: Calm down Shrimant.

SHRIMANT: I don't want this money. Money's at the root of all this. It
    taught me to use my body this way. From the time I was thirteen.
    And now it's too late. This is how I am. I was never fond of reading.
    Or art. Or studies. Or anything. Only things of the flesh. All I had
    was my body. That was the only truth. And there was no other
    alternative but to go on believing in it. And now it's my body that

has let me down. (*Pause.*) I wanted that child. It would have borne my name. People would never have known about me then.

(*Pause.*)

PANSY (*maliciously*): Flop. Then why were you running after me?

GARBO: Pansy!

SHRIMANT: Pansy, you are the only one who can give me back my body. Women are no use to me now. (*Pause.*) And he has nothing but contempt for me ...

PANSY: Garbo, he was trying to buy me. With watches, clothes, art school, records, discotheques ... things I would never have set eyes on otherwise;

GARBO: Do you want to go home?

PANSY: Eh?

SHRIMANT: No.

GARBO: Do you want to go home?

PANSY: I'll come to your place.

GARBO: Just tell me if you'd like to go home.

PANSY: But my parents won't have me now.

GARBO: They will. I'll tell them.

PANSY: Huh! They'll never listen to you. I'll stay in your flat. I'll only be a burden on them if I go home.

GARBO: So what?

PANSY: I'd rather not.

GARBO: You should go home.

PANSY (*irritated*): But I don't want to.

INTUC: You see? You'll never be able to leave this place now. You've been living in a colony of lepers. Without your knowledge, the bacteria have already made a home for themselves in your system. (*Pause.*) And this is our victory. We'll spread this disease everywhere. Pansy is our first victim.

(*Silence.*)

GARBO: I know something dreadful has happened that shouldn't have happened. But must you let it affect your minds like this? Suppose this boy does something awful to himself one of these days?

PANSY (*like a spoilt child*): I'll kill myself. (*Silence.*) Garbo, if he hadn't come to the station unexpectedly like that, I'd really have committed suicide that day. (*Pause.*) I don't like my parents one bit. Out of all my brothers and sisters, I was the one they disliked. I was the middle one. That's why. (*Pause.*) Well, not really disliked but ... (*Pause.*) I just don't love them. I love only you, Garbo. Truly! (*Pause. Annoyed at her silence.*) Do you think my running away upset them in any way? Do you think they bothered to make any enquiries about my whereabouts after I'd gone? Not even an ad in the papers. (*Pause.*) I saw the railway line gleaming in the sun, and I thought I'd like to kill myself. I've no one of my own. Shrimant has been making a nuisance of himself, and *you,* you are nice to me only when it pleases you. (*Pause.*) It was you who first said you'd take me to your flat Garbo.

(*Tries to hold her hands. She lets him, and stares fixedly at him for some time.*)

GARBO: Intuc, the disease has gone deeper in him than you think. (*Pause. Sighs.*) I am responsible for it also. It's all so terrifying. (*Pause.*) Initially I played around with him just for fun. Then it became a habit. An entertaining game. (*Pause.*) But he attached different meanings to everything. (*To Intuc.*) Do you know the kind of places he has followed me to in broad daylight? He became addicted, and I was responsible. He'd throw tantrums, cry, rage, threaten me into giving myself to him. I gave in each time, because I was either fed up, or annoyed, or in the mood for a lark. I should have hardened my heart at least once. (*Pause.*) Pansy, you're still too young.

PANSY: I love you.

GARBO: He came to me first because he was alone, without mother or father. Then all that remained was the body.

PANSY: We'll live together Garbo. You'll have a baby again. Yours and mine.

GARBO: The rot has eaten into him to the core. (*Pause.*) There's one more thing I must tell you. There's no possibility now of my conceiving again. (*Intuc begins to laugh uncontrollably.*) Intuc, don't laugh.

INTUC: What do you want me to do then? I'm full of admiration for this entire plot. (*Laughs.*) So Garbo, you are one of us now, incapable of creating anything. Now you fit beautifully into our world.

PANSY: You too ... You too ...

INTUC: Flop? No. The body still functions. Because it exists. Because it has to function. (*Picks up a book.*) Take this, Garbo.

GARBO: When did it come out?

INTUC: Fifteen days ago. Read the dedication. 'To the Creative Force.' That's you. Humbug. Look at the jacket. That's humbug too. And the poems inside.

GARBO: They are good poems Intuc.

INTUC: Do you remember I once read you my new poems?

GARBO: Oh yes!

INTUC: How fresh and untainted they seemed then.

GARBO: Those days were like that too.

INTUC: Like white flowers gently falling to the ground at the beginning of the rains .... Tender, fragrant, delicate, ready to wilt at the merest touch.

GARBO: It was the month of Shravan, remember?

INTUC: It had been drizzling all morning. I was reading while you stared through the windowpane at the rain outside.

GARBO: The poems drizzled through my mind like the rain.

INTUC: And mine.

GARBO: Even after you stopped I remained entranced. Remember? I only recovered my senses when you laid your head down on the table with fatigue.

INTUC: And you ran your fingers through my hair. (*Pause.*) You never did that to me again.

GARBO: How much we walked after that.

INTUC: Getting drenched.

GARBO: We had decided to get drenched. And the cups of tea we had in roadside cafes. And the way we splashed the water as we walked.

INTUC: The whole day. And when we got home exhausted at night, we were both shivering with cold.

GARBO: Hot black coffee then. And bread. Nothing more. Remember?

INTUC: We drank all the coffee sitting wrapped up in a single blanket. And you kept running your fingers through my hair, again and again.

GARBO: You were clinging to me like a child. You kept rubbing your head against me.

INTUC: Then you gave me all you had, like a flower that blooms joyously, scattering its abundant fragrance.

GARBO: I was so moved. (*Pause.*) Why did your eyes keep filling with tears?

INTUC: I felt so complete and fulfilled. Full to the brim. My mind dripped gently like rain-drops sliding off tree-leaves after a shower.

GARBO (*lost, inaudible*): I could understand it then. I could understand it.

INTUC: That is why you could hold me so close to yourself. I felt as if I was lying in the embrace of the sky.

(*Pause.*)

GARBO: Where are those days now?

INTUC: Lost forever.

GARBO: Are they?

INTUC: Destroyed by us.

GARBO: Is it all over then?

INTUC: All over. Killed. We've grown older. Our appetites have grown dull. Our palette jaded. Our minds hard. If we come together now, we callously ignore the ugly coarseness of our bodies and chew the cud of sexual pleasure.

GARBO: Don't say that.

INTUC: It's the truth.

GARBO: If you stubbornly insist on saying so, then it becomes the truth.

INTUC: Why deceive yourself? (*Pause.*) You'll never be happy with these people Garbo.

GARBO: I will not be happy with anybody now. It's too late for all that. Too late for happiness. For love. That is never to be. The mind has grown too calculating. If ever I feel a momentary tenderness for anybody, the mind rears its head and hisses, 'Are you in your senses? You are playing with fire. You know what suffering will follow. And what will you gain in return for all the suffering and the risk? Anything of value?' And so on and on. Is there anything to be gained out of such exaggerated cautiousness? Making a million subtractions to get something. I can't cope with this any more. I'm a low woman of no importance. Why do you burden me with impossible significance? It is not fair.

INTUC: Why are you telling me all this? We haven't committed any crime that we should gloss it over with sweet words. Garbo, these poems are all phony, and you know it. And nothing's going to stop me from saying so openly. Today is the day for confessions.

GARBO: Even when all the critics are ...

INTUC: There she is—Garbo the liar. How blatantly you can lie once an uneasy truth has been lost from your womb. Do you remember what you said when I once read you some of these poem? You said, 'Have you written yourself out?' I had picked on the wrong listener. Why did you have to tell me something I already knew? I was looking for false assurances, and they had to come from you. (*Pause.*) But the truth is not that I was finished, but that I had never started. (*Pause.*) I have not, in my whole life, written a single genuine line. I know it. The day you asked me that question, I decided never to write again.

GARBO: But you had written before that. If you decided to stop writing, please don't hold me responsible for it.

INTUC: I don't. I wrote because people wanted to read. They still read, but now I am overcome by disgust. How can they stomach such lies? They discuss and argue and write reviews which are equally false. That's why I stopped writing. I have nothing to sell or buy in this market of thieves.

GARBO: All this is fine if you can afford to stick by your decision. I can't. If I did, I'd starve to death. The only way for me is to continue facing the cameras again and again with phony postures and gestures. (*Pause.*) I sometimes feel I should have got married. (*Pause.*) I have no hopes left of ever doing a really challenging role. I've grown dry like bark of dead wood, waiting for a role or love to come my way. It is too late. Too, too late. Never again will I put forth tender green leaves. (*Pause.*) Do you remember the first time we met? We talked for hours. It was wonderful. But the wonder of it soon faded and all we were left with was our bodies. There are times when I feel a deep-down restlessness. This is what my life has been. And now I'm growing old and I'm left with nothing. Inch by inch I have lost ground without gaining anything.

INTUC: You should get married Garbo.

GARBO: Who will marry me now? Men who danced around me two years ago are now at the most willing to have me as a keep. The proposition has actually been made to me. (*Laughs.*) I must give it serious thought. Maybe two years from now they won't even want me this way. (*Laughs.*) Perhaps Pansy will marry me.

PANSY: I'll do anything for you. I'll stay by you for ever.

GARBO: Lovely. Charming idea. It's all very well your slobbering over me now. But it won't last long, when you grow a little older, you'll ditch me and leave, and I'll remain alone, an old hag.

(*Suppresses a sudden sob.*)

SHRIMANT: Garbo, you'll never be alone. We'll always be with you.

GARBO: Can you do anything to stop getting on?

PANSY: Garbo, do you think I'm such a cad that ...

(*Pause.*)

GARBO: You know that director chap I was talking about? I lied about
   him. (*Pause.*) He's just a kid, but he's nobody's fool. He's the first
   man who's spat contemptuously at me. He preferred an unknown
   starlet to me. Shrimant, Pansy, Intuc, don't you understand? Your
   Garbo is now even less desirable than an ordinary starlet. Your
   Garbo is nothing but an illusion you have built for yourselves.

INTUC: If it is an illusion, we wish to keep it intact, else it will be difficult
   to live.

SHRIMANT: Why live?

INTUC: Because we don't have the guts to kill ourselves. What will
   happen to us when we give up our bodies? Would you be able to
   commit suicide?

SHRIMANT: Intuc, do me a favour. Kill me.

PANSY: You're already dead.

GARBO: How cruel he's become.

INTUC: And he will grow worse as youth advances. And then suddenly
   one day he'll realize with a shock that he too has started slithering
   through mud. Nobody escapes ultimate disillusionment.

GARBO: Why do you need delusions? Don't you wish you could throw
   them all off and breathe freely?

INTUC: I used to think that way myself. But that's not the way. We need
   these chains to hold us. We don't feel free with their falling off. Just
   lonely. As our illusions fade one by one, our loneliness increases.

GARBO: So we end up with our body. There's no illusion there.

SHRIMANT: Kill me. Kill me.

INTUC: Is this how life has always been? For thousands of years people have been born, and have been dying. Like worms. Bodies beget bodies which wriggle and squirm for awhile, turn rigid, and die. I'm sick, sick of the whole thing. (*Pause.*) Even art becomes an illusory thing. What art can worms create? (*Pause.*) Nothing genuine seems to grow out of me. If something does come up, it is stunted, diseased. Instead of growing, its leaves drop off. What can I write? It is not just leaves dropping. It is the root that is rotten. (*Pause. With a laugh.*) There was a time when I pranced about like a Moharram tiger proclaiming myself to be an artist. It was a sad delusion. When I think of it now, I feel terribly ashamed. Thank God I've stopped writing. It's the only courageous act I have ever shown myself capable of.

GARBO: And the thought of it is enough to keep you going.

(*Intuc suddenly bursts into uncontrollable laughter.*)

What's the matter Intuc? Stop it. Stop it for God's sake.

(*Intuc controls himself with great difficulty.*)

I can't even bear to hear anybody laugh these days.

INTUC: You've started talking like a top-notch actress.

GARBO: And what about all the words you've been pouring out all this time?

INTUC: The words of a fake writer. Garbo, we are fakes. All of us. We are false all the way through. Oh ancestors in heaven, look down upon your false hybrid, castrated progeny who deluded themselves into thinking they were capable of producing something great. But here it will end—all self-deception. Garbo, I stopped writing because my poems were being rejected. I was clever enough to know when to stop, and I earned credit for it. Is this courage? (*Laughs.*) But the other chap, the one who dared reject my poems, he certainly had guts. He found somebody else. (*Pause.*) Have you ever seen a Moharram tiger at dusk? The editor who sent my poems back must have said, 'Oh you Moharram tiger, I've found some others like you, but freshly painted. Your paint is old. It's peeling now, and your black skin is beginning to show through. Why don't you quietly mingle with the crowd before it notices what is happening? That way you'll be safe, and we'll be safe.' Throw away that book Garbo. It is worthless. There's not a single honest line in it.

GARBO: You'll write. One day you'll write.

INTUC: No I won't. I'm not capable of writing honestly, because I've never lived honestly. I'm not strong enough for that. Every time the Principal looks displeased, I start shivering thinking I'm going to lose my job. I can't afford to buy books. So I borrow them from the library and forget to return them. Compromises and ignominious surrender all the way. Greed and temptation. And thefts and swindling. What right do I have to spit on the rest of the world or to talk of rebellion? A rebel's strength lies in his uncompromising adherence to his own principles. Garbo, at least I am able to confess to all this ugliness because of you. That's a cause for celebration. Let's go to bed. Let debilitated worms make lifeless love. If the body is the only truth, then let's stick to it and make life beautiful.

SHRIMANT: Intuc.

INTUC: Come Garbo, come ...

SHRIMANT: No. Not in my house.

INTUC: Garbo.

SHRIMANT: No. Never again will anybody find sexual happiness here.

INTUC: This is hardly happiness. More like penance.

SHRIMANT: Not in my house.

PANSY: Flop!

SHRIMANT: This is my house. My wishes are the law here.

PANSY: Flop! Flop! Flop!

(*Shrimant lunges at Pansy and catches him. Pansy struggles out of his grasp. Confused and furious, he hides behind Garbo.*)

SHRIMANT: Move, Garbo. I'm going to kill him.

(*Garbo moves away.*)

PANSY (*terrified*): Garbo!

GARBO: Let me go.

PANSY: He'll kill me.

GARBO: Leave me.

INTUC: Ha, ha, ha, Pansy. Do you understand now? Even you are alone.

SHRIMANT: Get out all of you. You have no right to torture me like this.

GARBO: Shrimant.

SHRIMANT: Don't call out to me like that, Garbo.

GARBO: Oh God. I feel so guilty. As if I am responsible for everything.

INTUC: But you are. Because you're a woman. Let's go to bed. Now that
you have grown barren, that is all you are good for anyway. Come.

GARBO: No.

PANSY: Garbo. Come away from here. I'll go with you. You'll conceive
again.

GARBO (*brutally*): No I won't.

INTUC: She said so once. Hurry, hurry, hurry. Come and see, a barren
woman in a world of eunuchs. Come Garbo.

SHRIMANT: Not in my house. I'll kill every one of you.

PANSY: He's jealous.

GARBO: I wish you'd all kill me instead. I can't stand this any more.
What can I do for you? Shrimant ...

(*Pause.*)

SHRIMANT: Come and live with me. I'll marry you. People won't guess
about me then. Garbo? (*Garbo is silent.*) You'll never get a better
offer than this. (*Pause. Shouting.*) You want to have them all I
suppose, all of them. (*Pause. Gently.*) This is the only chance
I have.

(*Pause.*)

GARBO (*trembling*): Shrimant ...

SHRIMANT: You find me repulsive. I know ...

GARBO: That's not true, but ...

SHRIMANT: I remember, so don't act. You saw my failing those two or three times and I instantly became repulsive to you. (*Pause. Raging.*) Have I not given you enough pleasure before this? How can you refuse me one more chance? I will take it by force. I want to see what happens. Come on.

GARBO: Intuc.

INTUC: Sorry.

GARBO: Shrimant, spare me. I feel terrified by all this.

SHRIMANT: I was going to look after your child..

GARBO (*angrily*): Not out of compassion. Only as a cover for your lost manhood.

SHRIMANT: But you were all the same calmly going to palm it off on me weren't you? A whore. That's what you are. A whore. How are you concerned with what I am? I'll fling a few paise at you and make you dance naked for me. Come on in ...

GARBO: Intuc.

INTUC: Don't call me.

GARBO: You're a coward.

INTUC: I know it.

GARBO: I'm glad that baby of mine was never born. I'm going.

PANSY: I'll go with you.

INTUC: Garbo, please don't go. We need you.

GARBO: You're asking for too much.

PANSY: Come, Let's go.

GARBO: No.

PANSY (*angry*): You're the same, aren't you? You moved away when Shrimant came to kill me a while ago.

SHRIMANT: Pansy, don't put your trust in her. She's a coward too. And she doesn't love you either.

GARBO: That's right. I don't love anyone.

PANSY: Let's get out of here.

GARBO: That's impossible. Pansy, I will have nothing to do with you from now.

SHRIMANT: Listen to her.

GARBO: Don't come to my place, I'll throw you out.

PANSY: I'll commit suicide.

GARBO: Do it.

PANSY: You've deceived me. You've deceived me.

GARBO: This is nothing. I've deceived you in a much bigger way. You deserve it. (*Pause.*) Listen carefully. There was no accident. I meant to kill my baby. (*Pause.*) Do you understand? I killed that baby.

(*Pause.*)

INTUC: Garbo!

GARBO: Now what have you got to say?

INTUC: That's not true.

GARBO: It is. The director was willing to use a dummy for the race sequence. But I insisted doing it myself.

INTUC (*muttering*): Why? But why?

GARBO: I wanted to punish him. He didn't come to my tent. I went to his one night, because I wanted a role in his next film. He sniggered. He laughed at me. (*Pause.*) I couldn't bear it. He'd been like that from the beginning, taking every opportunity to insult me. And when I went to win him over, do you know what he said? He pointed at the camels and said, 'Go to them. That's what you want.' (*Pause.*) I didn't even have a second heroine's role. I was playing the ageing elder sister. I had about three scene to do. (*Pause.*) When I did the camel scene my entire body was being churned up, and I kept praying, let it happen, oh God let it happen. And it did. When I felt the warm blood streaming down, I screamed. Now let me see. Just let me see his miserable face.

(*Pause.*) When I came to, there was nobody but a huge, coarse woman near me. I asked her where the director was. She said, he's shooting. They've found somebody to replace you.

INTUC: Garbo, this is not true. Say it isn't. Please.

GARBO: Every word of it is true. I felt then that I'd done wrong. I didn't know how to face the three of you. But ... now I've seen you for what you are. I'm glad it died. It has had a lucky escape.

INTUC: Escape? (*Pause.*) Yes, you're right. Even you are false. A coward. I'm glad it died. Make one worm less in this world. Dead before it was born. (*Pause.*) Garbo, go away. You have cheated me. You are dead to me.

GARBO: You deceived yourself. You should never have expected so much out of me. I'm an ordinary woman of flesh and blood. You burdened me with all sorts of imaginary virtues. I carried on for as long as I could. But I couldn't keep up the pretence forever. That doesn't mean I have done any wrong. And anyway, who are you to make demands on me?

INTUC: Get out.

PANSY: I'll go with you.

GARBO: No.

PANSY: Garbo ...

GARBO: I'll call for the police, Pansy.

PANSY (*enraged*): Whore ... whore ... whore ...

(*Garbo suddenly sits down sobbing.*)

INTUC: Who is crying? Garbo? She never cries. (*Pause.*) Stop it. Stop your crying. Your tears have no value now.

GARBO: Please don't be like that. I have nobody.

INTUC: She's beginning to sicken me. So abject!

SHRIMANT: Garbo, come to me, come. I'll kick them out of here.

PANSY: Me? Me?

SHRIMANT: You too. She will have nothing to do with you from now
   on. Garbo? Garbo? Stay with me. Come Garbo.

(*Garbo begins to leave, stumbling.*)

PANSY: She's cheating us. Kill her. Kill her.

(*As Garbo blindly struggles towards the door, Shrimant plunges a knife
into her. She collapses.*)

SHRIMANT: Pansy, Pansy. I have killed her.

PANSY: Killed ...

SHRIMANT: Killed her. Will you stay with me now? You'll stay won't you?

PANSY: Intuc.

INTUC: Garbo's gone. Murdered. Or did she die first and was
   murdered later?

PANSY: Is she dead? Is this blood? So much of it.

INTUC: Blood. The blood is real ... Garbo was false.

PANSY (*hoarsely*): Help!

SHRIMANT: Pansy, don't shout. Stay with me.

PANSY (*going to the window*): Help! Help! (*Silence.*) Nobody's coming.
   What now? What now?

CURTAIN

Desire in the Rocks

Vasanakand

Translated by
Shanta Gokhale

Characters:

Hemakant

Lalita

Five women

Scene One

A rambling old mansion. Pitch-black night. Enter Hemakant and Lalita. Hemakant carries a torch.

HEMAKANT: Here we are.

LALITA: Yes.

HEMAKANT: Yes.

LALITA: Here?

HEMAKANT: Right here.

LALITA: Is this our house? Ours?

HEMAKANT: Mansion.

LALITA: Mansion?

HEMAKANT: It's not a house. Mansion. Call it 'mansion'.

LALITA: Yes.

HEMAKANT: Just look at those beams. Teak. And pillars. Look at the carving on those pillars.

LALITA: It's dark here.

HEMAKANT: So what? Just feel it. It's as though the darkness has blossomed into flowers. Feel the carving. Rich. Pedigreed. Proud.

LALITA: It's dark here.

HEMAKANT: Are you afraid?

LALITA: Hem.

HEMAKANT: Come here.

LALITA: Hem!

HEMAKANT: Come to me Lalita.

LALITA: Hem! (*Pause.*) Are we going to live here now?

HEMAKANT: Yes.

LALITA: In this dark?

HEMAKANT: You decide.

LALITA: No, no.

HEMAKANT: Lali?

LALITA: You decide. Yes, you decide.

HEMAKANT: I won't do anything against your will.

LALITA: My will? Where's the question of my will?

HEMAKANT: No?

LALITA: No.

HEMAKANT: Then?

LALITA: You decide. (*Pause.*) You planned everything.

HEMAKANT: So I'm to blame.

LALITA: No. Not that. But after meeting you, I've no will of my own left. (*Pause.*)

HEMAKANT: You're just scared for no reason at all.

LALITA: I've come with you.

HEMAKANT: It's night. And dark. That's why you're scared.

LALITA: Hem!

HEMAKANT: Don't be afraid, Lali.

LALITA: Take care of me.

HEMAKANT: Haven't you come because you trust me?

LALITA: Yes.

HEMAKANT: Come here. Come close to me.

LALITA: Hemakant!

HEMAKANT: We've come very far. Broken away from the whole world.

LALITA: Will we never go back from here?

HEMAKANT: Go back?

LALITA: You decide.

HEMAKANT: I don't want to go. We won't ever go away from here. At least I don't want to. This place had been calling me for so long. I owe something to this place. To these rocks. I belong to this place now. To its rocks.

LALITA: How many rocks there are! What huge stones!

HEMAKANT: It's a village of rocks. An invitation to a sculptor. His dream space.

(*Pause.*)

LALITA: You'll be happy here.

HEMAKANT: You?

LALITA: I?

HEMAKANT: Won't you be happy?

LALITA: I? Does my happiness matter?

HEMAKANT: I want you to be happy

LALITA: I will be. (*Pause.*) Aren't there any people in this village?

HEMAKANT: Why?

LALITA: Didn't see any.

HEMAKANT: It's night.

LALITA: And why are there no trees here? Not one. Just burnt, stunted scrub.

HEMAKANT: There's no water here.

LALITA: How rocky the place is! Such huge stones. Like heavy, frozen shadows. Standing still in their places.

HEMAKANT: I'll carve a tree in each one of them. For you.

LALITA: Hemakant!

HEMAKANT: Lalita!

LALITA: You are my brother. Don't ...

HEMAKANT: What?

LALITA: Nothing.

HEMAKANT: Don't love me so much. Right?

LALITA: I'm not used to love.

HEMAKANT: Am I a stranger?

LALITA: Hem, I hardly remembered you. You were away in Europe for fifteen years. Did you remember me?

HEMAKANT: Yes. I remembered a fair-skinned girl. Five years old. Wearing a pink frock. Watching me from behind the ayah's *pallu*.

LALITA: But I remember one thing clearly. I was afraid of you even then.

HEMAKANT: Are you still afraid of me?

(*Pause.*)

LALITA: No.

HEMAKANT: You are.

LALITA: No.

HEMAKANT: Yes you are. You let the truth out. Look here.

LALITA: Don't.

HEMAKANT: Look here. Look. Tell me. What's to be scared of in me?

LALITA: Hemakant.

HEMAKANT: Tell me.

LALITA: Don't look at me like that.

HEMAKANT: Rubbish!

LALITA: You're older than me. By fifteen years. That's why I feel scared. I've spent all these twenty years of my life just being scared.

HEMAKANT: Were you were afraid of Dadasaheb?

LALITA: Petrified. After he died, I thought I was free of fear. But then the trustees and the solicitors came. I was afraid of them. I couldn't understand what they were saying. Then you came, Hem. And I felt really free.

HEMAKANT: Then why are you afraid of me? Say you won't be.

LALITA: I'll try.

HEMAKANT: Why should you have to try? I love you.

LALITA: That's what I'm afraid of.

HEMAKANT: Lali, that's because you have lived all alone.

LALITA: Alone? Yes. So alone. So terribly alone! From the time I was a small child. There were servants in the house, flunkeys, visitors. But I was always terribly alone. 'Missibaba, change your frock.' 'Missibba drink your milk.' 'Missibaba, time to go riding.' 'Missibaba, the master was asking for you.' That was it. That was all the contact I had with people. Dadasaheb would walk into the room on the stroke of seven: 'Have you studied? Did you bow before your mother's photograph? Good. Goodnight.' That was it. Over. After that, for a long while I could hear only the squeak of his slippers as he walked away, passing from room to room. I was completely alone, Hem. Terribly alone. I'd lie on my bed thinking. How huge this portrait of our mother is! Was she ever alive? Suppose she stepped out of the photograph now? All night the eyes in that photograph would stare at me. And smile that same frozen smile. I was terrified. But also attracted. Hem, Hem, why did you go away from home? Leaving me to endure it all by myself?

HEMAKANT: But I'm back now, aren't I?

LALITA: When I heard you were coming back, I didn't know what to do. I was scared, but excited.

HEMAKANT: Did you remember me?

LALITA: No.

HEMAKANT: I don't suppose Dadasaheb even mentioned my name.

LALITA: No. Even the servants were forbidden to. Your rooms were locked. I'd only seen an old photograph of yours. An ayah had shown it to me secretly. It was of you as a boy. The ayah lost her job.

HEMAKANT: Why?

LALITA: Dadasaheb heard about it.

(*Pause.*)

HEMAKANT: That's why I didn't come back while he was alive.

LALITA: Hem!

HEMAKANT: Hmm?

LALITA: Are you upset with me?

HEMAKANT: For what?

LALITA: Dadasaheb has left everything to me.

HEMAKANT: So?

LALITA: And I can't do a thing. Without permission from the trustees.

HEMAKANT: What do you think? That I care for those two-bit diamonds
and rubies? Or those villas in every village?

LALITA: I feel guilty.

HEMAKANT: Lali, you don't know me. For fifteen years I wandered
through alien lands. Starving. Driven by a single obsession—
Art. I fought against the bitter cold with nothing but rags on my
back. Not once did I think of the comforts of this place.

LALITA: Did he throw you out of the house? Dadasaheb?

HEMAKANT: I left of my own free will. He would throw a fit every time
he saw me with a chisel and hammer. Such things didn't go well
with our blue blood. One day he came at me with a whip. I caught
his hand mid-air and said, 'I'm twenty. And I'm leaving home.
For good.' So I left. With just whatever I had on.

LALITA: Are you very angry with him?

HEMAKANT: No. There was no way he could have understood my
obsession. (*Pause.*) Nor anybody else. (*Pause.*) Lali, nobody can
understand the passion that stones inspire in my hands. Nobody.
That's why it doesn't upset me. My world is different from yours.
It's a world that is mine alone.

LALITA: Yours alone?

HEMAKANT: Yes.

LALITA: Don't you feel lonesome?

HEMAKANT: Lonesome?

LALITA: Lonely?

HEMAKANT: I'm willing to pay that price. I will pay any price to realize my dreams. Always.

LALITA: Your dreams?

HEMAKANT: Yes.

LALITA: What are they?

HEMAKANT: They are embedded in these stones. Waiting for the touch of my hands. My dreams flower in stones, my queen.

LALITA: Hem!

HEMAKANT: Lali.

LALITA: Don't call me your queen. (*Pause.*) Or Lali. Lalita—my name is Lalita.

HEMAKANT: I love you. That's why, my queen, and Lali. And Lal. Lalan. Lalya.

LALITA: Don't.

HEMAKANT: I will. Else I'll stop talking. Completely. Forever. I'll go away from here. Would you like that?

LALITA: Why do you like to quarrel?

HEMAKANT: I'll go away. Would you like that?

LALITA: Did I say that?

HEMAKANT: You don't like anything I do. Or say.

LALITA: I didn't say that either.

HEMAKANT: Then let me call you queen. And Lali. Or whatever else I want to. I love you. Come to me.

(*Pause.*)

LALITA: Why?

HEMAKANT: I'm going to carve you in stone.

LALITA: Me?

HEMAKANT: Yes.

LALITA: Why?

HEMAKANT: Because you are ravishing. And because I love you.

LALITA: Don't.

HEMAKANT: Why not?

LALITA: Don't.

HEMAKANT: But why not?

LALITA (*faintly*): Don't carve me in stone.

HEMAKANT: What?

LALITA: I'll be imprisoned in them forever.

HEMAKANT: You'll become immortal. My hands will carve you in these rocks. And my hands too will become immortal with you.

LALITA: Please don't.

HEMAKANT: You're a coward.

LALITA: No Hem.

HEMAKANT: Of course you are. You're afraid of everything. Of houses, people, the dark. (*Pause.*) Of experience.

LALITA: I feel really afraid of this mansion.

HEMAKANT: Wait, I'll blow out this torch too.

LALITA: Please don't tease me.

HEMAKANT: I'm serious.

LALITA: Don't. (*Pause.*) Hem, don't imprison me in your sculptures.

HEMAKANT: Why?

LALITA: It would be a sin.

HEMAKANT: Sin?

LALITA: Yes.

HEMAKANT: How?

LALITA: Your eyes will see all of me. Your hands will mould me. My soul will be naked before you. That can't happen. I feel it's a sin.

HEMAKANT: Coward!

LALITA: How often are you going to call me coward?

HEMAKANT: For as long as you don't show the courage to live life.

LALITA: Where can I find it?

HEMAKANT: I'll give it to you. Will you take it?

LALITA: Yes. I need it badly. Really badly. (*Murmurs.*) Really. (*Pause.*) How will you give me courage? How will I take it?

HEMAKANT: You know how.

LALITA: No.

HEMAKANT: Yes.

LALITA: No truly I don't. I'm a silly girl.

HEMAKANT: You do know. You don't want to admit it.

LALITA: No.

HEMAKANT: Then why do you constantly avoid my eyes?

LALITA: I don't.

HEMAKANT: Look at me. Look ... no. You won't. Because you desperately want to.

LALITA: I'm looking. See. I'm looking at you.

HEMAKANT: Keep looking like this. Keep looking. Let me see.

LALITA: Yes I will.

(*Immediately averts her glance.*)

HEMAKANT: You are afraid, my queen.

LALITA: No.

HEMAKANT: Yes.

LALITA: No.

HEMAKANT: Yes. You need support. Lali, you don't love me.

LALITA: I do.

HEMAKANT: Then come to me. Close. I want to put my hand on your head.

LALITA: Put it. I'm not afraid.

HEMAKANT: Good girl. A sweet and good girl. Beautiful hair. How beautiful! Like a cascade of black silk. I will bring it alive for a second time. In my sculptures.

LALITA: Hem?

HEMAKANT: Hmm?

LALITA: Why did you choose this village?

HEMAKANT: Don't you like it?

LALITA: Tell me why you chose it.

HEMAKANT: It's our village. This is our land. (*Pause.*) Rather, your land. You are the mistress of this place.

LALITA: What kind of land is this? No water anywhere. No trees. Even the houses are like stone tombs. Like mysterious threats looming on either side of the road.

HEMAKANT: The whole region is rocky.

LALITA: How come this mansion alone is made of wood?

HEMAKANT: Because timber is rare. It's the arrogant pride of our wealthy ancestors.

LALITA: How far we have travelled to get here! Across a plain that seemed endless. And then through this jungle of stones.

HEMAKANT: Do you know something? People were buried alive under this mansion.

LALITA (*startled*): Hem!

HEMAKANT: Scared?

LALITA: You say such terrible things.

HEMAKANT: But true. The mansion wouldn't stand. Kept collapsing. Fires would start. Someone said, offer up a human sacrifice. A beggar woman and her child were buried under here. The mansion stayed up.

LALITA: Enough.

HEMAKANT: Why are you afraid? It happened two hundred years ago. Generations have lived here since.

LALITA: Were they happy living here?

HEMAKANT: No. Every single person had to adopt an heir.

LALITA: Couldn't they bear any children at all?

HEMAKANT: Of course they did. They say that the curse of the beggar woman was on them. Some children were still born. Others died at birth.

LALITA: Hem.

HEMAKANT: Lali.

LALITA: Hem, let's go back.

HEMAKANT (*taunting*): Coward.

LALITA: Yes. But let's go back.

HEMAKANT: You don't believe in such idiotic tales do you?

LALITA: I don't know. But wasn't that why Dadasaheb didn't stay here? Nor Mother?

HEMAKANT: Dadasaheb was the first man to leave this place. He went out for his education. Never returned. (*Pause. Teasingly.*) That's why we lived. Otherwise we too would have been still-born wouldn't we? (*A sob escapes Lalita.*) Dear, dear Lali. Braveheart Lali. I thought you weren't scared. Look up. Look up. Come on look up. No crying. No crying at all. Otherwise I'll go away.

LALITA (*shouting*): Don't threaten me all the time with going away. (*Pleading.*) Where can I go alone if you go? You know I have no one except you.

HEMAKANT: No one?

LALITA: And this is where you've brought me. I'm so terribly frightened, Hem!

HEMAKANT: Am I not yours?

LALITA: I've said so once. Please hold my hand tight.

HEMAKANT: Yes Lali.

LALITA: Hold it tight. Tighter. My heart's pounding.

HEMAKANT: Lali, Lali.

LALITA: Don't look at me like that. I'll die of fear.

HEMAKANT: What are you afraid of?

LALITA: No. I don't really know.

HEMAKANT: Why should you be afraid when I'm with you? Look at me. Am I afraid? Just lean on me with all your weight Lali.

LALITA: Will you always be with me?

HEMAKANT: Yes.

LALITA: Every moment?

HEMAKANT: Yes.

LALITA: You won't leave me?

HEMAKANT: No

LALITA: Truly?

HEMAKANT: Yes Lali.

LALITA: Because I'll have no one if you leave me. (*Pause.*) Don't leave me. (*He laughs.*) Why do you laugh? (*He laughs again.*) Don't laugh like that. It's terrifying.

HEMAKANT: Come. Let me show you around the mansion.

LALITA: No.

HEMAKANT: Why not?

LALITA: No.

HEMAKANT: But why not?

LALITA: No. Not just yet.

HEMAKANT: Because it's dark?

LALITA: No. Not that.

HEMAKANT: Because I'm going to eat you up? Or do you think you'll see ghosts?

LALITA: No.

HEMAKANT: You might too.

LALITA: Hem!

HEMAKANT: I'm sure you will. There's been a lot of sinning around here. Every soul in this place has remained unfulfilled. We'll hear breathing in every room if we go around. Deep sighs, screams, laughter, the tinkle of bangles. (*Lalita screams.*) What's wrong?

LALITA: Hem!

HEMAKANT: What's the matter Lali?

LALITA (*eyes lowered, pointing upwards*): Up there! Look up.

HEMAKANT: What's there?

LALITA: What's that Hem? Up there?

HEMAKANT (*laughs out loud*): Idiot! It's only a chandelier!

LALITA: Hem ...

HEMAKANT: It's wrapped in red cloth.

LALITA: I thought ...

HEMAKANT: What?

LALITA: It looks dreadful ...

HEMAKANT: Like a skinned animal strung up, right?

LALITA: Let's go back, Hem.

HEMAKANT: Back where?

LALITA: Anywhere away from here.

HEMAKANT: No.

LALITA: Hem ...

LALITA: No.

(*Drums being beaten, in the distance. Faint at first, then gradually growing distinct.*)

LALITA: I'll do anything for you. Honestly. Anything at all. Let's go away, please.

HEMAKANT: No.

LALITA: I'll die

HEMAKANT: You won't.

LALITA: Yes, Hem, I will.

HEMAKANT: While I'm here? (*Lalita sobs.*) There's one way out, Lali.

LALITA: What?

(*The sound of the drums draws closer.*)

HEMAKANT: Will you take it?

LALITA: Hem!

HEMAKANT: Will you do it?

LALITA: I'll die.

HEMAKANT: Look. Look into my eyes. (*Holds her tight.*) Look.

LALITA (*in a swoon*): Hem!

HEMAKANT: You want to look up. Why do you resist it? Look. Look!

(*The pounding of drums draws nearer still.*)

LALITA (*terrified*): What's this noise?

HEMAKANT: Look up, Lalita. Look up.

LALITA: What is it? What?

HEMAKANT: The Goddess.

LALITA: The Goddess? Goddess?

HEMAKANT: Yes. They take her out in procession every new moon and
     full moon night. To judge sin and virtue.

LALITA: Shut those windows, Hem.

HEMAKANT: No.

LALITA: Hem ...

HEMAKANT: No. The windows will remain open.

(*The procession of the Goddess on the road outside. The drums reach a
feverish crescendo. A woman possessed by the goddess sways in a trance.
The villagers in the procession carry torches and throw fistfuls of* gulal *in
the air.*)

LALITA (*paralysed with fear*): Shut it. Shut the window.

HEMAKANT: No.

LALITA (*trembling*): Hem ... Hem ...

HEMAKANT: Then look up once. Look.

LALITA: No.

HEMAKANT: Lali, Lali, don't deny it.

LALITA: No.

HEMAKANT: Look. Look up. You want it. Our eyes locked in our very
first meeting. This spark was lit in that moment. No words were
spoken. Look up. (*The procession stops in the middle of the road.
The woman in a trance sways. The drums strike up. Lali screams.
He holds her close.*) Don't be afraid, my queen. Don't be afraid.
Come. Come close. Very close.

LALITA (*clinging to him*): Hem, Hem!

HEMAKANT: Lali, Lali!

(*She clings to him in desperation. He fixes his lips on her throat. They fall
to the floor in each other's arms. His lips are still on her throat. The drums
pound on. The woman in a trance sways. Lalita and Hemakant freeze.
Lights dim. Darkness. The procession has moved on.*)

Scene Two

Lights come up. The two are still in the same position, in the same place. Many days have passed.

HEMAKANT (*moving away*): Get up, Lali.

LALITA: Hmm?

HEMAKANT: Get up.

LALITA: No, please ...

HEMAKANT: Up.

LALITA: So soon?

HEMAKANT: Yes.

LALITA: Is it morning?

HEMAKANT: I'm off.

LALITA: Hem!

HEMAKANT: Hmm?

LALITA (*raising her arms*): Help me up!

HEMAKANT: What?

LALITA: Please help me up.

HEMAKANT: Unhunh.

LALITA: Don't be like that.

HEMAKANT: That's enough. I'm off to work.

LALITA: Please help me.

HEMAKANT: Lali, enough of this madness.

LALITA: Is this madness?

HEMAKANT: Get up.

LALITA: I want to be mad.

HEMAKANT: Carry on.

LALITA: Look, Hem. I've raised both my arms. Now help me up. (*Pause.*) You're cruel. Stubborn. Self-centred. Selfish. (*Laughs out, seductively.*) How sweet you are! Cruel and sweet. (*He is about to leave.*) Hem, what will you take to smile a little? Don't go without smiling. Kiss me. Soothe this excruciating pain. Then leave.

HEMAKANT: Lali.

LALITA: I will not get up otherwise.

HEMAKANT: Stay put then.

LALITA: Watch me.

HEMAKANT: I am.

(*Goes closer.*)

LALITA: Now why have you come to me?

HEMAKANT: You want me to watch you. I'm watching.

LALITA: Go away.

HEMAKANT: What did you think? I came to help you up?

LALITA: You wouldn't. I know it. When I say something, you have to do the exact opposite. It makes you happy. Hey, get off.

HEMAKANT: Open your lips.

LALITA: No.

HEMAKANT: Open them.

LALITA: No.

HEMAKANT: Lali!

LALITA: Unhunh.

HEMAKANT: Lale, I'll eat you up.

LALITA: Go ahead.

HEMAKANT: Lal, Lal!

LALITA: Hem!

HEMAKANT: Close your eyes.

LALITA: No. Let me look at you. Into your eyes.

HEMAKANT: Aren't you afraid?

LALITA: Afraid?

HEMAKANT: Hunh. Like you used to be before?

LALITA (*laughs*): Afraid? I've forgotten the word.

HEMAKANT: So then? Open your lips, Lali.

LALITA: No.

HEMAKANT: Are you going to be stubborn?

LALITA: Aren't you?

HEMAKANT: Watch out. I'll scare you.

LALITA: Oh! Really? Scare me. Go on, scare me. I'll wind myself around you tight like death itself, before I fall.

HEMAKANT: You will surely take my life some day.

LALITA: No no. I will be the breath of your life.

HEMAKANT: What are you looking at?

LALITA: Hem, I want to enter your eyes. Deep into them. I'll become a tiny drop of blood and travel through your body. Through your heart, brain, mind, soul. I'll talk to all your secrets. Discover all your dreams. Then I'll turn into a tiny pupil and live in your eyes. Will you let me?

(*He stares at her for a moment.*)

HEMAKANT: Get up.

LALITA: What's this?

HEMAKANT: What?

LALITA: I'm saying such lovely things and you break me off like this.

HEMAKANT: Lovely?

LALITA: Hem, lift me up. Won't you do just this one thing to please me?

HEMAKANT: Open your lips first.

LALITA: Lift me up first.

HEMAKANT: Lips.

LALITA: No.

HEMAKANT (*moves away*): Fine.

LALITA (*laughs out*): You're suffering, aren't you? Good. Suffer. It amuses me.

HEMAKANT: Hmm?

LALITA (*gets up, stretches*): I'm up. By myself.

HEMAKANT: Wait, Lal. Hold it.

LALITA: What?

HEMAKANT: Stop. Don't move.

LALITA: Why?

HEMAKANT: Wait, my queen. You look bewitching!
(*Begins to sketch rapidly.*)

LALITA: I look bewitching? Like this?

HEMAKANT: Shut up.

LALITA: And if I move?

HEMAKANT: I'll kill you.

LALITA: Really?

HEMAKANT: Don't talk.

LALITA: You've sketched me all over that book. (*Pause.*) And sculpted me into those rocks outside the village.

HEMAKANT: Keep quiet.

LALITA: I say to those sculptures: 'Hello Lali, how are you. How do you feel out here in the sun?' (*Pause.*) Why did you make the sculptures outside the village where it's deserted? Who will come to see them there?

HEMAKANT: The whole world will come. Are stones things to be kept in houses to destroy their beauty? They must stand in the open air. On hills. Plains. I'm going to create a whole forest of sculptures, Lali.

LALITA: A forest of Lalis. See? How many images I've given you! Of me. And look at you. You won't do one tiny thing to please me. (*He completes the sketch. She moves.*) Done?

HEMAKANT: Hunh.

LALITA: Show.

HEMAKANT: What for?

LALITA: Well, it's my picture.

HEMAKANT: It's not yours.

LALITA: Not mine?

HEMAKANT: Unhunh.

LALITA: Then whose is it?

HEMAKANT: It's a picture of heavy, languorous, voluptuous youth. This moment and this mood will now be frozen in stone.

LALITA: But she's still Lali.

HEMAKANT: She has no name. You're merely the excuse.

LALITA: How distant you become as soon as you've got what you want. I'm the excuse. And suppose I hadn't existed?

HEMAKANT: Never mind.

LALITA: Tell me. Go on. What if I hadn't existed?

HEMAKANT: There'd have been someone else.

LALITA: Hem!

HEMAKANT: Don't quarrel now.

LALITA: Take those words back. What do you mean someone else?

HEMAKANT: I'm going.

LALITA: Yes of course. Your stones must be waiting for you. Stones are closer to you than Lali who's alive. Don't go.

HEMAKANT: Why don't you come with me?

LALITA: No.

HEMAKANT: Come. Stay there.

LALITA: I go mad there. With just the sound of your hammer and chisel. You forget me completely when you're working.

HEMAKANT: But I'm sculpting you, my queen.

LALITA: Without a thought for me? Or do you think I'm also lifeless, like the stones?

HEMAKANT: The stones are not lifeless.

LALITA: And I am?

HEMAKANT (*laughs teasingly*): Yes.

LALITA (*flaring up*): Yes? Yes? Say that again!

HEMAKANT: Yes.

LALITA: All right. Then I won't come anywhere near you now. You won't even see me.

HEMAKANT: I'll come to you.

LALITA: I won't let you come near me.

HEMAKANT: You will.

LALITA: No.

HEMAKANT (*aggressively*): Yes.

LALITA: Don't. Don't you come near me. (*Laughs.*) Brute. You know I'm weak. And so full of yearning. Hem, even if you don't come to me, I will. I'll follow you wherever you go. Like a shadow. (*Pause.*) Hem, how am I?

HEMAKANT: How are you?

LALITA: Tell me.

HEMAKANT: What am I supposed to say?

LALITA: Tell me how I am. Am I beautiful?

HEMAKANT: Hunh.

LALITA: Sweet?

HEMAKANT: Hunh.

LALITA: Tempting? Seductive?

HEMAKANT: Hunh.

LALITA: Hunh, hunh. Where are you lost? Tell me nicely.

HEMAKANT: You're mad.

LALITA: But you like me still.

HEMAKANT: Hunh.

LALITA: Hold me close.

HEMAKANT: Come here

LALITA: Unhunh. Feel the agony first.

HEMAKANT: Lali ...

LALITA: Shall I open my lips?

HEMAKANT: Lalan ...

LALITA (*holding out her foot*): There. Kiss my big toe. (*He kisses.*) Now the other toes. (*He kisses them too.*) The foot. (*He does. She laughs out.*) Slave! Slave! You're my slave. What shall I do? What can I do for you? I want to be your slave. Here. Kiss my hands. Thumb. (*He does.*) Fingers. (*He does.*) The palm. (*He does.*) Hands (*He does.*) I'm going to faint. My breath can't take the weight of so much bliss. (*He pulls her roughly to himself.*) Oh! Hem!

HEMAKANT: Lal!

LALITA: You've scattered live coals in my body. Quench them with your lips.

HEMAKANT: Wait. Stay as you are. You look like a self-willed palash tree flaming with red blossoms. This mood. One more mood. I'll catch it in my sculpture. You're trembling. How you tremble. This trembling will tremble again in my stones. Lali, you are beautiful.

LALITA: Say it again.

HEMAKANT: You are beautiful.

LALITA: Again.

HEMAKANT: You are beautiful.

LALITA: Again ... again. I'll give you anything to hear this over and over again. Hem, take me. Take me in my entirety. Take me in every place, at every moment. Here. In the house. In the open. Under crashing rain. With stabs of lightning burning our bodies. In the raging sun. On the hard, black ground cracking with the heat. Under dense trees dripping starlight. In mute, profound darkness. In thick forests. On the banks of streams. On enormous boulders. Among the tall, swaying grass. In old, deserted edifices. In ruined temples. On luxurious beds. Open plains. In all places. Take me in all places. Because I am yours. And you are mine.

HEMAKANT: Yes. In all places. At all times. I will take you in all your moods. I will store them up in every drop of my blood. And bring them alive again in stone upon stone. Lali of the brimming, vulnerable eyes. Lali tossing from side to side with the exquisite pain of fulfilment. Lali of the full, inviting lips, Lali of the breasts heaving with emotion, Lali of the navel as deep as desire. Lali of the long, long thighs trembling with irresistible lust. I'm going to embed it all in stone—the physical manifestations of pure desire. Primeval. Elemental. The eternal beauty and vitality of woman. The heady light of passion that surges and overflows through every pore of your body, will fill and flow out of every pore of my sculptures. The desire that palpitates in your every sinew will be seen breathing in my sculptures. This indestructible, eternal passion can be embedded only in another indestructible, eternal thing, Lali. In my sculptures. In art.

LALITA: Yes, yes, yes, Hem.

HEMAKANT: Lali, you will go, but you will be immortal. Your passion will be immortal.

LALITA: And?

HEMAKANT: And what?

LALITA: Just that?

HEMAKANT: What else Lali?

LALITA: And what about the call of the sea that roars through my body in the moment of union? And the soothing melody of the flute that resonates in my blood? And the myriad tiny silver bells that ring in unison? What about all those things? Will they not become immortal? Will you not build them into your sculptures?

(*Pause. He is staring fixedly at her.*)

HEMAKANT: What are you saying?

LALITA: Have you not understood?

HEMAKANT: What are you talking about, Lalita?

LALITA: You don't know? Don't you feel any of these things?

HEMAKANT: What things?

LALITA: The things I feel. Don't you feel them when you come down on my body?

(*Pause.*)

HEMAKANT: No.

LALITA: No?

HEMAKANT: No.

LALITA: Hem!

HEMAKANT: I smell the heady scent of your hair. I feel the exciting saltiness of the sweat off your face on my lips. I feel I'm burning as I sink deep into a red-hot fire. And then comes darkness. It envelops everything. Quiet, exhausted. A void.

LALITA: How different! What a difference!

HEMAKANT: What's different?

LALITA: Just this—between what you feel and what I feel.

HEMAKANT: What's wrong with that?

LALITA: That's why ...

HEMAKANT: That's why what, Lali?

LALITA (*murmurs*): That's why.

HEMAKANT: What, Lali?

LALITA: That's why you become a sudden stranger. Distant.

HEMAKANT: I'm always near you.

LALITA: You are. And you aren't. Now I understand. I've tried so often to hear the call of the waves in your body. I still do. And the flute. And the bells. I have never heard these sounds. I call out to them, but receive no reply. Why, Hem? Can you not hear the resonance of my mind?

HEMAKANT: Mind?

LALITA: Yes.

HEMAKANT: Where does the mind come into this?

LALITA: Doesn't it?

HEMAKANT: What?

LALITA: Doesn't it come in?

HEMAKANT: No. And if it does, it shouldn't.

LALITA: Why?

HEMAKANT: This experience is purely physical. It must be experienced in its purity.

LALITA: But the mind ...

HEMAKANT: Don't involve that in this.

LALITA: If it does? What then, Hem?

HEMAKANT: It'll corrupt the purity of the physical experience, Lali. Let the mind watch. Be vigilant. Aloof. So that you can live the experience. Fresh and full.

LALITA: I'll never be able to plan my life like that.

HEMAKANT: Do I not give you happiness?

LALITA: Of course you do.

HEMAKANT: Satisfaction?

LALITA: You do.

HEMAKANT: My body?

LALITA: It is beautiful.

HEMAKANT: Do you like it?

LALITA: I like it.

HEMAKANT: Do you yearn for it?

LALITA: I do. And how!

HEMAKANT: You find it attractive?

LALITA: I do, I do.

HEMAKANT: Irresistible?

LALITA: Yes, yes! Irresistible.

HEMAKANT: Then why do you ask meaningless questions, my queen? The body is the only truth.

LALITA: Yes. Yes. And how beautiful it is! How wondrous!

HEMAKANT: Yes, Lali. Beautiful and wondrous.

LALITA: You showed me. You told me. Can the human body be so beautiful? Filled with so much insane joy? I can offer up my life for this joy. (*The procession of the goddess appears outside the mansion, as in the first scene.*) The Goddess ...

HEMAKANT: Are you afraid?

LALITA: Me?

HEMAKANT: Hmm?

LALITA (*laughs*): Afraid? Me? Of whom? What?

HEMAKANT: Shall I shut the windows?

LALITA: Why? Why should you do that?

HEMAKANT: The Goddess is out there. And people.

LALITA: What Goddess? What people? And what sin am I guilty of? Let her see. Let the Goddess also see. She cannot have ever seen such a wild celebration of physical pleasure. Take me. Take me. Hold me close. I shall become one with you to the beat of these drums. Look. Look into my eyes before they close with happiness. Do you see fear? Doubt? Terror? You will see chandeliers of desire blazing there. Extinguish them one by one. With your lips. Hands. Body. Let only the burning torch remain. To prevent accusations. As witness to the uninhibited bliss of man and woman. A symbol of my eternally burning desire. Come to me. Come. Come.

(*They freeze as they did at the end of the first scene. The possessed woman sways in a trance. The drums boom. The light fades slowly. Darkness.*)

Scene Three

A veritable forest of Lalita's sculptures outside the village. Hemakant is working on a new piece. Lalita sits on the ground, staring fixedly at him.

LALITA: Hem!

(*Pause.*)

HEMAKANT: Hmm?

LALITA: Hem!

HEMAKANT: Hmm?

LALITA: HemHemHemHem!

HEMAKANT: Lali.

LALITA (*sighing*): I feel good. It makes me feel good to say your name again and again. The ache that rises in my heart with every beat becomes bearable when I say your name. I love you so much, so very much, that it chokes me. I feel faint. Hem! Hemakant! Hemchandra! Hemant! Hem! (*Pause.*) I know you will not answer me now. You're fed up. Irritated. Aren't you? But I'll keep calling you. Without stopping. Hem. Hem. Hem. What a lovely name. And how handsome the owner of the name! (*Pause.*) You look like a god. Hard. Aloof. Remote. And beautiful. My prayer doesn't reach your ears at all. I am a silly, simple, abject devotee. I am your slave. Oh Lord, my Lord. When you descend from there, I will spread my hair under your feet. Trample over me.

The seal of your authority has been stamped on every drop of my blood. My body is yours, my heart is yours, my will is yours. I am nothing but a pile of dried leaves without you; a mere sapless plant trailing on the ground. One glance from your eyes and I sprout tender green leaves. You blow life into my body with just your voice, your glance, your touch. (*Pause.*) Hem? Are you bored? Why don't you talk to me?

HEMAKANT: You talk.

LALITA: You think I say foolish things, don't you? Mad, childish. Isn't that so?

HEMAKANT: Carry on.

LALITA: How harshly you speak. It makes my heart bleed.

HEMAKANT: Then don't talk.

LALITA: And do what?

HEMAKANT: Look around. Sit quietly.

LALITA: Where can I look? I can't look at anything except you. How abject you've made me.

HEMAKANT: Have the accusations begun?

LALITA: No, please, no. That's not what I meant. Please don't be angry. But why are you so distant? So very far? My mind searches for you through the whole of space but you slip away. Why do you go so far away when you work with your chisel?

HEMAKANT: I concentrate.

LALITA: Can you concentrate forgetting me?

HEMAKANT (*pointedly*): Who are you?

LALITA: Hem! (*He laughs.*) Don't laugh so hurtfully. I can't bear to hear you laugh like that. (*Pause.*) Hem, what are you thinking about now?

HEMAKANT: What could it be?

LALITA: What is it?

HEMAKANT: Nothing at all.

LALITA: You must be thinking about something.

HEMAKANT: Nothing.

LALITA: How can that be?

HEMAKANT: I said nothing, didn't I?

LALITA: You're lying.

HEMAKANT: Fine.

LALITA: What do you mean fine? Tell me, what were you thinking about? (*Pause.*) Tell me. Tell.

(*Pause.*)

HEMAKANT: My mind was empty.

LALITA: Lies. Lies. All lies. You don't want to tell me. You were thinking about someone else.

HEMAKANT: No.

LALITA: Yes.

HEMAKANT: No.

LALITA: Yes. And you want to hide it from me. Isn't that right? Isn't it?

HEMAKANT: Fine.

LALITA: You accept that too? I accuse you of things and you don't even get angry? Tell me what you were thinking about.

HEMAKANT: I've told you once.

LALITA: That's a lie. You are saying it to make me suffer. You must have been thinking of something very ordinary. But you won't tell me because you want me to suffer. Isn't it?

HEMAKANT: Yes.

LALITA: So what were you thinking about?

HEMAKANT: That it's getting hot.

LALITA: Just that?

HEMAKANT: Yes.

LALITA: Truly?

HEMAKANT: Yes.

LALITA: Then why didn't you say so earlier?

HEMAKANT: I've told you now.

LALITA: But why not before? And you've just cooked this up. Right? You weren't thinking about it then. You are saying so now just to satisfy me.

HEMAKANT (*stopping his work for the first time*): Lali!!

LALITA: Don't shout.

HEMAKANT: Nothing satisfies you.

LALITA: Because you're deceiving me. You are being false to me.

HEMAKANT: Fine. So?

LALITA: You can't do that to me. You will not be like that with me. I must know. I must know everything. Everything that goes on in your mind. Every thought. Every feeling. I must know them all. I have a right over them.

HEMAKANT: Lalita.

LALITA: And how can your mind be empty? Why am I not there? Why are thoughts of me not there? Why are memories of me not there? Tell me. Tell me, you brute!

HEMAKANT: Tell me just once. Who are you?

LALITA: I'll claw your face.

HEMAKANT: Stop Lali. Just stop a little. This is too much. Just too much. There's a limit to my patience. Don't try to dominate me. You would like me to be your slave. Someone who will bow to you every moment ...

LALITA: I have given you my all ...

HEMAKANT: And you are making me pay full price for it. You want to swallow my soul itself. You want to pluck my life and wear it in your hair. You don't want me to draw breath without your permission. I must accept being imprisoned within your sight. Everything must happen under your watch. Every move must be made with your permission. You must understand the meaning of everything I do. If I look at the sky, why did I look? If I pluck a flower, why did I do that? For whom? For myself? Sure? If I wake up before you why did I do that? If I fall asleep before you, why? How could it happen? If I keep quiet, you're angry. If I talk, tell you my memories, you suddenly flare up. A simple mention of people you've not known, will not know, whom I will never meet again, makes you fly into a jealous rage. Because you have no place there. You insist that every part of my life where you don't exist, your name doesn't exist, your shadow doesn't exist, must be excised out of my life as well. It's ego! An arrogant ego! You are an egotistical, self-centred, jealous, petty woman! Don't you try to control me, Lali. You will find it difficult. Let me be free. (*Lalita begins to weep.*) Don't cry. (*Scolding.*) Don't cry Lali. (*He begins to come down. She spreads her hair out in his way.*) Idiot. (*Going around her*). I don't like this kind of idiocy. (*She hugs his foot. Puts her head on it. He frees himself.*) What's all this? Get up. Get up. (*Scolding.*) Get up. I said, get up. (*Moves away roughly.*)

LALITA: Don't please.

HEMAKANT: Don't what? Carrying on as if you have no spine! Don't become abject like a destitute dog.

LALITA: Don't you like it?

HEMAKANT: No.

LALITA: Because you feel guilty. You think you've brought me to this state.

HEMAKANT: If it makes you happy to think so, go ahead.

LALITA: Doesn't it make you sad?

HEMAKANT: No.

LALITA: But why? Why?

HEMAKANT: You are responsible for this yourself.

LALITA: I am responsible? True. It is true that I love you and you don't love me.

HEMAKANT: Is it my fault that you don't know where to stop?

LALITA: Can one choose to stop?

HEMAKANT: You must decide that. Don't involve me in this. And don't harass me.

LALITA: I don't harass you. I harass myself.

HEMAKANT: Stop doing it.

LALITA: It's not in my hands. (*He moves away.*) Hem, don't go. Don't leave me alone and go away. Without you I collapse on the ground, nothing but a ball of flesh. Merging with the soil. Wait here. Wait. I swear I won't trouble you. Won't harass you. You'll see. I won't even ask you stupid questions. I was wrong. I made a mistake. Forgive me.

HEMAKANT: Now don't go on about this forgiveness nonsense.

LALITA: Honestly I was wrong. I shouldn't have clawed at you till you bled. Won't you sit here? Please sit. Sit. If you sit beside me, I will take it that you've forgiven me. Otherwise I will suffer agonies. (*He sits down just to end her nagging. Pause.*) I feel terribly guilty.

HEMAKANT: Why?

LALITA: I've made you sit here against your will.

HEMAKANT (*looking at her with pity*): Not necessarily.

LALITA: Hem, you can go. Go alone if you want to. I'm not saying this in anger, my love! I don't want to be fetters round your legs.

HEMAKANT (*looking at her fixedly*): Lali ...

LALITA: Hmm?

HEMAKANT: Why do you suffer so much?

LALITA: Hem ...

HEMAKANT: You're an idiot.

LALITA (*with a sob*): Hem ...

HEMAKANT: Lali.

(*Puts his hand on her head.*)

LALITA: I am so grateful to you.

HEMAKANT: Don't cry.

LALITA: Yes I am grateful because you put your hand on my head. I needed this badly. Very very badly.

HEMAKANT: Come.

LALITA: Hem?

HEMAKANT: Come.

LALITA: Do you mean it?

HEMAKANT: What?

LALITA: You asked me to come.

HEMAKANT: I always say it Lali.

LALITA (*excited*): Yes, Hem, yes. You do say it. (*He takes her in his arms. She is trembling, incredibly exhausted. A few moments later—*) I want death.

HEMAKANT: Are you so sad?

LALITA: No. Happy. At this moment I'm completely happy. That's why ... that's why I want death. This minute ...

HEMAKANT: You are mad.

LALITA: What if we simply freeze as we are, where we are now? If we turn into stone?

HEMAKANT: Rot!

LALITA: Hem, hold me closer. (*He holds her close.*) Put your lips on my hair. Now on my forehead. Eyes. Chin. Lips. (*A long sigh.*) I really want death—I'm exhausted. I want to sleep. (*Long silence. She is in his arms.*) Hem!

HEMAKANT: Hmm?

LALITA: Hem!

HEMAKANT: Hmm?

LALITA: Hem?

HEMAKANT: Hmm.

LALITA: I'm very happy.

HEMAKANT: Hunh.

LALITA: Are you?

HEMAKANT: Hunh.

LALITA: Honestly?

HEMAKANT: Yes.

LALITA: Don't be angry.

HEMAKANT: Sleep.

LALITA: Hem?

HEMAKANT: Yes?

LALITA: Will you do one thing for me?

HEMAKANT: What?

LALITA: Tell me if you will.

HEMAKANT: What?

LALITA: Just say once, 'I love you'. (*He laughs.*) Please say it. 'I love you.' (*He laughs.*) Don't laugh. Say it. Please. Say it just once. (*He continues laughing. Lalita interjects angrily.*) Why are you laughing?

HEMAKANT: Have you started off again?

LALITA: Yes, but say it. Be false. Say it even if you don't feel it. I want to hear those words in your voice.

HEMAKANT: Right. I love you.

LALITA: No. Not like that.

HEMAKANT: I said it.

LALITA: No. Properly.

HEMAKANT: Don't torture me.

LALITA: But why are you so afraid of those words? Say them. I'll cling to them even if I know they are not true.

HEMAKANT: How should I say them?

LALITA: Not dryly, without feeling.

HEMAKANT: Okay, with feeling. (*Pause.*) I love (*Bursting into laughter.*) you.

LALITA: Bastard.

(*He moves away.*)

HEMAKANT: Enough. Come on. Upsydaisy.

LALITA: Bastard. You're a petty, ungenerous man.

HEMAKANT: Fine.

LALITA: Swine, brute, a selfish monster with no heart.

HEMAKANT: Fine.

LALITA: Calls himself an artist. There's not a single sign of the artist in you.

HEMAKANT: Fine.

LALITA: You're a leech. That's what. A leech that lives off sucking other people's blood.

HEMAKANT: Anything else?

LALITA: How dare you behave like this? I gave you my all without thinking twice. How dare you spit on it! You'll have to pay for it one day. You will have to pay the full price for this one day. My rage won't go waste. My curse is on you.

HEMAKANT (*splits his sides laughing*): Curse? Curse? Curse? (*Still laughing.*) The curse of the Goddess herself. Woe is me! What will happen to me now?

LALITA: Don't laugh. Don't hide your inadequacy under laughter. Artist indeed! Artist my foot! You aren't even human. Your body is filled sawdust. And a heart as lifeless as those stones of yours. Spends the entire day chipping at stones. You don't even have the skill of a mason in your hands. You're a mere stone-breaker.

HEMAKANT: Okay Lali. That's enough. More than enough.

LALITA: Why? Because I'm speaking the truth?

HEMAKANT: What do you know about it?

LALITA: What do I not know?

HEMAKANT: You're only good for that love stuff. Don't get into art and creation. It's beyond you.

LALITA: Why are you raising your voice?

HEMAKANT: Then don't talk like an idiot.

LALITA: You're scared of my knowing. I may be younger to you in age. But bigger in mind and heart. That's why you raise your voice. You're secretly jealous of me. Who are you anyway? What do you have? You're an impoverished man. You don't have a drop of feeling. You're like a rocky plain. Not a drop of rain stays on you. It all washes off on all four sides. What right do you have to talk about art? And creation?

HEMAKANT: Lali!!

LALITA: Don't shout. Truth is bitter, isn't it?

HEMAKANT (*shouting*): Shut up.

LALITA: I wasn't going to take these poisonous arrows out of their quiver. I was going to bear their pain alone. But I can't. It has become unbearable. What do you think? That only you can laugh at others? I could also laugh mockingly. And I will too. Dear me! These are supposed to be sculptures. Pure expressions of primeval, vulgar passion. All these—these revolting statues are works of art? Open your eyes and take a look.

HEMAKANT: They are yours.

LALITA: Not mine. Where am I in them? Where is Lali in them? They are all statues of shameless sluts, sitting in obscene postures. Lali is not a slut like them. Lali, who gives all of herself, is not like this—revolting, obscene.

HEMAKANT: Are you through? How much more important do you want to feel? However much it is, you'll never understand the agony of creation Lali. Nor the ecstasy.

LALITA: Why not? Why will I not understand?

HEMAKANT: You have to be born an artist for that.

LALITA: You have to be born a true human being. I am true. My blood is true. It's alive. Its impulses are true. They're alive. What can I not understand? Do I not merit even this much, having travelled through fire, burning everything behind me? Why are you deceiving yourself? You know it yourself. That is why you sit staring at your work for hours in despair. Creation is not such an easy thing.

HEMAKANT: You? Telling me that?

LALITA: Yes, I am.

HEMAKANT: And who are you anyway?

LALITA:There is something greater than your statues and creation.

HEMAKANT: Create something and show me.

LALITA: What?

HEMAKANT: A sculpture. A poem. A song. A painting.

LALITA: That's all?

HEMAKANT: Show me.

LALITA: Is that all?

HEMAKANT: It's not easy. You have to stake a lifetime of obsession. Turning your back on all other calls.

LALITA: Is that all? I am going to have a baby.

HEMAKANT: Oh great!

LALITA: Don't mock.

HEMAKANT: All women bear children. Not everybody is an artist.

LALITA: Then all women are greater than artists, Hem.

HEMAKANT (*gloomy*): Don't call me.

LALITA: This child is yours as well.

HEMAKANT: So?

LALITA: Aren't you happy? Proud?

HEMAKANT: No.

LALITA: You aren't?

HEMAKANT: Not a drop of blood stirs in me.

LALITA: It will happen when you see him. (*Tender.*) I need you very badly at this time. Really badly.

(*Pause.*)

HEMAKANT: You've trapped me.

LALITA: Why do you say that?

HEMAKANT: Are you happy because you're going to have a baby? Or because it's a way to put me in fetters?

LALITA: A mark of your vitality is growing in my womb, my darling. You will be immortal. This child will make you immortal. Not these sculptures.

HEMAKANT: Don't come back again and again to my sculptures.

LALITA: It's a big happening. Something for which one should be willing to pay any price.

HEMAKANT: You pay it then.

LALITA: I will, happily.

HEMAKANT: Let me be free.

LALITA: What does that mean?

HEMAKANT: Leave me alone.

LALITA: Shall I go away from here?

HEMAKANT: Yes.

LALITA: Where?

HEMAKANT: Wherever. You have houses in so many cities.

LALITA: You?

HEMAKANT: I'll stay on here.

(*Pause.*)

LALITA: You detest my sight. You're jealous of me.

HEMAKANT: Go.

LALITA: No. I will not leave you. I will be very worried for you.

HEMAKANT: Go Lali. I will lose myself in this forest of stones.

LALITA: My child needs you. (*Pause.*) And you him. (*Pause.*) What's come over you all of a sudden? Why has your face gone pale? Hem, tell me. Please tell me. I hurt you didn't I? Everything I said back then was lies. It was cruel. I don't understand anything.

(*Hemakant walks away.*) Where are you going? We need to hold on to each other now.

HEMAKANT: Let me go.

LALITA: Hem ... let me come with you.

HEMAKANT: No Lali.

(*He leaves.*)

LALITA: Hem, Hem ...

(*The sound of women singing in the distance. Lalita turns in that direction. Gradually, the words of the song become more distinct.*)

FIRST WOMAN: In the first month ...
> The mother-to-be looks golden
> The baby grows, a dark-skinned god
> Sleep my baby sleep.

SECOND WOMAN: In the second month ...
> There is silver on her green blouse
> The mother and father are happy
> Sleep my baby sleep.

THIRD WOMAN: In the third month ...
> Adorn the forehead with red and gold powders
> Enjoy a bounty of bliss
> Sleep my baby sleep

FOURTH WOMAN: In the fourth month ...
> Food and drink grow tasteless
> Fold lime and catechu in ripe betel leaves
> Sleep my baby sleep.

FIFTH WOMAN: In the fifth month ...
> The baby bows to the Goddess
> Pick up your fill of scattered pearls
> Sleep my baby sleep

(*The lights go off. The strains of the song linger on.*)

Scene Four

A temple. A woman with a baby in her arms. The notes of women singing songs drift in from a distance. Enter Lalita.

WOMAN (*smiling*): Come in.

LALITA: Did you say come in?

WOMAN: I did. Please come in. Why don't you sit? Where are you from?

LALITA: Oh, from nearby. And you?

WOMAN: From out that way. Some ten fields away from here.

LALITA: Have you come alone?

WOMAN: No, the others will be here soon. They've gone to the Shiva temple. I stopped back because I was tired.

LALITA: Why have you come?

WOMAN: With an offering to the Goddess.

LALITA: Was it a boon you'd asked for?

WOMAN: Yes. My folks live nearby and they said, this Goddess is compassionate and she answers prayers. I said to her, give me a child. I'll come and lay him at your feet. (*Holding out her baby.*) Want to hold him?

LALITA: May I really?

WOMAN: Why not?

LALITA: How sweet he is!

WOMAN: Yes he is, though I say it. A bit like his father.

LALITA: What have you named him?

WOMAN: I wanted him to be Lal but his father was keen on Gulab. So we've given him both names.

LALITA: Hasn't his father come?

WOMAN: No. Said he didn't want to get mixed up with us womenfolk. You should see how he dotes on the child though. Look at this peepul-leaf quilt. He had it made for him. And these anklets. And a girdle has been ordered at the goldsmith's.

LALITA: What did you get?

WOMAN: A gold chain. And his name is inscribed on the locket.

(*Pause.*)

LALITA: Was it very painful?

WOMAN: The pain is not worth talking about dear. What use is a soil that doesn't yield a crop? Look, he is stirring. Let me take him.

LALITA: Oh, let him be. He is not crying. May I sing to him?

WOMAN: Do. Can you sing?

LALITA: Oh yes. There is a song my ayah used to sing to me.

WOMAN: Was that your servant woman? Do sing.

LALITA (*singing very softly*):
> My baby, he lies in a jewelled bed
> A toy made of pearls hangs above
> This baby to me by the Goddess given
> Now wants to sleep, sleep dear love.
>
> My baby his eyes, they're heavy with sleep
> Heavy with sleep are his eyes
> His cradle is decked with jasmine sweet
> The fragrance comes with each of his sigh.
>
> Oh my baby, my baby is sweeter still
> Than the jasmine that decks the cradle sweet

My baby who came from my tender womb
Is sweeter than jasmine sweet.

Hush my baby, hush now and sleep
Hush now and sleep my dear
How long must I sing, sleep dear sleep
Sleep my sweet rose, while I'm near.

(*Enter five women. They start at the sight of Lalita.*)

FIRST WOMAN: Oh mercy my lord! What have you done!

SECOND WOMAN: Have you no sense at all?

THIRD WOMAN: Take the child back. Are you out of your mind? Given the child into evil hands?

WOMAN: Now evil eyes have fallen on the poor dear, for sure.

FIFTH WOMAN: Lady, go away, please. Don't stand here like a beggar.

FIRST WOMAN: Tear her hair out. She deserves to have her back broken.

SECOND WOMAN: If you want to sin, go sin in your cursed mansion. Don't come to defile this place.

THIRD WOMAN: These filthy rich have no shame.

FOURTH WOMAN: Lady, go away. Go home. Why don't you go away?

FIFTH WOMAN: Look at the child first. God knows what the slut has been up to?

(*Lalita slinks away and watches them without hostility. The light picks out only Lalita and the five women.*)

FIRST WOMAN: Good riddance.

SECOND WOMAN: Let her be, now that she has gone.

THIRD WOMAN: You will make the offering now.

FOURTH WOMAN: Let's resume singing, dears.

(*The five women sing. The stage becomes dark. Lights on Lalita alone. The notes of the song gradually fade. Lalita wanders, lost, returning once more to the jungle of her sculptures.*)

LALITA: Hush-a-bye-baby, rock-a-bye baby. Shall I go back there? They will call me a sinner and a beggar and drive me out. (*Looking at the sculptures.*) Where is your creator? Where is your master? I want to tell him. Sing to me. Give me green to wear. Give me a green sari and a green choli. Speak to me. Please speak to me. How dark it grows in this place. Hem! Hem! Where are you? Where are you? I'm choking with fear? H-E-M! (*She runs in and out of the sculptures in rising panic.*) Am I lost? Am I? (*Terrified.*) I'm lost. Lost. (*A sinister darkness fills the stage.*) Hemakant! Hem! (*Screaming.*) Hem, Hem! I'm lost. Lost.

(*She wanders blindly, calling out in mounting hysteria, her voice torn to shreds with terror. A solitary voice, lonely calls, answered only by their faint, far away echoes. Finally she collapses. Something within her has snapped, and she whimpers.*)

Scene Five

The mansion. Lalita with a baby in her arms. Hemakant stands beside her.

HEMAKANT: Give him to me.

LALITA: No.

HEMAKANT: Bring him here.

LALITA: No please.

HEMAKANT: Let's not waste time.

LALITA: How peaceful he looks. He's sleeping.

HEMAKANT: Lalita.

LALITA: May I sing to him once? Only once. Then you can take him.
    Just once.
        Cradle of emeralds, pearl toys above
        Boon child of mine, sleep my love
        Sleep sits heavy, on your baby lids
        Fragrant flowers make your bed.

HEMAKANT: Lalita.

LALITA: He is asleep.

HEMAKANT: Give him now.

LALITA (*looks at the baby*): Take him carefully.

HEMAKANT: Yes.

LALITA: Lay flowers under him.

HEMAKANT: Yes.

LALITA: And over him, and around him.

Hmekant. Yes,

LALITA: Don't let thorns and stones prick him.

HEMAKANT: Yes.

LALITA: Can I come?

HEMAKANT: No Lalita.

HEMAKANT: He didn't cry once. Nor smile once.

HEMAKANT: Lalita, give him here.

LALITA: Why have I been punished?

HEMAKANT: Give.

LALITA (*giving him the baby*): Take him. My arms are empty now. (*Exit Hemakant.*) Hem, Hem! Have you gone? My baby's gone too. Who will sing to you now? Not me. You didn't want me did you? You didn't want my songs either. I'm a sinner. You went before this sinner's shadow fell on you. (*Hemakant returns alone.*) Hem.

HEMAKANT: All the arrangements have been made.

LALITA: By whom?

HEMAKANT: The man.

LALITA: Didn't you go?

HEMAKANT: No.

LALITA: Hem?

HEMAKANT: I've paid the man.

LALITA: Why didn't you go?

HEMAKANT: How would that have helped?

LALITA: Hem, that man won't do it with care.

HEMAKANT: He will.

LALITA: Who was he?

HEMAKANT: Someone.

LALITA: Was he a good man? Loving? With tender hands?

HEMAKANT: Lali, all the people of this village are up in arms against us. You know that, don't you?

LALITA: So who was he?

HEMAKANT: A beggar.

LALITA: Hem ...

HEMAKANT: Do we have a choice, Lali?

LALITA: You gave my child to a beggar?

HEMAKANT: Even he wasn't ready. He agreed only when I offered him a big sum of money. That too in secret.

LALITA: What a pity! Oh what a pity!

HEMAKANT: Why?

LALITA: Like hushing up a sin ...

HEMAKANT (*flaring up*): It's not a sin.

LALITA: Then why didn't you go yourself?

HEMAKANT: I've told you. Once the baby's dead, what difference does it make who buries him?

(*Pause.*)

LALITA: You are not prepared to admit our sin.

HEMAKANT: This is not a sin. We didn't kill him

LALITA: It all turned out to be true.

HEMAKANT: What?

LALITA: What you told me. Children are born dead in this mansion.

HEMAKANT: It's pure coincidence ...

LALITA: It's the curse of the beggar woman. And of the child.

HEMAKANT: What child?

LALITA: The one that's buried here. These sins ...

HEMAKANT: Sins, sins. Have you sinned?

LALITA: Yes.

HEMAKANT: You held him to your heart. If he had lived you were going to bring him up with love. You were going to sing to him. Would it have been a sin then? Would you have been ashamed?

LALITA: It's like a patch of leukoderma that has spread over the whole body. A few days of shame, but when the whole body is covered, what shame can there be? Sin once. Then it's over. That's not how it is. Sin never ends.

HEMAKANT: You wanted him didn't you?

LALITA: Yes.

HEMAKANT: You loved him didn't you?

LALITA: Yes.

HEMAKANT: Then it is not a sin, Lalita.

LALITA: How not?

HEMAKANT: You were the only one who was going to suffer. Going to endure. The joy too was going to be yours alone. How would it have troubled or harmed anybody else?

LALITA: And so it isn't a sin?

HEMAKANT: It isn't.

LALITA: Then why do I suffer so much pain? Why do I feel such anguish?

HEMAKANT: You felt that even before.

LALITA: Which means I was doing wrong.

HEMAKANT: It's how you are.

LALITA: So why have I been punished?

Hmekant. How?

LALITA: Why did my baby die?

HEMAKANT: Coincidence.

LALITA: Isn't it a punishment for my sin?

HEMAKANT (*lost in his thoughts*): What does sin mean?

LALITA: I don't know.

HEMAKANT: Even I don't know, Lalita.

LALITA: I only know grief, agony, anguish.

HEMAKANT: Lalita ...

LALITA: You? Do you ever feel sad? Do you suffer?

HEMAKANT: Why do you ask?

LALITA: Tell me.

HEMAKANT: Don't ask.

LALITA: What does it all mean then? Why did we come close? What was the invisible attraction? Why did it give us only pain? This is a punishment, Hem. Retribution. If it isn't, then explain these things to me.

HEMAKANT: Coincidence.

LALITA: Why do coincidences occur?

HEMAKANT (*uneasy*): Lalita, your mind isn't at peace.

LALITA: Is yours?

HEMAKANT: Yes.

LALITA: You're hiding it.

HEMAKANT: No. Why do I need to?

LALITA: You are an egoist. And you really believe it is a sin. That's why.

HEMAKANT: No.

LALITA: Yes. You are denying it because you're stubborn.

HEMAKANT: Why are you at such pains to make me admit it?

LALITA: I'm not.

HEMAKANT: Yes. You are trying desperately to make me say I have sinned.

LALITA: No.

HEMAKANT: Yes. You want company.

LALITA: No. There's no company in sin. Ever. (*Pause.*) I never had your company.

HEMAKANT: And you want to push the blame for what happened on me.

LALITA: No, never.

HEMAKANT: Lalita.

LALITA: It's really not like that.

HEMAKANT: Tell me one thing. Will you?

LALITA: Yes.

HEMAKANT: Tell me the truth.

LALITA: Yes.

HEMAKANT (*trying hard to convince himself*): Did I ever force you? (*Pause.*)

LALITA: No.

HEMAKANT: You also wanted me, didn't you? (*Pause.*)

LALITA: Yes.

HEMAKANT: You felt attracted to me even before I spoke of it? (*Pause.*)

LALITA: Yes.

HEMAKANT: Did I drag you here against your will?

LALITA: No.

HEMAKANT: Did I make you happy?

LALITA: Yes.

(*Pause.*)

HEMAKANT: Give physical pleasure?

LALITA: Yes.

HEMAKANT: You wanted it, didn't you?

LALITA: Yes.

HEMAKANT: Then I haven't sinned.

LALITA: You are my brother.

HEMAKANT: So?

LALITA: However weakly, I did resist. Not you. Myself. Why didn't you help me? Instead you crushed all my attempts.

HEMAKANT: So it was all my responsibility?

LALITA: No it wasn't. But it is a sin. We have committed a sin. A terrible sin. The whole village has risen in anger against us.

HEMAKANT: Because we don't live according to their conventions.

LALITA: Why not?

HEMAKANT: Because we live according to our own impulses.

LALITA: And so we suffer.

HEMAKANT: You make such a big deal of suffering.

LALITA: I don't make a big deal of it. I've gone beyond that. I'm merely stating what has happened.

HEMAKANT: Then just accept it. Why discuss it?

(*Pause.*)

LALITA: Doesn't anything get through to you? Are you afraid of words too?

HEMAKANT: Why should one trouble oneself with irrelevant things?

LALITA: It happens automatically. Don't you feel the need to find out why it happened?

HEMAKANT: No.

LALITA: Don't any questions bother you?

HEMAKANT: No.

LALITA: How dryly you allow life to wash over you!

HEMAKANT: Not dryly. I stand apart. I observe life dispassionately.

LALITA: Do you understand life by observing it like that?

(*Commotion outside. Shouts. People drag the beggar away. Some of them stop and pelt stones at the mansion in great fury.*)

LALITA: What's happening?

HEMAKANT: Don't worry.

LALITA: They threw stones.

HEMAKANT: They will harass us for a few days.

LALITA: They want to punish us. The Goddess has commanded them to.

HEMAKANT: Who told you?

LALITA: I know it. The Goddess came to me in a dream.

HEMAKANT: Lalita, don't begin to imagine idiotic things. You'll go insane.

LALITA: I don't mind. I don't. I'd prefer that to these persistent pangs that destroy my mind from within. (*Pause.*) Who was that man, Hem?

HEMAKANT: Which?

LALITA: The one they caught and took away?

(*Pause.*)

HEMAKANT: The beggar.

LALITA: The beggar?

HEMAKANT: Hmm.

LALITA: The one you ...

HEMAKANT: The same.

LALITA: Where has he abandoned my baby? On some dump? (*Slipping down, on her knees.*) My breasts are heavy with milk. It will pour on the ground, in the soil.

HEMAKANT: Please rest, Lalita.

LALITA: No. There will be no rest now. (*Pause.*) And what was the beggar's crime?

HEMAKANT: He helped us.

LALITA: Hem!

HEMAKANT: Hmm?

LALITA: Will you not go to free him?

HEMAKANT: What's the use?

(*Pause.*)

LALITA: I'll go. I'll tell them.

HEMAKANT: Don't. The people are mad with rage.

LALITA: Because we have broken all their conventions. They are not to blame.

HEMAKANT: Not because of that. They are jealous. They feel a secret attraction for you. They hate us for our wealth.

LALITA: We must be punished for our sins, Hem.

HEMAKANT: Sin sin sin. I've had enough of it. Do you hear? We have not sinned. Just remember that. We have not sinned.

(*Pause.*)

LALITA: If I could have simply believed your words!

HEMAKANT: What then?

LALITA: I would have put my head on your shoulders and slept peacefully.

HEMAKANT: Come. (*Lalita shudders.*) Come, Lali. (*She shakes her head.*) Lalita!

LALITA: No.

HEMAKANT: Why not?

LALITA: No.

HEMAKANT: Come to me.

LALITA: No. It makes my flesh creep. I feel revolted.

HEMAKANT: Lali ...

LALITA: Everything inside us is dead. It has smouldered within itself and burned down. To ashes. Ash is all that's left. A heap of ash. Not now. Never again.

HEMAKANT: Lalita!

LALITA: No Hemakant.

HEMAKANT: I need you.

LALITA: What can I do for you?

HEMAKANT: Do you know? They smashed all my sculptures to smithereens in the night.

LALITA: Who?

HEMAKANT: The people. Every sculpture has been broken.

LALITA: What can I do?

HEMAKANT: Why did this happen?

LALITA: How can I give you your answer, Hemakant? You must look for it yourself. Our paths now lie in different directions. (*Starts walking away.*)

HEMAKANT: Where are you going?

LALITA: Somewhere. Outside.

HEMAKANT: Don't go.

LALITA: I cannot bear to be in this mansion.

HEMAKANT: Don't go.

LALITA: I'll come back. Of course I will. (*Pause.*) Where else can I go? (*She goes away. Hemakant goes away too. Lalita wanders all over the place.*) How many days have gone by! How many nights. How many seasons. How many months. I wander ceaselessly. Through valleys. Over rocks and crevasses. I wander like a sad, lost spirit. How alien is the sky overhead. How alien the ground beneath my feet. All eight directions, vast and alien. Why do my eyes grow wet where I stand? And why is my mind like a broken shell— cast off on a desolate beach? In orphaned solitariness like breath cut off from body. How is it that the body doesn't fray and fall off the barren mind? Why does my restless foot not stay in any place? Why can I not bear to lay my head anywhere? Why does the mind not grow dizzy with this aimless wandering? Go. Keep going. You must keep walking, without a break, with no respite. There is nothing now for you, dear friend, except walk. (*Hemakant comes from the other direction in a similar state. They stand, looking at each other like strangers.*)

HEMAKANT: You look like a stranger. So unfamiliar. And yet so known. But the mind will not hold on to anything now. It will not hold tight to familiar signs ...

LALITA: Hem!

HEMAKANT: Hmm?

LALITA: Where are you going? Tired, exhausted?

HEMAKANT: Nowhere.

(*Darkness.*)

Scene Six

The forest of sculptures. Hemakant sits, absorbed. Enter Lalita, dressed gaudily, like a prostitute.

LALITA: Hemakant!

HEMAKANT: Hmm?

LALITA: You are very quiet.

HEMAKANT: Hmm.

LALITA: Why are your tools lying orphaned in the dust?

HEMAKANT: Let them be.

LALITA: How exhausted you look!

HEMAKANT: I am exhausted Lalita.

LALITA: Hemakant ...

HEMAKANT: I see everything clearly. But it is all meaningless now.

LALITA: No. It's not like that. There is so much meaning. So much.

HEMAKANT: What?

LALITA: I can't fathom. But there is meaning. It lies beyond our comprehension. It is much larger than us.

HEMAKANT: The soles of your feet are cracked.

LALITA: Because I wander so much.

HEMAKANT: Your eyes are bloodshot.

LALITA: I don't sleep.

HEMAKANT: Your skin is burnt.

LALITA: And stale.

HEMAKANT: Your appearance ...

LALITA: I've become a prostitute.

HEMAKANT: Lalita!

LALITA: Yes. The Goddess commanded me. In my dreams. This is my retribution.

HEMAKANT: I'm the one who should be punished.

LALITA: How are you involved?

HEMAKANT: I have destroyed you totally.

LALITA: I have done that to myself.

HEMAKANT: You were alone. You had no protection. (*Pause.*) I didn't want any other woman. My heart would have got entangled there. (*Pause.*) And I didn't believe in sin and virtue. (*Pause.*) Also, you used to be afraid of me. (*Pause.*) I was going to use you without getting involved. I thought this was what being aloof meant. This was strength, to look at everything dispassionately. (*Pause.*) Get out of those filthy clothes first.

LALITA: No they will remain on me. They are part of my retribution.

HEMAKANT: Nobody can punish you.

LALITA: I am inflicting this on myself. I have sinned. Mustn't I be judged? I am going to burn myself in this fire of retribution, Hem. I want to be pure again. Hem, I have laid this body under so many bodies. As retribution. Even then my heart won't stop breaking. Why doesn't it stop? Hem, Hem, the retribution for sin is to remain in sin forever. To continue to sin.

(*Pause.*)

HEMAKANT: Lalita ...

LALITA: Yes Hem?

HEMAKANT: Take me in your arms.

LALITA: That is what I've come for. That is why I'm here. I was happy in you. I cannot be absolved of my sin if others enjoy my body. I must hand it over to you now. Even as my mind revolts. Because it does.

HEMAKANT: You are revolted by me?

LALITA: Yes. Terribly. My heart and my body cries out against it in protest. Every line of your body once made my blood surge and grow hot. Those very lines now fill me with pure disgust. That is why. That is why I will give myself to you.

HEMAKANT: I don't want you like this.

LALITA: How can I change now?

HEMAKANT: I needed you so much.

LALITA: Are *you* saying that?

HEMAKANT: Yes.

LALITA: Can you ever need anybody?

HEMAKANT: Lalita!

LALITA: I am curious. Simply curious.

HEMAKANT: You were right, Lali.

LALITA: How?

HEMAKANT: These sculptures ...

LALITA: What about them?

HEMAKANT: They are not true. (*Pause.*) I'm not true either. I'm very false. It came to me suddenly. That night. When the people were smashing them one by one. (*The scene is enacted at the back. Only Hemakant's voice is heard.*) I was watching from afar. The enraged mob was breaking the sculptures limb by limb. Not once did I feel that I should rush in to save them. I was so terrified. I ran for my life. Afraid that they would take my life too. Finally I stopped somewhere. My head cooled down. Then my mind stirred and posed the question: 'Why did you do that?' The answer was easy. I was a coward. I did not myself believe in what I had created. (*The light comes up again.*) Those sculptures are false. False. That is what they are. Ugly. Loathsome. I see that now. Suddenly. I am defeated Lali. (*Pause.*) Why? Why did this happen? (*Pause.*) I wanted to depict pure desire in all its aspects. But what came out was mechanical, hideous, filthy. Totally unconnected with what had been in my mind. Can there be such a difference? Between what the mind sees and the hand does? Why does this happen? (*Pause.*) Yet these naked statues are alive. Their falseness is alive. Their obscenity is alive. They look back at me tauntingly and say: we are yours. Part of your blood, your mind, your life. You cannot deny us. And I don't. There is no place now where I can lay my head.

(*Pause.*)

LALITA: You are fortunate.

HEMAKANT: Lalita ...

LALITA: You at least know that your creation was false.

HEMAKANT: It is painful. I understand now how you must have felt when you gave birth to a dead child.

LALITA (*overcome with emotion*): For the first time. The very first time.

HEMAKANT: What Lalita?

LALITA: You have understood my pain.

HEMAKANT: Why do we suffer so much?

LALITA: That is what I once asked you, Hem.

HEMAKANT: You have found the answer.

LALITA: No. My mind has run helter-skelter but I still haven't found it. We will breathe our last holding this tattered, empty bag to our chests. But I do not fear it now.

HEMAKANT: I do. For the first time.

LALITA: You are involved for the first time. You cannot stay aloof now in this moment of defeat.

(*Pause.*)

HEMAKANT (*fearful*): Am I so weak? Was I playacting all my life when I thought I was unattached?

LALITA: You had erected a wall around yourself in self-defence. You refused to get involved. You were always guarded, aloof to make sure that you didn't suffer a single scratch. You wanted life's warmth without burning your fingers. But life always has its revenge in the end Hem. Its blow has fallen on you all on a sudden. That's why you have collapsed.

HEMAKANT: I wanted to observe everything. Embed it in my sculptures.

LALITA: You only observed the objective reality. You never ever reached the pure light of truth that lay buried under the outer shell of reality. You weren't willing to pay the price of burning yourself up totally in the process of getting there. Like the pain in the heart, there is an aching truth at the centre of every reality. You never laid your lips to it to absorb it. Because you did not wish to pay the price of giving up your life to the agony of that poison. Hem, it doesn't help to deny life. You must accept it first, and then cut the strings. Otherwise it sits on your back forever.

HEMAKANT: Was I false with you?

LALITA: Not with me. With yourself. You struggled to make sculptures of physical desire. But you didn't go to the source from where that desire surges. You did not discover the truth about desire. (*Pause.*) Perhaps you avoided it. (*Pause.*) That truth was here. In Lali's heart. In her mind. Not in her body alone. To reach there you would have had to suffer and endure everything that Lali did. Hemakant! All you did in life was to collect the empty shells of things.

HEMAKANT: Art ...

LALITA: You made your choice without knowing. Between living guardedly or burning to ashes in the search for truth. In the end, what is art, Hem?

(*Pause.*)

HEMAKANT: Would I have found the truth?

LALITA: Who says so? Where have I found the truth? Perhaps nobody finds it at any time. But that doesn't mean we are permitted to deny it. Our ineluctable destiny is to wander in search of it forever.

(*Pause.*)

HEMAKANT (*defeated*): I don't have the strength.

LALITA: And there's nothing I can do for you.

HEMAKANT: Lalita, give me strength. Hold me close.

LALITA: No no, I can't do anything. I stand in the same darkness where you stand. I've been there longer. That is all. Just that.

HEMAKANT: Lalita, Lalita, hold my hands tight. Hold my head close to you.

(*He holds her hands tight. She looks at him with compassion. The villagers come carrying torches. Their faces are vindictive, violent. For a moment they stand still, watching. Then slowly but steadily they come forward to surround Hemakant and Lalita. Lalita goes towards them. Kneels down and bows her head.*)

LALITA: I surrender myself to you.

HEMAKANT: Lalita!

LALITA: I have done wrong. I have sinned.

HEMAKANT: Lalita.

LALITA: Punish me as you will.

HEMAKANT: Lalita, don't leave me and go.

LALITA: Punish me. I have sinned.

HEMAKANT: Lalita, Lalita!

(*As the mob moves forward, Hemakant raises his hammer. He musters all his strength and then drops the hammer on the ground. Silence. Then the people pick up stones, coldly vindictive. Some of them drag Lalita away by the hair. Someone throws the first stone. It draws Hemakant's blood. There's a shower of stones after that. Darkness.*)

Scene Seven

The mansion. Night. Lalita in tatters, her head shaved. A moment later, Hemakant comes crawling in. Battered, blood-soaked, a few breaths away from death.

LALITA: Hem, Hem. You're here at last.

HEMAKANT: Lali!

LALITA: Look at your state. Like a cobra with its hood crushed.

HEMAKANT: Lali!

LALITA: Yes, yes. We have been dreadfully humiliated. We have endured a great deal.

HEMAKANT: Lali!

LALITA: No. Don't grieve Hem. It was not your fault. You weren't aware of what you were doing. But they didn't see that.

HEMAKANT: You ... you ...

LALITA: No. No. I am not angry with you. Nothing angers me. I don't even regret anything. Hem, Hem. We will not feel anger. We will not feel grief. We will forgive life. We will forgive destiny. (*Hemakant grows weak and lays his head on the ground.*) You're tired aren't you? Terribly exhausted? Wait Hem. I'll take your head in my lap. You are suffering terribly aren't you? Feeling sad?

We will put an end to it. An end. Just wait a while. Wait. (*Picks up a torch and sets fire to the whole mansion.*) We'll end it all. Everything. We'll burn down everything. I will hold you close. I will stroke your head. (*She takes his head in her lap, full of compassion.*) Hem ... Hem.

(*The whole mansion bursts into flames.*)

CURTAIN

Old Stone Mansion

Wada Chirebandi

Translated by
Shanta Gokhale

Characters:
Dadi
Aai
Bhaskar
Sudhir
Prabha
Chandu
Vahini
Anjali
Parag
Ranju

Aai: mother; Aaji: grandmother; Dadi: grandmother; Bhavji: brother-in-law, husband's brother; Wance: sister-in-law, husband's sister; Tatyaji, Baba: father; Bhau: elder brother; Vahini: elder sister-in-law; Soonbai: daughter-in-law; Kaka: uncle, father's brother; Kaka, Kaki: aunt, father's brother's wife; Bai: term used to address older women.

Act One

Scene One

The ancient, respectable but dilapidated mansion of the Deshpandes of Dharangaon, a small village, somewhere in Vidarbha. There is a verandah in front, and a bedroom to the left (A). To the right of the verandah is a room (B) which also serves as a drawing room. A middle room beyond the verandah, and a suggestion of more rooms further behind. A number of chairs—old, half broken, assorted—stand on the verandah, and a swing. A very old carpet on the floor. A few bolsters in a sorry state. A carved mahogany bed and a magnificent mirror in room A. There is an antique iron chest in B. Old steel trunks are piled in the middle room behind the verandah. The apron of the stage is the courtyard.

The Time: about ten-thirty at night. A lantern burns in the central room where Aai sits on the floor, resting her chin on her knees, lost in thought. Dead silence. Dadi sits on the verandah, back to the wall. Her voice rips through the silence.

DADI: Vyenkatesh ... *Arrey* Vyenkatesh! Where has he gone *bappa?* ... What time is it? (*Sound of a man's rhythmic snoring.*) Time moves so slowly, the pest.

(*Ranju comes out on the verandah, a lantern and a copy of* Filmfare *in hand. She ignores Dadi, goes past her into the middle room and looks at herself in the mirror. She is totally engrossed in arranging wisps of hair on her forehead. Prabha walks in with her bedding, glances at Ranju, then spreads it beside Aai on the floor. The sound of snoring continues.)*

PRABHA: How much longer will you keep waiting for them? Go, lie down.

AAI: What time is it?

RANJU (*starts reading aloud*): 'Does Hema Malini get midnight calls? Who was recently seen prowling around her spacious bungalow?'

PRABHA: Ranju!

AAI (*to Prabha*): Tell Chandu to take another look at the bus stop dear ...

PRABHA: The last bus must have come and gone, Aai. Why don't you sleep? They'll be here tomorrow. (*Aai gets up and starts walking out.*) Now where are you off to in the dark!

AAI: I left the back door open.

PRABHA: Wait Aai, I'll shut it.

(*Aai sits down. Someone whistles outside. Ranju starts. She is about to get up when Chandu enters. She promptly sits down and starts reading.*)

RANJU: 'Are Zeenie baby's vital statistics changing?'

CHANDU: What's that you're reading, girl?

RANJU: *Filmfare.*

CHANDU: Good way to study!

RANJU: Teacher says, read a lot of English. Then my English will improve.

CHANDU: Clever fellow—your teacher!

(*Sound of snoring.*)

DADI: Is there nobody around bappa? Vyenkatesh ... have you abandoned this poor blind woman? (*Chandu goes to Dadi. Touches her.*) Are you there, son?

(*Chandu calms her down, then goes in. Aai lies down on the bed. Prabha sits by her, reading a book. Ranju continues reading aloud.*)

PRABHA (*to Ranju*): Read to yourself.

(*Silence. Rhythmic snoring. Then suddenly a whistle ... Ranju rushes to the door.*)

PRABHA: What's at the gate?

RANJU: Nothing.

PRABHA: Then get back in, this minute!

RANJU (*grumbling*): That's right. Scold me all the time! All of you!

VAHINI (*passes through the middle room to her bedroom, carrying a lantern*): Gets scolded by everybody, the pest. Go study. Miss Failure!

(*Vahini goes to the bedroom. Puts down the lantern. Looks at the snoring Bhaskar. Starts putting cream on her cracked feet. Enter Ranju.*)

RANJU: Why do you keep calling me Miss Failure?

VAHINI: Ui! Aren't you that? You should study hard, dear.

RANJU: Aai, may I sleep in the locker room today?

VAHINI: No. Kaka-Kaku will sleep there, if they turn up. Sleep near Dadi.

RANJU: Not me. She keeps calling out all night.

VAHINI: Then go sleep in Parag-bhau's room.

RANJU: I'm not going to sleep alone in a man's room!

(*Bhaskar turns on his side. A filigree-work brass box kept under his pillow falls down. Startled, Bhaskar wakes up. The sound has reached Aai and Prabha too. Aai becomes alert.*)

VAHINI: Ui! What's this now?

BHASKAR: Nothing. Go to sleep.

VAHINI: Where did you get this old box from?

BHASKAR: It's some old paan-box of Tatyaji's. Thought I could use it. It was just lying around upstairs.

RANJU: A paan-box under your pillow! Ui Bai!

BHASKAR: Stop blabbering. Go sleep.

(*Exit Ranju.*)

VAHINI: Why are you sleeping on the bed when we are in mourning? I'll have to wash the whole bedding now.

BHASKAR: So? They haven't come, have they? Your darling brother-in-law and sister-in-law?

VAHINI: Chandu-bhauji says the bus got cancelled. Wonder if they're stranded somewhere.

BHASKAR (*sarcastically*): Of course he'll come. Full of love that he is! (*Bhaskar goes towards the pooja room with the box. Vahini is surprised. He passes Aai and Prabha in the middle room. Aai gives him a hard stare. Bhaskar hurries past. Comes back immediately without the box. Aai continues looking at him. He is flustered.*)

BHASKAR: Why don't you sleep? Sudhir won't show up today.

(*Aai is silent. Bhaskar goes back to his room. Vahini looks at him curiously.*)

BHASKAR: Who left the pooja room open? The rats have knocked everything down.

VAHINI: You went in again! Why did you go when we're in mourning? What will Aai say? Really!

(*Bhaskar throws himself down on the bed. Vahini goes through the middle room to the back door and calls.*)

VAHINI: Chandu-bhauji, will you stop fetching in the firewood so late at night! First carry Dadibai to her bed. (*She returns to the middle room. To Aai.*) Do you need anything more?

(*Silence. Vahini goes to her bedroom. Aai gets up and starts going in.*)

PRABHA: Now where are you off to?

AAI: She may have forgotten to shut the kitchen window.

PRABHA: Why do you bother about these things now? (*Before she has finished speaking, Aai has gone.*) Wait, I'm coming. Don't go alone in the dark.

(*Exit Prabha, taking the lantern with her. Vahini lowers the flame of her lantern and lies down. Long silence. A flash of torchlight outside. The sound of a scuffle. A female voice cries, 'My God!' Male voice: 'Careful'. Enter Sudhir and Anjali warily, carrying suitcases. They stop. Sudhir looks at Dadi. Anjali's palav has caught on something. She is trying to hold its torn strips together.*)

SUDHIR: Looks as if they're all asleep. You go in first.

ANJALI: I won't go in first.

SUDHIR: Dadi hasn't even noticed we're here.

ANJALI: Will you go in first and meet Aai please? It's already five days now.

SUDHIR: I just don't have the courage. You go in.

ANJALI: I've told you. This is one time you must go in first.

(*Silence. Both come on to the verandah. Bhaskar comes out. For some time no one speaks.*)

BHASKAR: When did the telegram reach you?

SUDHIR: Day before yesterday. We left immediately.

BHASKAR: Hmm. I was wondering what happened. It was already past ten. I thought perhaps you hadn't got the telegram at all.

SUDHIR: The train reached Amaravati late. The last bus had left by then. We had to take a taxi.

BHASKAR: Tatyaji gave us no time at all. He got up from his evening pooja and collapsed on the spot. I shouted, 'Tatyaji! Tatyaji!' But it was all over.

SUDHIR: How is Aai?

BHASKAR: As well as she can be. She's had her eyes fixed on your coming. It's not as if we aren't around her every moment. But it's you she's talking about all the time.

(*Vahini enters. She sees Sudhir and draws the end of her sari to her eyes. Anjali also dabs at her eyes.*)

VAHINI: So you couldn't see him before the end, could you Sudhir-bhauji? How he kept talking about you and Abhay in his last days!

(*Pause.*)

SUDHIR: How could you have let him go on with that routine—baths, prayers ... when he was so ill?

VAHINI: You know what he was like. Fever or no, he had to have his daily bath—though he didn't have the strength even to break a *papad*. But we must be happy that he died in the pooja room, purified with his bath and his prayers. Such an auspicious death. (*Pause.*) Why didn't you bring Abhay? Tatyaji was so proud of him!

SUDHIR: He's having his unit tests. He's in the twelfth grade this year.

BHASKAR: Aai will be disappointed.

ANJALI: Train bookings are also difficult these days.

SUDHIR: I'll send him over for Diwali.

BHASKAR: Do that. We should try to come together at least for funerals and festivals.

VAHINI: Put your bags away and meet her first.

BHASKAR: You're sleeping in the locker-room today.

SUDHIR: Why? We'll be fine upstairs.

BHASKAR: You're saying that because you haven't been upstairs lately. (*Aai has entered the inner room. Sensing her presence, everybody on the verandah falls silent. Finally Sudhir and Anjali muster enough courage to go in. Aai looks at Sudhir, then sits on the floor and stares at the ground. Sudhir sits in front of her. Silence.*)

SUDHIR: We got the telegram very late.

(*Suddenly Aai begins to sob as if a dam has collapsed.*)

AAI (*weeping*): Our shelter's gone.

(*Silence. On the verandah, Vahini wipes her eyes. Bhaskar is expressionless.*)

BHASKAR: Your darling brother-in-law didn't feel like bringing his son. They've come like strangers, five days late.

VAHINI: Let it be. They're here now, that's what matters.

BHASKAR: 'We'll send him for Diwali,' he says. What is he talking about! Doesn't he have any sense of the occasion?

VAHINI: Will you please not say a word now.

BHASKAR: I'm just telling you.

VAHINI: You do everything, then spoil it all with the things you say.

BHASKAR: Makes me furious. Her father-in-law lies dead, and these people worry about train bookings! What do you say to that?

VAHINI: Look, she's a Bombay girl. Born there, lived there, before marriage and after. And daughter of a Konkanastha. How could she bond with your people? Now don't say or do anything till the rites are over.

(*Enter Chandu.*)

VAHINI: Ui! Where are you coming from?

CHANDU: I was giving water to the cow.

VAHINI: Weren't you supposed to go to the bus-stand?

CHANDU: I went long ago.

VAHINI: And Sudhir-bhauji didn't come?

CHANDU: Because they said the bus got cancelled.

VAHINI: You don't say!

(*Chandu notices the suitcases.*)

CHANDU: Arrey! They're here, are they?

VAHINI: Of course they are. Did you really ask? Or just settled down for a chat in somebody's courtyard?

(*Enter Sudhir. He ignores Chandu as he flops down.*)

VAHINI (*laughing out aloud*): They came by taxi, see? You think they travel by bus like us?

SUDHIR: Aai's suddenly stooping, isn't she?

VAHINI: It's a big *shot* to bear for any woman Bhauji!

ANJALI (*bringing Sudhir his medicine*): Take your pills, please.

VAHINI: What are those for?

ANJALI: His blood pressure shoots up at the drop of a hat these days.

VAHINI: Is money piling up in the bank Sudhir-bhauji? Rich people's diseases getting friendly!

ANJALI: Here, take them. You missed a dose on the journey.

VAHINI: Oh my! What nervousness! How pit-a-pat you are, remembering to bring those pills along in all that rush! Goodness! How did you tear your sari?

ANJALI: It caught on the tractor as we came in.

SUDHIR: That tractor ... really! I don't know how long it's going to stand in the courtyard, rotting.

VAHINI: It has to be there, where else? It's like the Nandi in front of a Shiva temple. You bow to the tractor before you enter the Dharangaonkar Deshpande *wada*! Come. Have a bite, both of you.

SUDHIR: No, please ...

VAHINI: But the food's all ready ...

SUDHIR: Don't feel like it.

VAHINI: He was destined to go. He's gone. Does that mean people stop eating and drinking? Come now. Get up. Those who are left behind have to keep life going. Get up.

DADI: Vyenkatesh! What time is it, son?

SUDHIR: Have you told Dadi that Tatyaji's no more?

VAHINI: What do we tell her even if we want to? Her hearing's gone, her sight's gone. Nothing reaches her. That's how she sits all day, not moving. But every now and then it's: 'What time is it? What time is it?' Actually she's no trouble at all. Carry her to her plate when it's time to eat; carry her to her bed when it's time to sleep. There's been such a tragedy in the house—her own son's gone—but do you think she understands? Happy soul. I mean that. Will you have tea at least? Or not even that ...

SUDHIR: We'll have tea.

VAHINI: Just asked in case tea takes your sleep away. Anjali, could you have your bath meanwhile?

(*Both go in. Sudhir stares fixedly at Dadi. Suddenly, some dust falls on Dadi.*)

DADI: Arrey bappa! Is there no one around here?

(*Sudhir makes a move to go to her, changes his mind and remains where he is. Enter Prabha.*)

SUDHIR: Where have you been all this time?

PRABHA: In the storeroom. Waiting till you were through. You're the grief-stricken ones. Not me.

SUDHIR: There you go as usual.

PRABHA (*in a choked voice*): Tatyaji didn't speak to me till the very end.

SUDHIR: Now don't start crying, please ...

PRABHA: Don't worry, I won't. Vahini's the one who cried when Tatyaji died. Even more than Aai. And Bhaskar collapsed. I was at the Panchayat library. They couldn't send me a simple message. Although Parag and Ranju were at home.

SUDHIR: Probably didn't think of it.

PRABHA: Go on, take their side.

SUDHIR: I've barely got here and you've started off.

PRABHA: When the father dies, the daughter must look out for herself.

SUDHIR: What do you lack?

PRABHA: I must live off whatever crumbs you brothers throw me now. You're all right. You'll take your share and go off to Bombay. But let me tell you Sudhir, it's not even five days since Tatyaji died. Five days. And Vahini has changed already. The house keys moved instantly into her keep. And Aai went instantly into the shadows of the back room. When Tatyaji was alive, you couldn't hear Vahini's footfall on the verandah. But within five days her orders are heard way outside the wada.

SUDHIR (*bored*): I'll have a bath.

PRABHA: Your wife's in the bath. Sit down. Have you brought my books?

SUDHIR: Prabha, just think ...

PRABHA: Yes or no?

SUDHIR: You're an idiot. Is this the time or the occasion?

PRABHA: I'd sent you a list long ago so you could get me the books on your next visit. I thought you'd bring them if you'd already bought them. You don't come more than once every three or four years anyway.

SUDHIR: I'd bought shawls for Dadi and Aai. I didn't bring them either. At such times ...

PRABHA: For Dadi! Who's ever given her anything new to wear! Her shawl will go straight into Vahini's trunk. Dadi doesn't need more than some tattered old rug thrown over her. Save me from such old age!

SUDHIR: You think you can escape it?

PRABHA: I don't intend living that long.

SUDHIR: As if that's in your hands!

(*Enter Anjali.*)

ANJALI: I've drawn water for your bath. Are you going?

(*Exit Sudhir.*)

PRABHA: Dear me! Why are you reduced to wearing tatters?

ANJALI: My sari got caught in the tractor.

PRABHA: .... or is it just to show us ...

SUDHIR (*off*): Give me my towel, will you?

ANJALI: Coming!

(*Exit Anjali. Silence. Dust falls on Dadi's body.*)

DADI: Vyenkatesh ... just see how the mice run around ... Vyenkatesh ... Vyenkatesh!

(*Prabha stands looking at Dadi. Then sinks into her own thoughts. Lights fade gradually.*)

Scene Two

Lights come up. Next morning. Everyone is having tea. Enter Ranju, pushing back her dishevelled hair.

RANJU: Tea for me.

BHASKAR: Tidy that mane first.

SUDHIR: Go and wake Parag.

RANJU: My tea first.

VAHINI: Parag went out early after his tea.

SUDHIR: Some exercise routine or something?

BHASKAR: Sure! Running wild round the village dung-heaps.

VAHINI (*changing the subject*): Anjali, why don't you mend that sari? That's a huge tear. She was blessed by the tractor as she came in.

BHASKAR: Arrey baba Sudhir, see if you can find somebody in your Mumbai to buy that tractor.

VAHINI: Uie! You think people ride tractors to work in Mumbai? Really!

BHASKAR: Is there anything that doesn't sell in that city?

SUDHIR: Who'd want to buy a tractor in Mumbai? And anyhow, there isn't much left of it now. It's half buried in the ground. Every time I come, it's sunk a few inches more. The body's rusted and rotting.

BHASKAR: Nobody's used it in twenty years.

SUDHIR: Money down the drain. You should have sold it long ago.

BHASKAR: You think we dared suggest any such thing to Tatyaji? It was nothing but a whim. 'We'll buy a tractor, we'll buy a tractor', he went on. And bought it one day. Fine. We thought it might be useful. Nothing of the kind. First of all, our land was tilled by the tenants. 'Now the landlord has bought a tractor, he'll till the land himself', they thought. They were dead set against it. Worse, it would break down all the time. Once broken, it stayed that way.

VAHINI: You think you get good *mechanicals* in the village? So there it stands!

SUDHIR: You could have hired it out to other landlords.

BHASKAR: Who's got that kind of land around here? Two to five acres. Twelve is the limit. Who needs a tractor for that? It's not as if I didn't try, but people should be able to afford it. Mind you, I'd already told Tatyaji that we should buy fifteen buffaloes instead of the tractor and start a dairy.

RANJU: Why didn't you buy a posh car, instead?

BHASKAR: Because your father doesn't know how to milk a car. *Bhaitaad*.

VAHINI: Remember rich people used to have elephants swaying before their gates in the old days, Bhauji? The Deshpandes decided to be modern and put a tractor there. Forget about usefulness. As long as we can make a show of wealth. So we have the tractor in front and the palanquin at the back!

BHASKAR: Your bridal procession came in that palanquin. You seem to have forgotten that.

VAHINI: How could I? We've both been dumped in the backyard ever since. More tea?

SUDHIR: No.

VAHINI: Call out if you want some. I'll get back to my cooking.

SUDHIR: You do the cooking now?

VAHINI: Who else will?

SUDHIR: Where's Gaja?

VAHINI: Dear me, he left three years ago. Cooks for the restaurant at the bus-stand, they say. The pest. Not to have a cook is such a *handicraft*.

RANJU: You know what? Parag chews tobacco with Gaja.

BHASKAR: Ungrateful bugger. This fellow's father and grandfather spent their lives in the Deshpande kitchen. This fellow couldn't care less.

VAHINI: Who does? They all left one by one. There used to be four servants to every one of us then. Can't blame them either. Do we pay the kind of salaries they get outside?

BHASKAR: But who stood behind them in their times of need? We'd have continued to do that. I sent word to that Gaja: 'We're in mourning. Help out till the rites are over.' Didn't show up, the bastard!

SUDHIR: Aai doesn't mind your cooking during mourning?

VAHINI: She puts up with it, that's all.

BHASKAR: Aai gets really upset over all this pollution business. You've no idea. You're sitting pretty in Bombay. (*Looking at Dadi.*) No such problems there. She's gone beyond pollution and stuff like that, poor soul!

VAHINI: I don't feel good about it either. But what can you do, the pest. (*Rising, to Ranju.*) Get up. Don't sit there unwashed, uncombed. Go have your bath and come to help me in the kitchen.

RANJU: I want to hear 'Listeners' Choice'.

VAHINI: Look at the girl!

ANJALI: Let me help.

VAHINI: No dear. You'll find our *Deshasthi* ways confusing.

SUDHIR: She's not new to them anymore Vahini. We've been married twenty years.

VAHINI: Forget old and new. You can put away the groceries in the store-room when Chandu-bhauji brings them. (*With a meaningful glance at Bhaskar.*) You must get the groceries today, do you hear, Chandu-bhauji?

CHANDU: I will.

VAHINI: And Bhiva's chopped the firewood but not brought it in, the rascal.

CHANDU: I'll bring it in.

VAHINI (*to Bhaskar*): You'd better send Chandu-bhauji to Nagarmal for the groceries. Give him a note.

BHASKAR: Why? (*Awkward silence.*) What's happened?

CHANDU: Bansilal is asking for arrears.

VAHINI (*to Sudhir*): Chandu-bhauji went to get two boxes of matches yesterday and he sent him back.

BHASKAR: Tell that bugger the Dharangaonkar Deshpandes have never died on their debts. So what if Tatyaji is dead? We're all here. Tell him I'll sell the tin off the roof to repay him. When this fellow's father came from Marwar with nothing but a *lota*, he made his home in our stable. He's forgotten those days now. Why did you take what that two-bit man said?

VAHINI: Does he ever open his mouth before anyone? Really Sudhir-bhauji, tell us how we're to manage! (*Silence. Bhaskar, Sudhir look uncertain. Vahini sizes up the situation*). I'll put the grocery bags out. (*Speaking as she goes in.*) It's nothing but spending and more spending for the next fifteen days.

BHASKAR (*getting up*): I'll go ahead. (*To Chandu.*) You come with the bags. And get a sack for the sugar.

(*Exit Bhaskar. Chandu goes in.*)

RANJU: What time is it, Kaka?

SUDHIR: Eight.

RANJU: Eight? Oh no! Missed my 'Listeners' Choice'. Where's the transistor?

(*Rushes in. Bumps into Chandu who is coming out with the bags.*)

SUDHIR: Do we need to buy a lot of groceries?

CHANDU: Everything we need for the last rites.

SUDHIR: Hm. (*Chandu goes.*) Do you get it?

ANJALI: Softly ...

SUDHIR: They expected me to say I'd pay.

ANJALI: Please don't drag me into this.

SUDHIR: What do they think? And how do they manage when we're not here?

ANJALI: Why are you going on at me? You don't have the guts to speak up at the right time, and then you pester me.

SUDHIR: I'm going to speak up this time, come what may.

ANJALI: I've been hearing the same cracked record for the last ten years.

SUDHIR: But Tatyaji was alive then.

ANJALI: It's Aai now!

(*Enter Chandu.*)

SUDHIR: Weren't you going to the grocer's?

CHANDU: No. Came back halfway. Bhau sent me back.

SUDHIR (*getting up*): Can you get my shaving kit out?

CHANDU: Sudhir ... (*Sudhir looks at him enquiringly*). I mean ... Bhau's sent me to you ... (*Faltering.*) ... he's asked for seven or eight hundred rupees ... if you have it.

(*Sudhir looks at Anjali. She's looks at him, but looks away as soon as their eyes meet.*)

SUDHIR: Seven or eight hundred? Where will I suddenly produce that much from? We left in such a hurry when the telegram came, there was no time even to go to the bank.

CHANDU: Let it be. I'll ask Vahini.

(*Sudhir goes in. Chandu is in the back room where Aai is sitting on a mat.*)

AAI (*calling him as he passes by*): Chandu ...

CHANDU: Coming.

AAI: Have you brought the groceries?

CHANDU: No, not yet.

AAI: Have you eaten anything since morning?

CHANDU: No.

AAI: Have a few bites, son. Parched rice, or something. How long will you starve?

(*Vahini suddenly emerges from inside.*)

VAHINI (*voice slightly edgy,raised*): Nobody else has eaten either.

AAI: Yes dear. I only said it because he was fasting yesterday, Thursday. He didn't eat at night.

VAHINI: Was he the only one fasting? Now give up all these worries, please. Really!

CHANDU (*to Vahini*): Vahini we'll have to arrange for some money somehow.

VAHINI: What's this now?

CHANDU: Bhau sent me to ask Sudhir. He doesn't have that much.

VAHINI: And where should I get it from?

CHANDU: Everything will have to be paid for. Bansilal won't give credit. We'll need at least seven or eight hundred rupees.

VAHINI: Knock my teeth out and take them.

AAI: Why do you talk like that my dear? These are the last expenses for him. Shouldn't the rites be completed properly?

VAHINI: Of course they should be. But can't everybody share the cost? Wasn't he everybody's father? Or are we alone responsible for keeping up the Deshpande name? (*To Chandu.*) Tell him to come home and take whatever ornaments his wife is wearing.

AAI: Wait a bit dear. Let me see.

(*Gets up. Opens a trunk lying in a corner. Takes out a few notes from the folds of a sari and gives them to Chandu.*)

AAI: Will that be enough? It's all I have, son.

CHANDU: It's your money, Aai. Keep it.

AAI: What do I need it for? He gave it to me before he died. I had kept it aside for an emergency. It was his money. Let it be spent on him.

(*Vahini watches all this, then flounces out.*)

CHANDU (*as he goes out*): You shouldn't have done it.

AAI (*in a low voice*): Try and eat something at the bus stand.

(*Chandu leaves with the bags. Prabha has been observing everything silently. Darkness in the backroom. Light on the verandah.*)

PRABHA: See how quietly he went? Slogs all day like a menial.

ANJALI: Why don't they find him a job?

PRABHA: Who'll slave here then? You come like a guest for a few days, every four or five years. You don't know what goes on here. (*Pause.*) This time I'll go with you to Bombay.

ANJALI (*alert*): Won't Aai need someone here with her?

PRABHA: Let's take her along too. It would be a good change for her.

Didn't you see? Vahini waited for Aai to take out her money. If she stays here alone, they'll tear her apart and devour her.

ANJALI: Speak to your brother. It's not for me to say. Whatever he decides ...

PRABHA: You're quite under my brother's thumb, aren't you!

ANJALI: You know his temper. He's a Deshpande through and through. Plus he has high B.P. (*Pause.*) You think it's all fun and games for us. But let me tell you, only we know how we manage. Pull the sheet over your head and your feet are uncovered. Pull it down and your head's uncovered. First it was a battle to find a two-room flat. Now it's a battle to pay off the loan. At least here you own the roof over your head—and the food comes off the land.

PRABHA: Don't give me that sob story about your poverty, please. Nobody's going to visit you, all right? You're a proper Konkanastha, aren't you?

ANJALI: I didn't mean it that way. Stay with us and see for yourself. That's why I never speak. Everything gets twisted around.

PRABHA: It's surprising how your sister stayed with you for so many years then.

ANJALI: Goodness! It's simply that our place is near her college, so she used to stay over once in a while. She wasn't living with us. God knows who carries such stories to you.

(*Sudhir at the door of B.*)

SUDHIR: Where is my shaving kit?

ANJALI: It's in the suitcase, left-hand side.

SUDHIR: Get it out for me. Can't find it.

(*Goes back in.*)

ANJALI (*in an indulgent tone, to Prabha*): A Deshpande through and through! Won't do a thing on his own!

PRABHA: Quarrel on!

(*Exit Anjali. Lights on Sudhir and Anjali in B.*)

ANJALI: Here it is.

SUDHIR: Don't stand there chatting. Vahini has already lit the stove.

ANJALI: She doesn't like me meddling around. A little more or less of anything in the cooking and the barbs start flying. That's how it's always been.

SUDHIR: Words don't kill. It's just some people's way of talking.

ANJALI: She brings up my Konkanastha roots all the time. I'm used to cooking according to the proportions I use in Mumbai. There are so many more people here. I can't gauge quantities correctly. If something falls short by mistake, you can be sure my Konkanastha ancestors will get packed off to heaven.

SUDHIR: But Vahini is good at heart.

ANJALI: Only with you. You don't know what happened in the back room a while ago. You should ask Chandu-bhauji about her goodness. Why does he slog so much, like a coolie?

SUDHIR: What happened in the back room?

ANJALI: I'm not going to tell you. You'll say Konkanasthas carry tales.

SUDHIR: You have a complex about being a Konkanastha.

ANJALI: Don't you have one about being a Warhadi Deshpande?

SUDHIR: So what of it?

ANJALI: Ugh!

SUDHIR: What's ugh about it?

ANJALI: That accent!

SUDHIR (*imitating her accent*): Then how should one speak? We two make a deadly combination.

ANJALI: Go around the house just once. The rooms upstairs are locked up. There are huge cracks in the walls of the back verandah. There are supports all over. I don't understand how they are not scared. Such a massive mansion—but there's neither care, nor repairs, nor a coat of paint.

SUDHIR: It's nearly two hundred years old! When you first saw it, your mouth fell open and wouldn't shut.

ANJALI: That's how the wada was then. Tatyaji loved looking after it. Now every time I come, I find a few more things gone. There used to be at least twelve haandi-lamps hanging in the verandah. Not one remains. All broken, they say. A few years ago I'd asked for just one of them, as an antique piece. You should have seen how it rattled Bhauji. You're not the people who should talk about Konkanasthas!

SUDHIR: What would that haandi have looked like in your ten-by-twelve room in Mumbai? Things look good where they belong.

ANJALI: There were four enormous durries—carpets, mirrors, copper vats, huge serving vessels. Where do all these things go?

SUDHIR: What do you want with those huge vessels? You're not planning to start a catering agency for weddings are you?

ANJALI: I don't want a single thing from your house.

SUDHIR: Then stop grumbling. (*Pause.*) For the last ten years Tatyaji came into the house only for his prayers. He didn't bother about anything else. This is all my brother's doing.

ANJALI: There's hardly anything left now. God knows whether they've sold the stuff or given it away.

SUDHIR: Let it be now.

ANJALI: I care about such things only because they are antiques. Every one of them would have fetched thousands of rupees in Mumbai.

SUDHIR: Really, you Mumbaikars! Always waiting to turn everything into money.

ANJALI: I was just telling you.

SUDHIR: Next you'll tell me how much money the family jewellery will fetch.

ANJALI: If it's still around.

(*They exchange looks.*)

Scene Three

Around noon. Prabha and Dadi are on the verandah. A low whistle is heard outside. Prabha sits up, then quickly gets up and goes out. Returns after a few minutes. Vahini comes out of the back room.

VAHINI: Who was that?

PRABHA: Ranju's teacher.

VAHINI: Why did he go away? Ranju ...

PRABHA: I asked him to go.

VAHINI: But her lesson—

PRABHA: Are you blind, or what?

VAHINI: It's her final year at school. She's failed twice. She must get through at least this time, the nuisance!

PRABHA: Get rid of that smart-alec first. Comes whistling here.

VAHINI: What's wrong with him?

PRABHA: He teaches gratis. Ranju is seventeen. Put the two together.

VAHINI: Stuff and nonsense.

PRABHA: You'll regret it. Ranju is flighty to begin with. She's either in front of the mirror or gadding about in the village. We didn't dare step over the threshold of the house in the old days.

VAHINI: Let me also tell you, Prabha-vansa. Don't you pick on Ranju all the time.

PRABHA: Why would I do that?

VAHINI: Only you know why. But it's not good to be suspicious of people all the time. I know my children well. I do!

(*Sudhir at the door of the verandah.*)

SUDHIR: Prabha—

PRABHA: Don't you interfere.

VAHINI: Look at her! When she was small, she wanted only me, no one else, to plait her hair. And look how she quarrels with me now!

SUDHIR: Can't you stop blabbering? Think of what's happened, of the mood in the house.

(*Parag comes from outside. Sees his uncle and quickly goes indoors.*)

VAHINI: Aren't you going to speak to Kaka? (*To Sudhir.*) Otherwise it's Kaka, Kaka all the time.

SUDHIR: What's the matter with Parag this time? He's constantly out.

VAHINI: He's embarrassed to show his face to you. Abhay is younger, but he's gone ahead.

SUDHIR: I heard something a while ago.

VAHINI: Like?

SUDHIR: Nothing much.

VAHINI: That he drinks? How nosey people are—carrying tales all the way to Mumbai!

SUDHIR: Is it true, Vahini?

VAHINI: Well, it happened just a couple of times. And promptly all the relatives branded him a no-gooder. But he's like your Abhay, Bhauji.

SUDHIR: Something must be done.

VAHINI: There's nothing to do here after the tenth grade in school. If only he could have studied with Abhay in Bombay!

SUDHIR: Vahini, I tried very hard to get him in after his results. But which college would take him with such low marks. Even the eighty and eighty-five per cent-wallahs queue up for hours for admission.

VAHINI: Then where do the duffers in Mumbai go? I feel really worried. He doesn't do a thing. Doesn't even take an interest in the farm.

SUDHIR: Isn't Bhau strict with him?

VAHINI: Over-strict. That's what's made him like this. If you lash out at the children every time you see them, they aren't going to stay home, are they? Out all day, he got into bad company, what else! That's his kind of strictness, see? It's his nature. How can I alone run around everywhere and look into everything?

SUDHIR: Parag looked startled.

VAHINI: He's so good when he's himself. And so affectionate, I tell you. It was his job to pound Tatyaji's paan for him.

SUDHIR: He was always affectionate—used to be all over me. He'd come running the minute I stepped in.

VAHINI: He still adores you. Kaka, Kaka, Kaka's house, Kaka's letter, This happened to Kaka, that happened to Kaka. He's been ruined by this village. Bad company; and not being too bright at his studies to begin with. So there it is.

SUDHIR: I'll take him to Mumbai for a few days.

VAHINI: Take him. He's your son.

ANJALI: But he should want to come.

SUDHIR (*sternly*): Will you go and draw my bath water for me first.

(*Anjali makes a face and goes to the middle room.*)

SUDHIR: He'll be fine after he spends a few days with Abhay.

VAHINI: How he admires Abhay—his looks, his clothes, the way he plays cricket! When Abhay tops his class in Bombay this boy dances happily here. That's how love works.

SUDHIR: Abhay's also very fond of him.

VAHINI: That's natural. There's just the two of them, brothers. They have only each other. If your letter says 'blessings to Raghoba', that's enough to send him into ecstasy. None of us is allowed to call him 'Raghoba'. That name's reserved strictly for Sudhir-kaka. For us he's 'Parag'. That's how it is. How's Abhay?

SUDHIR: Totally changed in the last three years. You'll never recognize him if you see him now. He's not seventeen yet, but he's almost six feet tall.

VAHINI: Has he put on any flesh, though?

SUDHIR: All muscle. He can't bear to miss even one day at the gym.

VAHINI: That's wonderful. And he's got Anjali's looks. That's good too. Why didn't you bring him along? If he becomes too much of a Bombaywallah, he'll have no feelings left for us.

SUDHIR: Oh no. He talks about this place all the time. Especially about Parag. Parag taught him to swim in the pond here. That's a strong memory. They used to run riot all over the wada, remember?

(*Enter Bhaskar.*)

BHASKAR: Has the crown prince come home?

SUDHIR: Bhau—

BHASKAR: Take a good look at your Raghoba's ways. I warned him—if you dare step out, you'll have to face me. He couldn't stay indoors even for these ten days of mourning. Where's the scoundrel?

VAHINI: Sleeping. He looked startled when he saw Bhauji. Felt ashamed to face him. Now don't start shouting at him. He's feeling miserably guilty as it is poor soul.

BHASKAR: This ... this is how you shield him! That's what's spoilt him. If his ass had been whipped at the right time, things wouldn't have come to such a pass.

VAHINI: Sudhir-bhauji's taking him to Bombay. He'll improve in Abhay's company.

BHASKAR: He? Improve? Hah! Abhay will get spoilt in his company.

VAHINI: I wish you wouldn't lash out at him like this all the time.

BHASKAR: You think it makes me happy to say such things? What a fine body he had! Like a piece of gold! And now his ribs stick out all over.

VAHINI: Please!

BHASKAR: We kill ourselves working all day, and this fellow loafs or sleeps like a buffalo. If anybody's to bring credit to the Dharangaonkar Deshpande name, it'll be your Abhay. Don't let even the shadow of this family wastrel fall on him.

SUDHIR: Let it be. Don't get angry—at least not while we are here.

BHASKAR: You won't understand how it hurts.

SUDHIR: Sit down for a while, please. You too, Vahini. You've been so busy since we came, we haven't even talked properly.

VAHINI (*sits*): So, what shall we talk about? (*Silence.*) Ui! That's what happens. When you want to talk, nothing comes.

SUDHIR: The house needs repairs. It's looking ...

BHASKAR: Repairs? Are we talking of a two-room house? That could be easily done. But with a hulk like this, where do we begin? It would take a full tin of oil just to oil the woodwork. (*Pause.*) It's something we should all think about together.

SUDHIR: With us five hundred miles away?

(*Anjali enters.*)

BHASKAR: That's what I mean. Here problems descend on us everyday like guests turning up one after the other. There was Tatyaji's illness. And in the midst of all this chaos, the boy is going astray.

VAHINI: Bhauji says he'll take him to Bombay.

BHASKAR: If you have any sense, you won't take this light of our eyes anywhere. Both our children have turned out badly. Your son's a good boy. Let him stay that way.

ANJALI: How can you say that! They are brothers after all.

BHASKAR: Yes, but how different! We'd first rejected your proposal because you were a Konkanastha. And then Abhay is born with the brains and fair skin of Konkanasthas. He'll get a first, eh Sudhir?

SUDHIR (*subtly boastful*): He's expected to be in the merit list.

BHASKAR: There.

ANJALI: At least he's working hard for it.

BHASKAR: Another Konkanastha trait. Not like us. We tilled our fields lounging on swings; we lost whole estates, while we chewed paan. If the servant didn't get us our spitoon in time, do you think we got it for ourselves? No sir! Out went the jet of tobacco juice straight into the corner of the room.

ANJALI: *Chee!* (*To Sudhir.*) Can you ...

(*Exit Anjali. Sudhir follows.*)

VAHINI: I think they wanted to start the talks.

BHASKAR: How do you know?

VAHINI: They've been hovering around since morning.

BHASKAR: Let them.

VAHINI: We are the elders. Why don't you broach the subject and get it over with?

BHASKAR: Can't you wait even till the thirteenth day is over? I tell you!

VAHINI: Please talk things over with them before you plan to do anything.

BHASKAR: You really are ...

(*Enter Ranju.*)

BHASKAR: Where were you all this time, young lady?

RANJU: Studying.

BHASKAR (*sarcastically*): Your love for studies is brimming over, isn't it?

VAHINI: Your teacher was here.

RANJU: Met him. He says, come to my house for lessons from tomorrow.

BHASKAR: No.

RANJU: He says, you won't be able to study in your house because you have guests.

BHASKAR: I said no.

VAHINI: Let her go if she wants to. The teacher's mother is always at home.

BHASKAR: Deshpande girls don't run around to people's houses. Married for thirty years and you still don't know that!

VAHINI: I'm also the daughter of a Deshmukh. I know what's done and not done. But if the girl passes this year, we can marry her off. Poor man, he's teaching her for free because he hasn't forgotten past favours he says.

BHASKAR: Some teacher! Loafs all over the village with his hair in puffs like some eunuch of a Hindi film hero. Any time of the day, he's at the bus-stand paan shop, spewing paan juice all over the place. With that transistor slung around his neck twenty-four hours like a sacred thread! Is this a teacher or a buggering nautch-boy?

VAHINI: Everybody's like that nowadays. Why should the bright boys stay back here? Leftover dregs stay. We must make do with them. What else?

BHASKAR: Your tuition stops from tomorrow. You don't go there. He doesn't come here. Why are you snivelling?

RANJU: My English is weak.

BHASKAR: Let it be. You're not going to have tea with the Queen of England! And get that hair out of your eyes. Look at her sari! Look at her hair! Needs to be thrashed!

(*Exit Bhaskar.*)

VAHINI (*to Ranju*): Go inside, Ranju. Haven't I told you to cover yourself properly! How did you get to be so wild? You don't listen to anybody. What were you fidgeting around in the pooja room for?

RANJU: So it's okay if Baba goes in there?

(*Enter Chandu, bent under the weight of the groceries he is carrying.*)

VAHINI: The groceries at last. (*Noticing blood on Chandu's foot.*) Now what have you done to your foot?

CHANDU: Hurt myself on the tractor as I came in.

VAHINI: Put some turmeric on it first thing, all right? That tractor's a real pest. It should be thrown out. (*Going into the middle room.*) Bring the groceries in here. (*Instead of giving him a hand with the groceries, Ranju hangs on to Chandu's arm.*)

CHANDU: Ranju ... stop it, Ranju!

RANJU: Chandu-kaka, you're looking just like a hero.

CHANDU: Go on! Move off!

RANJU: No. *Hum nahin door honge.* In *Coolie* Amitabh carries sacks just like this. Why don't you go into films?

CHANDU: Then who'll carry the sacks here?

RANJU: Me? If I get even half a chance, I'll be in films.

CHANDU: Right. But first help me carry these.

RANJU: *Nahin.* No. I'm a naughty girl, I am. *Hum natkhat ladki hai.* (*Again she clings to him. He staggers. Some things fall. Enter Anjali.*)

ANJALI: Wait, let me carry that. How did you hurt your foot?

RANJU: *Thes lagi thes.* His foot bleeds. My heart bleeds.

ANJALI: Stop being vulgar, Ranju. Chandu-bhauji, please go put something on that cut. Do we have Burnol?

(*Chandu goes in.*)

RANJU: Hey Anju-kaku, have you seen Amitabh?

ANJALI (*busy*): Hm.

RANJU: Really?

ANJALI (*startled*): What? Why should I go to see him?

RANJU: When he was ill, I fasted five Saturdays, you know. If anything had happened to him I'd have killed myself. (*Sudhir comes in. Ranju is now all over him.*) Sudhir-kaka!

SUDHIR: Why would you have killed yourself?

(*As they talk, Ranju and Sudhir move into the other room. Anjali follows.*)

ANJALI: What's this, Ranju? Move away. Let him change his clothes.

RANJU: He's my darling uncle.

SUDHIR: Listen my darling niece. Move. Let me take my shirt off.

RANJU: Have you seen Amitabh, Sudhir-kaka?

SUDHIR: Sure. He comes to our milk booth everyday to buy milk.

RANJU: What lies!

SUDHIR: Really! Even Jaya comes over to borrow this and that!

RANJU: But the stars are so rich!

ANJALI: Not as rich as the Deshpandes. Now go and get some tea for your Kaka.

RANJU: Right away. *Ji haan.* Where's Rajkamal Studio, Kaka?

SUDHIR: Oh, Rajkamal? Right behind our house! Now go, get that tea!

RANJU: At once. Ji haan.

(*Pulls his hair and runs off.*)

SUDHIR: This is something new this time.

ANJALI: Too much touching and clinging!

SUDHIR: She's playing the naughty village belle.

ANJALI: She's wild!

SUDHIR: Noticed how they avoided the issue?

ANJALI: Hmm.

SUDHIR: The minute I touch on it, off they go, 'We have this problem, we have that problem.' Huh!

ANJALI: Hmm ...

SUDHIR: He just doesn't want to talk about it.

ANJALI: You two brothers sort it out between yourselves. I want to stay right out of it, okay?

DADI: Vyenkatesh ... Vyenkatesh ... Why is nobody talking to me ... (*Sudhir goes up to her and puts his hand on her knee.*) Vyenkatesh, my son ... I've been calling for so long. Fed up with the old woman, are you?

SUDHIR: Dadi ... Dadi (*Shouting.*) It's me, Sudhir. Not Tatyaji.

DADI: Vyenkatesh ... Is it night? Why am I hungry in the middle of the night?

SUDHIR (*shouting*): It's not night. (*Realizes the futility of shouting.*) Oh well, come, have something to eat. Chandu!

(*Chandu picks up the old woman like a bundle and carries her to the middle room. Aai stands in the doorway.*)

AAI (*to Sudhir*): Don't shout dear. There's more to come.

(*Lights fade.*)

Act Two

Scene One

The same day. About ten o' clock at night. A lantern in each of the four rooms. The wick in the one on the verandah is longer. Everybody is out on the verandah. Prabha sits on the threshold between the middle room and verandah; Chandu sits in a corner, far away from the others, like a servant. Aai is in the middle room. Parag sits in his room, embarrassed. The women are cutting beans. The men are preparing paans.

BHASKAR: No sign of the rain stopping.

VAHINI: Look at it. Pouring as if the sky has been ripped open.

SUDHIR: It was quite clear this morning.

VAHINI: My heart just sinks when it rains like this. The upper floor is so shaky, it could collapse any moment.

SUDHIR: But why don't you have it repaired?

BHASKAR: With what?

VAHINI: It's nothing to you Bombay people. Ranju! What are you doing out there by the gate?

RANJU: Looking at the rain.

VAHINI: Come in at once!

RANJU (*coming in*): Sudhir-kaka, rain scenes—do they shoot them in real rain?

SUDHIR: Vahini, her head's full of nothing but films. She's been on like this all morning.

VAHINI: You're telling me? Her daily dose starts the moment the touring talkies tent goes up for a new film. Once, twice—there's no limit to how many times she can see the same film.

SUDHIR: But why do you let her go?

VAHINI: What other entertainment does this place have for children? They get bored, poor souls. When she starts sniffing and snivelling, I say go, don't pester the life out of me.

SUDHIR (*blurting out*): We've just stopped going out to see films since we got our TV.

(*Realizes his mistake immediately. Glances at Anjali. She behaves as if she has not heard. Everybody tense.*)

RANJU: You've bought a TV?

SUDHIR: Yes. Quite recently actually. I was paid some arrears due to me ...

RANJU: Colour?

BHASKAR: Must have cost ten-fifteen thousand at least.

SUDHIR: No, no. Just five.

ANJALI: And on instalment. That's one good thing about Bombay, you can buy anything on instalment.

VAHINI: Good for you Anjali. You're collecting things one by one for the home. There's going to be no TV here while we're alive. Even if we did get one, we'd have to start by getting an electrical connection.

SUDHIR: Why don't you get a connection anyway? It's so dark around here.

BHASKAR: It's not dark or anything. It's all a question of habit. We don't find it dark. And you think it's any good having a connection? Four days of the week there's no power. People installed pumps in place of their waterwheels. Now they are regretting it. Half their orchards have dried up. The government is happy because

it has given electricity to the village, and the people are happy
because they have connections. But if you ask me, there's more
loss than gain in it.

PRABHA: As if you'd buy a TV if the power supply was assured!

VAHINI: Why not? We might.

BHASKAR: She doesn't think her brother's capable of buying a TV. He's
only good at ruining the family. Right, Prabha?

VAHINI: Ranju! At the gate again? Come in at once!

PRABHA: All those big vessels you sold off by weight—that money could
have easily fetched a TV.

SUDHIR (*shocked*): Have you really sold them off?

VAHINI: They were all broken. No use to anybody. Nothing but clutter
in the store-room, pest.

SUDHIR: There were two enormous copper bath vessels.

VAHINI: Gone. Bath vessels gone. Brass buckets gone.

SUDHIR: Actually, Anjali wanted one.

ANJALI: Indoor potted plants look so pretty in them.

RANJU: See see! Anju-kaku's decor ideas, all film style!

VAHINI: Decor with old crocs! What *nonsenseness*!

SUDHIR: Vahini, you could have dropped us a line to ask! Forget decor. Do
you have any idea what the price of copper and brass is these days?

VAHINI: Didn't think of it, I must say.

SUDHIR: Didn't what of it? Really!

BHASKAR: You think we were happy to sell them? Each one with an
ancestor's name engraved on it? But circumstances were
such that ...

SUDHIR: You should have informed me at least.

BHASKAR: All right, I didn't do it this time. But other times when I did,
what did you do about it? Do you even reply to my letters? We're
desperate for money here in the sowing season. We spend a

hundred or two hundred rupees hard cash every day. Then Tatyaji falls ill. You think that cost us a small sum? So we sold the old pots.

SUDHIR: For how much?

BHASKAR: We didn't make a fortune out of them, let me assure you! When we sell old pots, you think we can go out into the open market with them, like others? It's all hush-hush by the back-door. We mustn't show cracks in the facade must we?

SUDHIR: We should forget about facades and things like that now.

VAHINI: Easily said for people living in Bombay, Bhauji. You can't afford to do that in the village. Only we know how we manage.

SUDHIR: Do you think it's roses all the way for us in Bombay?

VAHINI: At least you don't have to strain to make ends meet.

BHASKAR: Your clothes, why, even your suitcases, dazzle us.

SUDHIR: You have to do these things if you live in the city. You don't expect us to come here with tin-trunks on our heads do you? You talk about our clothes. But we just about manage with both of us slogging from seven in the morning till nine at night. Still, you won't see as much as a drop of butter or milk or curds in our plates even one day of the year. You should try living in Bombay and coping. Every step costs money.

PRABHA: Oh! By the way, Sudhir, the villagers are supposed to be in the dark about our real circumstances. Never mind that old Bansilal won't let us touch a thing unless he sees hard cash.

BHASKAR: She's in her element! Doesn't have to do a thing, except take swipes at whoever passes by.

PRABHA: I'm going to say something, now that both of you are here. Tatyaji didn't let me study. Tatyaji's gone. Now let me go to college in Amaravati.

SUDHIR: Now? At your age?

PRABHA: I got a first in my matriculation. Twenty years ago. I wanted to be a doctor. But the Deshpande girls weren't supposed to live anywhere by themselves to study. All for their family prestige and honour—never mind if our lives were reduced to dust.

BHASKAR: Prabha, Tatyaji took all the decisions affecting you. Why harass us with these things? Fact is that Sudhir was also studying at the time. It wouldn't have been possible to send money for both of you. And what do you think my life is? Not mud but gold? I've been buried alive permanently in this soil. If I'd had a job, I'd have been a superintendent by now.

VAHINI: It's all a matter of luck and destiny.

BHASKAR: That's how it is. Now didn't I try my best to find a match for Prabha? But nothing worked at first. When it did, Prabha turned up her nose.

PRABHA: They were all bullocks off the farm. Not a single educated man amongst them.

BHASKAR: Two of your brothers are farmers as well.

PRABHA: I wanted an educated husband.

BHASKAR: Why would an educated man marry you?

PRABHA (*almost shouting*): That's right! First stop me from studying and then blame me for it! Weren't you, as brothers, responsible in any way? You, Sudhir. Every time you came here you said you'd look for a match in Bombay. You never found time for me did you? You couldn't even manage a simple thing like sending me books. Don't think I'm panting to get married. It's done with now. It's too late. But don't think that'll stop me from holding a mirror up to your faces.

VAHINI: That's enough please, Vansa. Not in front of the children.

BHASKAR: Let her talk.

SUDHIR: What do you mean, let her talk?

BHASKAR: This kind of scene is quite normal with her Sudhir.

PRABHA: You call this a scene?

VAHINI: Why scold Ranju then? She'll naturally behave the way you do, won't she!

BHASKAR: That's enough. Aai's sitting in there. How will she feel?

(*Restless, Ranju has again gone off to the gate. Vahini shouts. Ranju comes back and starts crying.*)

VAHINI: Why are you crying?

RANJU: You are always scolding me.

VAHINI: What's there at the gate for you this time of night? Idiot.

PRABHA: Her teacher must be coming—for a lesson.

VAHINI: Prabha-vansa!

SUDHIR (*changing the subject hastily*): Where's Raghoba? Haven't seen him since the morning.

(*Parag is listening from his room. He shrinks into himself. Silence.*)

DADI (*very loudly*): What time is it son? Vyenkatesh ...

VAHINI: What time do we tell her it is? It's the same question every fifteen minutes. Nobody should live this long, the pest.

ANJALI: That's what we think. She may not think the same way.

VAHINI: But it's so hard on those who have to look after them. (*Noticing Chandu, she feels a tinge of shame.*) Of course, that's Chandu-bhauji's department.

BHASKAR: He used to look after Tatyaji as well. I was so busy with farm work. So he took the brunt. There's a lot of work for you for the thirteenth and fourteenth-day rituals Chandoba. Your last service to Tatyaji.

SUDHIR: A lot of work? Why?

BHASKAR: Won't it be? With the whole village coming for a meal?

SUDHIR (*tense*): What?

BHASKAR: What do you think?

SUDHIR: The village?

BHASKAR: Come on. That's the custom here. We have to feed the whole village on the thirteenth day or we lose face.

SUDHIR: So you're going to feed all the four or five thousand?

BHASKAR: Is there a choice? The sittings will start in the morning and go on till ten or twelve at night.

SUDHIR: And no thought for the expense! Five thousand plates means at least twenty or twenty-five thousand rupees. Where will you get that?

BHASKAR: That's what I wanted us to discuss. Tell me if you have an idea.

SUDHIR: I won't give anything.

BHASKAR: Whether you do or no, we'll have to manage as best we can.

VAHINI: Bhauji, this is the last expenditure for a family elder. Do we refuse it and get closer to hell?

SUDHIR: What old-fashioned ideas, Vahini!

VAHINI: Say what you like. But it's not right. Was Tatyaji nothing to you?

SUDHIR: That's not what I meant. But I won't be able to give anything much. Where do you think I can get that kind of money from all of a sudden?

BHASKAR: And where do we get it do you think?

SUDHIR: I can't say anything about that.

BHASKAR: I'll have to pawn her bangles.

VAHINI: I've kept them for Ranju. I won't give the bangles. When we're faced with her marriage, won't we need to put some gold on her? Or are we going to palm her off with nothing? Who'll marry your daughter without gold? Her face isn't exactly her fortune. No. No bangles.

RANJU: Is that all you're going to give me—bangles?

BHASKAR: Then we'll have to mortgage the orchard.

VAHINI: You sort that out. I won't give the gold.

SUDHIR: The farm belongs to all three of us, doesn't it?

BHASKAR: He was father to all three of us.

SUDHIR: The orchard will not be mortgaged. When have we ever been able to redeem mortgaged land? This strip of twelve acres is all that remains. Let's keep it. We'll never be able to buy such fertile land again. Also, if I suddenly need money in the future, I must have my share of the land.

BHASKAR: So you're suddenly talking about rights!

SUDHIR: Is that wrong Bhau? We'll have to talk about these things sooner or later.

BHASKAR: You're talking about rights, Sudhir, but you're forgetting your education—you think it came at no cost?

SUDHIR: Tatyaji spent that money.

BHASKAR: Only in name. You know that as well as I do. He passed on the whole responsibility of your education, your marriage, to me and sat back. Did that cost nothing? And here you are demanding your share!

SUDHIR: Look Bhau, I've had this thrown at me a little too often. My education, my marriage. Now let me tell you something. You didn't spend out of your pocket for my education and marriage. Didn't I have anything here twenty years ago? Wasn't there enough land in my name? Expenditure on me came from the income off that land. But that ended twenty years ago. Since then, you've been living off that income. What about that? Why go on with 'I did this, I did that'? Rubbish. Did you ever give me a single paisa from my land or even a measure of grain?

BHASKAR: You should come and take what's yours.

SUDHIR: Are we beggars to come and take things? The question is whether you were big-hearted enough to give me anything? Earlier, I used to spend my leave here. But you kept hinting I was saving my salary staying here. So I swore not to come too often and, even when I did, not to stay for too long. I kept away for years at a time. But you couldn't stand that either. Why are you calling me greedy then?

VAHINI: Please don't lose your temper Sudhir-bhauji. Not in front of the children.

SUDHIR: I've been wanting to say this for a long time, Vahini. Let your children know the facts too; or one day they might say uncle used to come here for free meals.

BHASKAR: Are you through? Yes. I agree with everything you say. I didn't give you your income. Neither cash, nor grain. True. But did you ever feel like asking me even once in all these years how the land was doing? I took Aai to Amravati for her operation. I had to set up house there for two months. Then came Tatyaji's illness. You think that didn't cost money?

SUDHIR: The same thing again! Why do you think it was your money that you spent on Aai and Tatyaji? Everything belonged to them. Why do you make out that they were obliged to you?

BHASKAR: Come here once and see for yourself. If the harvest's good one year, it's bad for the next three.

SUDHIR: How can there be a bad harvest on such well-watered land?

BHASKAR: Then the land went to the tenants. We had to fight it out in the lawcourts. The minute a hearing was announced, I'd drop everything and rush to Amaravati. I lost so much money doing that. From top to bottom, they were all Brahman-haters, every one of them. Didn't allow a single verdict to go in our favour. Wining and dining top officials isn't something I can do. You don't know how difficult it is for Brahmans to survive as farmers nowadays.

SUDHIR: So, how do the others manage?

BHASKAR: Have you seen how? There were seven Brahman families in this village. Three left long ago; there's no one left to light a lamp in their homes. Of the remaining four, two are priests and one a teacher. All deep in debt. With us, the facade is big and the debts are big. Other castes are doing fine. They open a liquor shop and soon they've built a large house. Some have bought trucks. Others are in brokerage. And there's always politics as the last resort. Are we capable of doing any of these things? Times have changed, but our expenses remain unchanged—festivals, family rituals, annual death rites. You've left all this to me and gone off. The Ganapati-Gauri festival alone costs a good seven or eight hundred rupees.

SUDHIR: Cut down on everything.

BHASKAR: Easy to say. Come here and show me how.

SUDHIR: I don't have to. You can do it yourself. Look at the way you spend. Take lunch this morning—we had four vegetables on our plates!

VAHINI: You think people aren't fussy around here! One doesn't like this, another doesn't like that!

SUDHIR: What nonsense!

VAHINI: And I'm not happy either if I don't serve a full plate. I'll never manage Konkanastha thrift in this birth at least!

SUDHIR: Then sink.

(*Long, angry silence. Aai comes to the door.*)

BHASKAR: There's the wada ...

SUDHIR: What are you saying!

BHASKAR: I am not talking of selling. Just mortgaging it will fetch us the amount we need.

SUDHIR: No.

BHASKAR: Then what do we do for heaven's sake?

SUDHIR: We come here because of this house. This is what pulls us here. If we lose that, we lose our home.

BHASKAR: By wada I don't mean the whole place. We'll mortgage just the part at the back that's broken. We talked and talked but never got around to repairing it. And now it's sinking. Bansilal's had his eye on it for years. In fact, he has offered to buy it.

SUDHIR: Why should he even suggest it?

BHASKAR: We haven't paid his bills for three years. We have no standing with him now. That's why he dares to look us in the eye and suggest such a thing.

SUDHIR: You've already discussed it?

BHASKAR: No ... nothing's been finalized.

SUDHIR: I really don't know what to say.

BHASKAR: The problem is, that part is in Aai's name. This part, where we live, is in our name—four of us, brothers and sister. That's how Tatyaji arranged it. His plan was to build two-room flats on Aai's portion and rent them out. That would have brought her some income of her own. But it couldn't be managed till the end.

SUDHIR: If it's mortgaged, who'll do the repairs?

BHASKAR: Why would Bansilal bother? He's just waiting for the day we're in a real mess so he can step in and grab the place. But let me tell you frankly, when we redeem it you'll have to bear half the cost. I don't have the capacity to carry the whole load by myself.

SUDHIR: But where will I get so much money from? (*Pause*). Better to reduce the scale of the whole thing.

BHASKAR: And lose face? Not possible.

AAI: Bhaskar. (*They start.*) Why don't you sell the part at the back?

CHANDU and PRABHA: Aai!

AAI: What will I do with that place, tell me?

BHASKAR: People will say the sons cheated their mother.

AAI: Why should people say anything? They'll have things to say even if we don't feed them. This is the last bit we'll be spending on him. I won't be able to rest all my life if things are not done the right way. Let's decide it once and for all. Sell off that part.

PRABHA: What do you mean decide once and for all?

AAI: I'm telling him to do it, dear. Where will he find the money otherwise?

PRABHA: My dear able-bodied brothers! Why don't you wear bangles?

Selling the morsel from your mother's mouth! And these two women, pretending as if they don't know what's going on!

VAHINI: Don't scold us for no reason, Vansa. We knew nothing till this moment.

AAI: Prabha, my child, please be quiet. Nobody is forcing me.

CHANDU (*suddenly*): Bhau, mortgage my share of the farm.

BHASKAR: Your four acres?

CHANDU: Let Aai have her rightful place.

BHASKAR: Think carefully. Or next thing we know, you've changed your mind.

AAI: Chandu, my son, don't do that. How many years are left to me now?

PRABHA: Let the older ones sell the orchard. Let them sell their shares.

BHASKAR: We'll do it. Then tell me what you'll eat.

AAI: It's not even ten days yet. What do you think we look like? Does it suit us to bicker like this?

CHANDU: Don't pay attention to Aai, Bhau. Mortgage my four acres.

BHASKAR: You're being very generous today Chandoba. Tomorrow you'll go around the village yelling that I forced you. What Aai says is right. Sudhir?

SUDHIR: Don't pretend to consult me now. Everything was decided beforehand anyway.

VAHINI: That'll do now, Bhauji. Twenty years of living in Bombay hasn't rid you of your Deshpandeness. Your temper's just the same as ever.

DADI: Vyenkatesh, Arrey Vyenkatesh ...

VAHINI: Look at her. Beyond our quarrels.

SUDHIR: Almost everyone in our family lives till a ripe old age.

BHASKAR: Look at our health! You're free to criticize us for having four vegetables at a time, but we've never needed to take a paisa's worth of medicine. Look at you Bombaywallahs! Blood pressure already and God knows what else! Oh well, I'll go lie down.

RANJU: Aai, my heart's pounding.

VAHINI: Maybe it's your blood pressure. Idiot! Why are you clinging to me? Do you have a fever? Why is she behaving like this since the morning!

(*Parag comes out suddenly and sits exactly behind Sudhir so he cannot see his face.*)

SUDHIR (*without turning round*): That's Raghoba isn't it? Mr Bashful.

(*Parag rests his head against Sudhir's back. Sudhir tries to hold his head but Parag won't let him.*)

VAHINI: The mouse is out of its hole.

SUDHIR: Raghoba, you ass. Abhay is cross with you because you don't write to him.

PARAG: I do. He doesn't.

Sudhir now gets hold of Parag's head, and pulls him forward.

SUDHIR: Look at this thatch. Hack down this jungle first thing tomorrow.

RANJU: Oh, but that's his *Mithun Chakravarty* style!

PARAG: Rot!

RANJU: But it is!

PARAG: I don't like film actors and all that.

SUDHIR: Exactly like Abhay. He doesn't either. His heroes are Gavaskar, Kapil Dev ...

PARAG: Kaka, does Abhay still play cricket?

SUDHIR: He does. But we don't allow him to play too much. It's his final year at junior college.

PARAG: Abhay would have made a terrific player.

SUDHIR: He wants to be a terrific engineer. What terrific thing do you want to be?

BHASKAR (*gets up to go in*): He's going to be a terrific drunkard.

VAHINI: Please ... (*Exit Bhaskar.*) See, that's how he treats him.

PARAG: Can I come to Bombay, Kaka?

SUDHIR: What will you do in Bombay?

PARAG: I'll study.

SUDHIR: Sure?

PARAG: You just see.

SUDHIR: Raghu, you need to be thrashed.

PARAG: Do it.

VAHINI: Do it! Even a thrashing is sweet if uncle's doing it!

SUDHIR: Why do you drink? (*Parag tries to get up. Sudhir pulls him down by his hand.*) Don't run away. Tell me.

PARAG: Let it be.

SUDHIR: No letting it be. Tell me, come on.

PARAG: I won't drink now.

SUDHIR: I'll be watching you while I'm here.

PARAG: Watch. Then will you take me to Bombay if I behave myself?

SUDHIR: I will.

(*Vahini has tears in her eyes. Wiping them, she picks up the basket of beans and gets up.*)

VAHINI: Come, go to bed now. It's nearly eleven o'clock.

(*A soft whistle outside. Ranju is agitated.*)

ANJALI: Did someone whistle?

VAHINI: Maybe a bird. Sleep now. It's late.

SUDHIR (*to Anjali*): Will you come out into the yard for a bit? It's so warm in here.

(*Sudhir and Anjali go out. Everybody retires to their respective rooms. Parag and Chandu spread their mattresses on the verandah. Ranju drags her bedding out of the middle room to the verandah and spreads it near Chandu's.*)

CHANDU: What are you doing here? Go and sleep next to Aai in the middle room.

RANJU: Dust keeps falling there and mice run around all night.

CHANDU: Ranju, didn't I tell you to go sleep near Aai?

RANJU: It's hot in there.

CHANDU: Will you move your mattress over there then. Go on, pull! Don't stick so close to him. Pull it further ...

RANJU (*bending over Parag*): Gavaskar's asleep eh?

PARAG: Just shut up, you *Dhema Malini*. Sleep.

(*Chandu carries Dadi in. Lights dim for a moment.*)

Scene Two

Some time later. Light on the yard. Sudhir and Anjali are sitting on a stone ledge.

ANJALI: How hot it is! It gets hot as soon as the rain stops.

SUDHIR: Sit near me.

ANJALI: Don't get ideas.

SUDHIR: Ideas?

ANJALI: What else? Out here in the open ...

SUDHIR: I wasn't even thinking that way. It's all in your mind.
(*Pause.*)

ANJALI: We are in mourning. You should remember that.

SUDHIR: Have we stopped eating and drinking because we are in mourning? Hunh?

ANJALI: Don't get so desperate.
(*Laughs.*)

SUDHIR (*fuming*): What's making you grin?

ANJALI: Ranju is also another abnormal creature.

SUDHIR: How does Ranju come into this?

ANJALI: You might think she's stupid, but she's interested in things she shouldn't be at her age. (*Pause.*) She was asking me about birth control today.

SUDHIR: You should have shut her up. The *bhaitaad*.

ANJALI: Bhaitaad! Why do you start on this dialect the minute we come here. Only Prabha-vansa speaks correct Marathi around here. Because she reads, I suppose.

SUDHIR: Oh you Konkanastha, you! How will you ever appreciate the sweetness of Warhadi.

ANJALI: Have you really made up your mind about Parag?

SUDHIR: Let's take him for a few days.

ANJALI: Parag is sweet. I like him too. But Abhay's at an impressionable age. And his studies ...

SUDHIR: But I've already promised him.

ANJALI: Really, the moment you think of something, you have to blurt it out. No thought for the consequences. Where will you go searching for him if he falls into some gutter, drunk? The risk of it!

SUDHIR: Do you really take him for a drunkard? He's been dying to come to Bombay for the last four years. Where will he stay if not with us?

ANJALI: It's up to you now. I've told you how I feel. I will not be responsible for him.

SUDHIR: He'll be so disappointed if I say no now.

ANJALI: Just for a while.

SUDHIR: Anyway, enough about Parag. We'll see.

(*Pause.*)

ANJALI: Have you noticed the pillows?

SUDHIR: They are greasy. Put a towel over them.

ANJALI: Not that. I'm talking about the covers. Noticed them? Made of the material we got Ranju for a skirt last time.

SUDHIR: You astound me! You still remember that material after all these years!

ANJALI: A gift is something given with love and this is how it's valued!

SUDHIR: Perhaps she didn't like it.

ANJALI: How she harasses Chandu-bhauji! Did you notice his foot? How bad the swelling is. But even with that foot he was working all day storing firewood.

SUDHIR: What's wrong with his foot?

ANJALI: Hurt himself on the tractor. (*Pause.*) Tomorrow you must take him for a tetanus injection at least. He only put some turmeric on the wound today.

SUDHIR: Hmm.

(*Sudhir is lost in his own thoughts.*)

ANJALI: Let's take Chandu-bhauji to Bombay for a few days, instead of Parag. Some rest for him and a bit of help for me.

SUDHIR: Hmm.

ANJALI: All he does here is slog.

SUDHIR: Hmm.

ANJALI: What's wrong? Why are you grumpy all of a sudden?

SUDHIR: Actually, we should take Aai to Bombay for a few days.

ANJALI: She won't come. I asked her this afternoon. She said she won't step out of the house for a year at least. (*Pause.*) Besides, I won't be able to cope with all her pollution-non-pollution business.

SUDHIR: What ornaments of yours have we left back here?

ANJALI: Quite a few. Why?

SUDHIR: We'll take all our things with us this time.

ANJALI: That's for you to decide.

SUDHIR: Aren't you interested?

ANJALI: That gold belongs to your family. What can I say?

SUDHIR: You don't want the gold, but you want a broken bath vessel. You women are really strange creatures!

ANJALI: And here's Mr Braveheart all set to take our gold away! Let's hear you ask your brother first. Then plan.

SUDHIR: It's your rightful property.

ANJALI: I'm not even sure how much there is. Have you Deshpandes ever taken me into confidence? I'm going to ask you something now because you have broached this subject yourself. Otherwise you'd have had something to say about Konkanasthas. What is ours by right here?

SUDHIR: Four acres of farm land and a share in the house.

ANJALI: Why don't you settle things once and for all?

SUDHIR: Meaning?

ANJALI: Just divide, distribute, and be done with it. We don't come here for years together and Abhay's not in the least bit interested in this place.

SUDHIR: Do you realize what you are saying?

ANJALI: I'm saying it only because you're perpetually worked up over it. Don't take the money if you don't want to. Why not just hand everything over and be free.

SUDHIR: I'll do nothing of the kind. The only reason why I can come here as a matter of right is because I own a share here. Otherwise one day even Parag might look at me as a stranger. Some day we'll leave those two cluttered rooms in Bombay and come and stay here. (*Pause.*) And whatever else Bhau might do, he won't keep your gold. He's really fond of you.

ANJALI: Chee ...

SUDHIR: Isn't he?

ANJALI (*serious*): Why does he comment on my looks all the time? I don't like it.

SUDHIR (*absently*): You're silly.

ANJALI: Let's go back as soon as the rituals are over.

(*Both leave. Darkness in the courtyard. Light on the verandah. Ranju is crying.*)

CHANDU: What's the matter with you?

RANJU: Nothing.

CHANDU: Then why are you crying? (*Ranju sobs even more loudly.*) Come on, tell me. Is something hurting you? (*Ranju shakes her head.*) Then? You want me to call Vahini?

RANJU: I want to die, just like Tatyaji.

CHANDU: You're a real bhaitaad. Go to sleep now.

RANJU: I feel so frightened, Chandu-kaka.

CHANDU: Of what? Death?

RANJU: I have no one in this world. Nobody cares about my feelings.

CHANDU: What's happened to make you say that?

RANJU: Baba says my English tuitions must stop. (*Sobs.*) Suppose I fail again? Then everyone will start scolding me again, right and left.

CHANDU: Does your English improve if you cry?

RANJU: My life is nothing but a blank page. Will all of you miss me terribly when I'm dead?

CHANDU: How can I say that now? Go to sleep.

RANJU: Then everyone will realize how good I was. I wish I could just go off somewhere.

CHANDU: Where will you go? Into films, in Bombay? Or run off with that teacher?

RANJU (*taken aback*): No. Never!

CHANDU: Then go to sleep, crackpot.

(*The verandah is dark. Light on the middle room. Aai and Prabha are sleeping there. From the movement of Prabha's body, one can make out that she is crying. Aai sits up.*)

AAI: Prabha ... (*Prabha is silent.*) Prabha, what's the matter dear?

PRABHA: Nothing.

AAI: Look this way.

PRABHA: Go to sleep, Aai.

AAI: Look at me.

PRABHA: What's going to happen to us, Aai?

AAI: It's all in their hands my dear.

PRABHA: You simply gave away your part of the house.

AAI: Prabha ...

PRABHA: Now you'll live like a hanger-on in your own home.

AAI: What else could I have done? You tell me.

PRABHA: You're so gullible.

AAI: Say that if you like, dear. But tell me one thing. Where would I go if I hurt my children? Do you really think I don't know what's going on? But things were different when He was alive. (*Pause.*) Prabha, let me tell you one thing. Don't fret. My day is over. Now it's your sister-in-law's reign here. Let that guide your behaviour. If you expect me to intervene, I will not do it. After all, they are responsible now. I am going to spend the rest of my life with them. How you scold dear! It's not nice.

PRABHA: They are selfish, all of them.

AAI: Has anyone ever escaped self-interest? Once you have a family, you become selfish automatically, whether you want to or no.

PRABHA: Your heart always goes out to your sons and their wives.

AAI: Call it selfishness, or anything else. But I can't afford to offend them. No.

PRABHA (*wounded*): I want to study. Let me do my BA at least.

AAI: It's not in my hands, Prabha.

PRABHA: See me through my four years in the city.

AAI: My dear, even when He was alive, I didn't have the power to give anything to anybody. Now I'm altogether dependent.

PRABHA: How much will you endure? When Tatyaji was alive, not a day went by when he didn't yell at you. You bottle up everything, for how long?

AAI: Prabha, is sorrow something you show others? You keep it to yourself. If it gets too unbearable, there are enough dark rooms in this wada. You go there and let the tears flow quietly. That's what all the Deshpande women have done.

PRABHA: I won't. I'll grab happiness for myself—and for you.

AAI: Prabha, I said a contented farewell to happiness long ago, when I saw I wasn't meant to have it. One should willingly give up what one cannot have.

PRABHA: Let me study, Aai. Let me stand on my own feet. We can live together then. We won't have to look to anyone for charity. Let me go to Amaravati.

AAI: What will Bhaskar say?

PRABHA: Let him say what he likes. Aai, don't you understand? They'll devour you bit by bit, and when they're done, they'll throw you aside like junk. They are putting up with you now because you work. What will you do when you're worn out? Those two cannot see beyond their wives and children.

AAI: Love always runs forward, dear. I have no expectations from anybody. All I ask is that God close my eyes soon. (*Silence.*) But my heart is heavy for Chandu. He toils like a beast, poor soul. He has no education, no wife, no children. No one he can call his own. He stayed single because you weren't married. There's time, a whole future—he might be sick, in pain ... the worry eats me up inside.

PRABHA: And whom do I have?

AAI: Prabha, we really ruined your life, dear. You were the cleverest of them all. And you loved your studies. But that was his nature. Nobody could act against his word. For him it was just one thing—why do girls need education? How much I pleaded with him, I swear to God I did. Times have changed now. So many girls of your age have gone ahead and studied. They work. They earn. I admire them so much. But we village people just didn't have the vision in those days.

PRABHA: Tatyaji hadn't spoken to me for years when he died. Yes, I did turn down proposals. But you tell me Aai, what kind of men were they? Like us, all of them—empty show of wealth, no education. Debauched louts.

AAI: Prabha, he didn't stop talking to you because he was angry with you.

PRABHA: He would leave the room the moment I stepped in.

AAI: How can I make you understand? He felt ashamed to face you. In his last days he used to say, I have ruined this child. My soul will not rest. (*Prabha weeps.*) He had become very emotional. But what was the use? (*Pause.*) Will a thousand or two be enough?

PRABHA: For what?

AAI: For your education.

PRABHA: What is a thousand or two these days, Aai?

AAI: What do we do then? I don't have any more. You know that. Whatever I had went this morning.

PRABHA: You shouldn't have given away that money. They'd have managed for themselves.

AAI: Think of the fuss there would have been if that money had been found in my trunk. You know how Bhaskar pries around opening trunks. So I gave it.

PRABHA: Aai, there's my gold.

AAI: That's with Bhaskar dear.

PRABHA: There's at least thirty *tolas* of mine. Give me that.

AAI: Prabha ...

PRABHA: Let me get out of here, Aai. This wada will devour me. I feel so stifled in this darkness. Let me go to Amaravati.

AAI: Everything is with Bhaskar. The first thing he did when your father died was to untie the keys from his sacred thread and take them.

PRABHA: Where's yours?

AAI: That's also with him.

PRABHA: You can take it as lost then.

AAI: How can you say that! He's your brother, isn't he?

PRABHA: I know him only too well. He will cry thief and swallow the gold himself. You'll see. I won't let him. Ask him for my gold and give it to me tomorrow.

AAI: The brothers are bound to settle things once the rites are over. Ask for your share then.

PRABHA: But you must tell him first, tomorrow.

AAI: Not tomorrow. After the thirteenth day.

PRABHA: You're going to be intimidated all your life.

AAI: I won't be this time, all right? You'll see. If it makes everything right for you, I'll fight with them for you. Yes, Prabha. (*Pause.*) What will you do with all that gold? Sell it?

PRABHA: Yes.

AAI: I'm asking because I'm ignorant. Will you really sell it?

PRABHA: I'll put the money in the bank. That much gold will fetch fifty–sixty thousand. I can study on the interest. I'll take a small job on the side. Give tuitions. Do anything at all. You watch. You'll come and stay with me.

AAI: How old that gold is! All the honour of our family is contained in it dear.

PRABHA: Once I get my degree and a job, you'll leave this village, this wada, everything that's here and come and stay with me. Honestly Aai, gold, husband, family, I've lost interest in all of that. Let's be free. How you drudge in this house! You are past seventy now. How much longer will you sit blowing into the chulah, getting smoke in your eyes?

AAI: You work as long as you can.

PRABHA: Once I have a job, I'll buy back all that gold for you. Then you can deck your daughters-in-law in it to your heart's content. (*Laughs.*) Put millstones of gold round their necks if you like!

AAI: My Prabhu! How long it is since you've laughed. We will sell the gold, we really will. How old those ornaments are! They belonged to great grandmother-in-law and grandmother-in-law. The

Deshpandes sold their lands, but never touched the women's gold. Lakshmi wasn't ever taken out into the market. You know Prabha, gold is not just money. One generation passes it on to the next and that one to the one after. So it goes—our link with our ancestors. When you put on the ornaments, you think of all the hands and necks they have touched! You sense all the Deshpande women standing around you, gazing upon you admiringly. When I first entered this house, how radiant Dadibai looked in those ornaments, how resplendent. She named each one and told me its history—who had made it and when .... (*Sighs.*) But I will give yours to you, come what may.

(*Light fades. It comes up in Bhaskar's room. He is snoring. Vahini wakes up with a start. She sits up.*)

VAHINI: Listen ...

BHASKAR (*startled*): What is it?

VAHINI: Can you go and take a look outside? I think Chandu-bhauji is moaning dreadfully.

BHASKAR: Why should he moan? Didn't our father die as well?

VAHINI: He's hurt his foot, for heaven's sake. He might be running a temperature. I wish he hadn't fetched in all that firewood. Please take him to the doctor tomorrow morning first thing all right? We don't want the wound turning *septum* and all.

BHASKAR: Can't he go to the doctor by himself? He's not a child.

VAHINI: That doctor won't even look at you if you don't put your money down first. Makes no difference to him whether you are a Deshpande or something else.

BHASKAR: We'll see.

VAHINI: We are the elders. We must behave that way and do what we should. What will people think of you otherwise? I sit here worrying and fretting that people might say nasty things about you.

BHASKAR: Will you let me sleep now?

VAHINI (*softly, fearfully*): And once the rituals are over, give everyone their share.

BHASKAR: Give what?

VAHINI: All those arguments today. What a scene in front of the children! After all, they're the only family our children will have when we are gone. Give it away.

BHASKAR: Give away what for heaven's sake?

VAHINI: Give each one his share. And let's be free.

BHASKAR: Shares out of twelve acres, and what will you eat?

VAHINI: I'm not talking about the land. Look at other families. Our people are really good at heart. Even Anjali is all right. It was very nice of her to get that skirt material for Ranju last time she came. Of course I didn't tell her people don't go about this village kicking bare legs in the air. But she did bring it didn't she? So I kept it and quietly made pillow-covers out of it.

BHASKAR: She is very cunning.

VAHINI: Not at all. A Konkanastha she may be, but she's never asked for her share. She's not too fond of people, that's all. Even Sudhir-bhauji said, nobody goes around wearing ornaments in Bombay and left them behind. But that's when Tatyaji was alive. It was different then. It's different now.

BHASKAR: Don't teach me what to do.

VAHINI: Suppose something happens? We don't want such responsibilities, the pest. There's no bank nor nothing here. That safe of ours belongs to 1857. One jerk and a thief will have it open. (*Bhaskar laughs.*) Why do you laugh?

(*Bhaskar takes out a filigree work brass box from under his pillow.*)

BHASKAR: Here.

VAHINI (*shocked*): What?

BHASKAR: You're a fool. Bhaitaad!

VAHINI: Will you please leave it where it was?

BHASKAR: Look. Everyone's share is here. Aai's, Prabha's, Sudhir's, Chandu's, mine. I'm not going to show it all to Sudhir.

VAHINI: You think he doesn't know how much each one has?

BHASKAR: What can he do if I say Tatyaji sold it? Let him see for himself when I open the safe on the thirteenth day. I put this in the pooja room day before yesterday.

VAHINI: Did someone see you do it?

BHASKAR: Ranju was snooping around asking, what's that, what's in it? I gave her such a scolding! I bring it out every night and keep it under my pillow.

VAHINI: It's not right. Don't invite anybody's curse on yourself.

BHASKAR: Everything is right. This is what will save us in the end. Not your darling brother-in-law. (*Opens the box.*) Wear them. Let's see how they look on you.

VAHINI: We are in mourning for heaven's sake.

BHASKAR: Oh dear! You're turning out to be a big mourner for your father-in-law aren't you! Wear them. Come on. Haven't seen you in those ornaments for years. (*Bhaskar holds out a fistful of ornaments towards Vahini. Her eyes glitter.*) Here's a Chandrahar. Thirty tolas. Wear it. (*Vahini wears the ornaments one by one. This scene should be played at a very slow pace, trancelike. The mood is charmed, heavy with emotion.*) A five-strand Mohanmal, fifteen tolas. A Pohehar, fifteen tolas. Chapalahar, fifteen tolas. Putalya, twenty tolas. Thhushi, five tolas. A Siree, five tolas. A Chinchpeti, ten tolas. A pair of Waki, ten tolas, a pair of Tode, twenty-five tolas. A pair of Jodgoti, twenty tolas, a pair of Gujarati Tode, twenty tolas. Patlya, ten tolas. Nuth! Look at the diamonds and rubies! Can't take your eyes off them! A gold rose hairpin, a Vajratik, a Bindi, chain, a Gopha. Three rings. This one set with diamonds, this with emeralds, and this with nine gems. (*Vahini is covered in ornaments from head to foot. Her whole personality has undergone a complete transformation. Glowing and throbbing with radiance, serene, inscrutable. A very icon of timeless feminine beauty.*) You look like the mistress of untold wealth!

(*Vahini gets up slowly. Goes to the mirror and looks at herself intently.*)

VAHINI (*in a voice charged with emotion*): Shall I tell you how I feel? I feel this is not just gold. It's something more. I sense all the Deshpande women standing around me gazing upon me admiringly. Dadi's mother-in-law, Dadi, Aai ... I feel their warm, affectionate touch on me. How many have worn and guarded these ornaments! How many hands and necks they have adorned! One day my Parag's wife will wear them. She too will feel my loving touch. When I first entered this house, how radiant Aai looked in these, how resplendent. She named each ornament, and told me its history—who had made it and when. How blessed I feel to be a link in this line.

(*Long silence.*)

BHASKAR: You're in a proper trance.

(*Vahini heaves a deep sigh. She quietly takes off each ornament one by one, replacing it gently in the box. She closes the box and gives it to Bhaskar.*)

VAHINI: Put it in the pooja room. (*Bhaskar is speechless.*) First thing tomorrow, give each one his share.

(*Bhaskar goes to put the box back. Dust falls on Vahini from the ceiling as the lights dim. The light comes on, only on the courtyard. A crazy, mysterious light. Dadi sits huddled in it.*)

DADI: Vyenkatesh! Arrey Vyenkatesh. Why have you brought me so far? Why are you behaving like a child? Are you playing a prank on this old woman? I am so tired son! Time just won't move, the pest. How many more days must I live? Why are you laughing? I am so full of dread I can't tell you. Something is going wrong here. The Deshpande household is not doing well. How the mice trouble me all night. They run all over the house. The wretched creatures have dug through the whole wada. Nobody's filling up their holes. How much can I alone do? Daughters-in-law, grand-daughters-in-law, great-grandsons, they've all come. It's time I went. I have lived my life. Nothing remains. Why are you laughing like that? Why my son ...

(*Aai comes in looking terrified. She notices Dadi. She moves forward and touches her. The light changes.*)

AAI: Dadibai ...

DADI (*groping*): *Who is that?* Soonbai is it?

AAI: How could she have got here? Chandu, Chandu ...

DADI: Wasn't Vyenkatesh here just now? Where did he go all of a sudden? Wasn't he standing there, near the engine? Vyenkatesh ...

(*Chandu comes in limping. His foot is swollen.*)

AAI: How did she get here, near the tractor? Carry her in, will you?

(*Chandu lifts her up.*)

DADI: Who is it? Why are you taking me away? It isn't Vyenkatesh. I saw him just now. Where did he go then?

(*Suddenly Dadi comes to herself and cries out aloud. Chandu carries her in.*)

AAI: Careful, Chandu. (*To herself.*) Why did she talk as if she was seeing things?

(*Aai stands dazed. Chandu comes back.*)

CHANDU: Aai ... (*Pause.*) Aai.

AAI: Do you think Dadibai saw something Chandu?

CHANDU: No Aai. Nothing. Come in now.

AAI: How did she get as far as the tractor in the middle of the night? (*Pause.*) No one is at peace. (*Folding her hands.*) Forgive us if we have made any mistakes. They are your children after all. Don't trouble any one. Has some wish of yours remained unfulfilled? We will fulfil everything. Don't let your heart linger behind.

(*Darkness.*)

Scene Three

Lights. Enter Anjali. Goes to the middle room. Vahini is lying there. She feels Vahini's forehead. Tells Parag who is sitting there to go and eat. Peeps out on the verandah.

ANJALI: Aai ...

AAI: Yes, dear ...

ANJALI: Tell Vahini to eat a little.

AAI: It's no use till the girl comes back.

(*Anjali returns to the middle room. Sits near Vahini.*)

VAHINI: Anjali ...

ANJALI: We'll find Ranju. I'm sure we will.

VAHINI: Whose curse do you think we have brought on ourselves?

(*Light on the verandah.*)

AAI: Chandu, my dear, I feel as if my spirit's gone right out of my body.

CHANDU: Come into the house. It's very late. Past midnight.

AAI: No, you stay here. We cannot talk in the house. (*Pause.*) Have they
   traced Ranju? No one is telling me anything. It's four days since
   Sudhir left. Where could the girl have gone!

CHANDU: Sudhir has gone to Bombay to look for her.

AAI: She's gone; but they say she's taken everything with her. Is that true?

CHANDU: That's what Bhau says.

AAI: Let the gold go, the pest. Let the girl be found. Dear God, don't let
   the Deshpande honour be torn into shreds any further.

CHANDU: Aai everything's gone.

AAI: Good it's gone. Root-cause of quarrels. The last link has been
   cut. Good.

CHANDU: What will we do now, Aai?

AAI: Chandu tell me. Had we earned it? The Deshpandes lived off other
   peoples' sweat, didn't they? So it's gone where it belonged.

CHANDU: Prabha has not opened her door for four days.

AAI: She lost her share with the rest. What hopes she had! (*Pause.*)
   Chandu, the others will manage somehow. But you are left
   without any protection.

CHANDU: Come into the house.

AAI: How hard you work. In the house, in the fields. You balance the
   whole house on your shoulders. (*Pause.*) Does your foot hurt?

CHANDU: It does, Aai.

AAI: Go to the doctor, please. Your brother isn't going to tell you to go.

CHANDU: The doctor wants his fee first Aai.

AAI: How swollen it is!

CHANDU: Aai, you mustn't tend to my foot.

AAI: Why not?

CHANDU: I feel bad. I should be pressing your feet.

AAI: Oh my son. Be like this all your life. It doesn't matter if everything else is lost. Let it go. Just keep your heart as it is and you will never want.

(*Sudhir and Ranju enter from outside.*)

AAI: Oh thank God. You're back. Ranju, my child …

(*Nobody has slept. They all come out on the verandah, except Prabha. Deep silence. Then Vahini collapses to the ground and breaks into sobs.*)

SUDHIR (*to Ranju*): Go on in.

(*She goes.*)

BHASKAR: Where did you find her?

SUDHIR: In Bombay.

BHASKAR: And the fellow?

SUDHIR: Couldn't find the teacher. I inquired at all the police stations as soon as I got to Bombay. The hotel owner had just brought her to the Bandra chowki when I got there. That was lucky. What a dreadful neighbourhood it is Bhau!

BHASKAR: And the fellow?

SUDHIR: Ran off. They spent the whole of the first day and night in a lodging house. They were asking the owner about film studios— where they were and that kind of thing. In the middle of the night, he left her by herself and ran off with the ornaments. She was sitting in the room, frightened. I have filed a complaint. Let's see if they find him. Even if they do, who knows if we'll get back any of the stuff he's taken.

(*Long silence. Then Bhaskar goes in. Locks the door from inside. Vahini looks at the closed door fearfully. Bhaskar takes down a whip and hits Ranju. Ranju screams. Then he goes on lashing her like a man possessed. She continues to scream. Vahini struggles to get up. Goes to the door, but collapses there. Stuffs the end of her sari in her mouth to stop herself from screaming. Anjali goes up to her and holds her. Parag clings to Sudhir, holding him tight. A little later, Bhaskar throws down the whip. Sits on the cot. Sobs soundlessly. Silence. Then Bhaskar comes out on to the verandah. Ranju goes up to the mirror crying to see what she looks like in tears. Vahini goes up to her and holds her close. Light only on the verandah now.*)

BHASKAR: Sudhir, how can I ever repay you for what you've done?

SUDHIR: Let's just forget it, Bhau. It's over and done with.

BHASKAR: The younger brother has become the elder and the elder younger today.

SUDHIR: We have found Ranju. Nothing else matters.

BHASKAR: Two more days and I'd have had to hide my face from the village. Just as well you came at night. Did anyone see you?

SUDHIR: No, I purposely took a taxi from Amravati. Decided to avoid the bus. I'd have run into dozens of familiar faces.

BHASKAR: Good you did that. We have not stepped out of the house for the past four days.

SUDHIR: Do you think people don't know about it in the village?

BHASKAR: I'm sure they do. But we weren't forced to tell them with our own mouths.

SUDHIR: The police station?

BHASKAR: It's four miles away. In the next village. No, I have not reported anything. Why should I report my own disgrace?

SUDHIR: The teacher has cleaned us out completely. We'll have to report it to the local police.

BHASKAR: That's one thing you mustn't ask me to do Sudhir. I beg you. People will spit on us. Let the gold go. It'll come back. But not our honour if it's lost. (*Sudhir sighs in despair.*) It's a blessing you are back in time. Tomorrow is the ninth day. The Brahmans will start arriving. They would have started asking questions.

SUDHIR: Has Bansilal given the money?

BHASKAR: Yes. Such a valuable piece of land! Went at the price of dirt. Finally you get just what you are destined to get.

SUDHIR: We must also have made mistakes. We reap as we sow.

(*Bhaskar isn't sure whether this is a barb or not. He looks at Sudhir for a moment. Then gets up.*)

BHASKAR: Go to bed now. You must be exhausted.

(*Bhaskar goes in.*)

SUDHIR (*to Anjali*): Get me some water Anjali.

AAI: He mustn't have eaten, dear. There is some food.

SUDHIR: No, Aai. We ate something on the way.

(*Anjali goes in.*)

PARAG: Kaka, did you meet Abhay?

(*Anjali returns with the water.*)

SUDHIR: Yes, I dropped in for a few minutes. I asked him to come with me. He said 'no'. He gets bored in this village.

PARAG: But I'll meet him when I come to Bombay anyway.

SUDHIR: Parag ... (*He takes time drinking water.*) Parag, don't come to Bombay this time.

PARAG: Why?

SUDHIR: Shouldn't somebody be with your parents at such a time?

PARAG: But Ranju is back.

SUDHIR: Yes I know, but ...

PARAG: And I've really behaved myself. Ask Kaku. In all these days I haven't once touched ... Kaku?

ANJALI (*putting her hand on his back*): Of course we're taking you. Kaka's just teasing you.

PARAG: Yes Kaka?

SUDHIR: Go to sleep now. We'll see later.

PARAG: No. Tell me first. Aaji, see how ...

AAI: Didn't Kaku say she'd take you?

PARAG: No. Kaka, you tell me.

SUDHIR: Okay. We'll take you. Sleep now. (*Parag lies down, still doubtful.*) Aai, go and sleep.

AAI: A load has been lifted.

(*Sudhir and Anjali go into B. Darkness on the verandah. Light in the room.*)

ANJALI: So you met Abhay.

SUDHIR: Yes. (*Pause.*) Phew! What a relief!

ANJALI: We could hardly swallow anything—worried sick as we were! Is Abhay studying?

SUDHIR: Yes, very hard.

ANJALI: We'll take Parag with us.

SUDHIR: Wait a minute ...

ANJALI: It's true, he didn't stir out of the house for four days. He was hanging about me, all the time. When you said you wouldn't take him, his face really fell.

SUDHIR: But weren't you saying no to begin with?

ANJALI: Yes. But look at the atmosphere here. He's totally mixed-up, poor soul.

SUDHIR (*surprised*): What's that phrase you used?

ANJALI: It just slipped out. I hear it all the time around here.

SUDHIR: That's my Warhadi woman! (*Pause.*) No, we can't take Parag. Abhay told me outright—don't bring him.

ANJALI: He's never cared for Parag. I knew it. He's always made fun of him. Never in front of you, because he wouldn't dare. But he's still young I thought.

SUDHIR: Then why were you shouting from the rooftops here about his great brotherly love?

ANJALI: They are all so fond of him. What was I supposed to tell them? That he makes fun of them?

SUDHIR: This time all I said was Parag is coming. And he just raved and ranted. I was stunned. He is ashamed of Parag, of his clothes, the way he speaks. He said he'd tell his friends he was a servant from the village.

ANJALI: You should have slapped him.

SUDHIR: He's as tall as me now. If he'd caught my hand mid-air, I'd have looked a real fool. If we take Parag with us, this fellow will treat him like dirt. Best not to. Parag's going to be very disappointed. But for a short while. We'll take him one of these days. Pass me that pillow.

(*Pause.*)

ANJALI: Before you do anything else tomorrow morning, take Chandu-bhauji to the doctor. I think his wound has turned septic. You know how tense we were. Nobody had any time for him. It didn't even strike us. I tried giving him some money, but Vahini burst into tears. Do you think we don't care for him, she said.

SUDHIR: Why do you get so involved in all this?

ANJALI: It's not right to say that. When Ranju ran away, I was worried sick about Abhay. All by himself for such a long time. Was he eating well? Or was he collecting his friends together and swigging beer! My mind was running really scared. This Ranju affair has been a bit of a bother but ...

SUDHIR: What do you mean, a bit of a bother? I am down by a thousand rupees. Had to pay the police. We aren't going to ask Bhau to return that. And the gold's gone too.

ANJALI: Don't even think about it at this time. You know, when Bansilal came to give the money, Bhauji just couldn't stop the tears coming.

SUDHIR: How much did he give?

ANJALI: Fifteen thousand, I think. The deed will be signed after the rituals are over. (*Pause.*) He's going to start a saw-mill here. He has already sent off to Amaravati for a bulldozer. Bhauji pleaded with him, wait a few days more. Let us finish all this and then you can bring in your bulldozer. But do you think the wretched pest would hear of it! This is an auspicious time he said.

SUDHIR: I've had enough of this. We aren't going to be much help around here. As soon as the rituals over, we'll leave.

(*Darkness. A mysterious, hazy light on the verandah. Chandu is lying in a corner and Dadi sits by the wall. The chanting of the ninth day mantra can be heard. The word 'spirit' is heard again and again above the rest. When the mantras are halfway through, the rumble of the bulldozer begins. Then the sounds of the bulldozer and the mantras mingle.*)

VOICE (*off*): Having cleansed the mouth, having time and place in mind, having resolved to perform the ninth day's Shradh for the release of Venkatesh, departed spirit of the Atri *gotra*, from a ghostly existence, having turned towards the south according to ancient practice, having offered a blade of *kusha* grass, and water for the washing of the feet, and a seat, having placed a kusha and a *til* to the left of the kusha, and another kusha in front of oneself to the right, having placed a vessel before one, and placed a sacred blade of kusha in it, having sprinkled water on it in silence, and cast a til in it in silence, having made an offering in silence, for his foothold, one should spread a covering of kusha on Vyenkatesh, departed spirit of the Atri gotra on this day, for the ninth day's Shradh.

(*The rumble of the bulldozer continues even after the mantras have ended. It drops to a hum when the dialogue begins, but it remains audible. Lights on Sudhir and Anjali's room. They are packing.*)

SUDHIR: Have you packed my shaving kit?

ANJALI: Yes.

SUDHIR: Towel?

ANJALI: Yes. (*Pause.*) I have left one of your shirts for Chandu-bhauji.

SUDHIR: He'll have to be taken to Amaravati.

ANJALI: Will you extend your leave?

SUDHIR: How can I do that, Anju? I have told Bhau. If there is any delay, the leg will be lost.

(*Vahini comes in.*)

VAHINI: Here, keep this.

ANJALI: What is it, Vahini?

VAHINI: Ladoos. For Abhay. From the offerings for Tatyaji.

SUDHIR: When are you coming to Bombay?

VAHINI: Next blue moon. You just have to call and we'll be there! Bhauji, say goodbye to Vansa.

SUDHIR: I've tried several times. She won't come out.

(*Bhaskar looks in.*)

BHASKAR: Time to go. Are you ready? The bus will be here any minute.

(*Sudhir goes in. Lights on the verandah, the side room and the middle room. Aai, Dadi, Chandu, and Ranju are on the verandah. Parag is in the side room, lying on a cot on his stomach. Sudhir disappears into the interiors of the house. Soon his voice is heard calling, 'Prabha, Prabha, open the door, Prabha'. A few moments later, he returns.*)

SUDHIR: Aai ...

(*Bhaskar comes out with the suitcases. Vahini and Anjali follow.*)

BHASKAR: Now come along ... come along.

VAHINI: He is always in a hurry.

BHASKAR: I'll go ahead and keep the bus waiting.

SUDHIR (*touches Dadi's feet. Anjali does the same*): Dadi ...

(*Dadi suddenly starts weeping.*)

VAHINI: She's stopped talking these days and has started this new thing.

SUDHIR: Aai ...

(*Both touch her feet. Also Vahini's. Vahini lifts the end of her sari to her eyes.*)

SUDHIR: Vahini, Chandu must be taken to the hospital in Amaravati tomorrow. Don't delay it.

VAHINI: Don't worry.

SUDHIR (*to Ranju*): Now be a good girl. Where is Parag?

RANJU: Sleeping.

SUDHIR: Where?

VAHINI: Let him be, Bhauji.

(*Silence. Then Sudhir goes into the side room, sits on the cot near Parag. He watches him for a moment, in numbed silence. Then puts his hand on Parag's hair. Returns to the verandah.*)

SUDHIR (*to Anjali*): Come. I'll be back soon. We will all come.

VAHINI: You must. This is your home.

SUDHIR: Let's go.

ANJALI: Vahini ...

(*Sudhir and Anjali go ahead. Then Sudhir stops.*)

VAHINI: Bhauji, come soon. But don't look back now. The more you
    do, the more your heart will tug at you. Write once in a while.
    Come whenever you can.

(*Sudhir and Anjali are at the end of the courtyard. Sudhir can't take the next step. He swallows, and turns to look back.*)

SUDHIR: Goodbye.

(*Just as he begins to walk away ...*)

CHANDU (*in a feeble, broken voice*): Sudhir ...

(*For a moment Sudhir stops, shaken, rooted to the spot. Then he and Anjali go out slowly. The light dims, then fades. Only one spot remains, on Aai, leaning against the wall. Gradually Aai begins to look like Dadi. The sound of the bulldozer rises. Darkness.*)

CURTAIN

Reflection

Pratibimb

Translated by
Shanta Gokhale

Characters:

Woman

He

Flags

Girl

Act One

A pleasant room of the paying guest kind. It is seven-thirty in the morning, but the curtains are still drawn and it is dark. He is fast asleep on the bed. There is total silence on the stage for a long time, for so long in fact that the audience should begin to wonder what's happening without actually beginning to shuffle and whisper. Suddenly the alarm clock near his pillow goes off shrilly. He doesn't move. The alarm keeps going till it is fully wound down. Again there is silence for a few moments. Suddenly He starts and gets up. For a few moments his movements are quite directionless. Then He stumbles over to the clock, peers at it and says, 'My God'. He puts the clock down in a rush, puts on his slippers and is hurrying to the bathroom when the telephone rings. He stumbles back to the clock, realizes his mistake and goes to the telephone. As he is about to pick up the receiver, the telephone, in sheer malice, stops ringing. Even before he can take his hand off the receiver, the second alarm goes off. While He is rushing to the clock a third bell peals. The doorbell. Confused, He makes for the telephone, realizes it's the doorbell and goes to the door. He opens the door and looks out. There's no one there. He shuts the door in disgust and returns to sit on the bed. There is a brief silence. The telephone half-rings, teasingly. He starts up and looks at it. Then He gathers himself together like an animal waiting to pounce, and stands watching all three—the alarm clock, the telephone, the doorbell—none of them ringing now. Gradually his tension disappears.

He relaxes on the bed. He is calmer. He gets up, draws open the curtains and throws open the window. Instantly the thunder of the traffic enters the room. He slams the window shut. He picks up his towel and goes to the bathroom. He squeezes toothpaste on to his brush and comes out brushing his teeth. He switches on the radio casually. The radio goes ting-tong and belts out three shrill jingles one after another. The fourth is about to begin when He turns off the radio utterly disgusted. He continues to brush his teeth, eyeing the audience thoughtfully. He glances at the newspaper. It is blank. There is not a sign of print on it. He reads the paper with great concentration, till a meddlesome, coquettish woman of enormous proportions enters through the back door, with a cup of tea in one hand, a broom in the other. She bangs the tea before him. He doesn't even glance up.

WOMAN: Your tea. (*He is startled.*) How can you sleep for so long, holding up my work and all? (*Starts sweeping the room, continuing to talk without looking at him.*) I get up at four in the morning all ready for the day's work. Who do you think you are? You get up any time you like and expect me to get your tea? Even a paying guest must have some discipline. Is it because I put up with all your nonsense? I had made it quite clear right at the beginning that I am a woman who believes in doing the right job at the right moment. You were fine the first few days. But now? It's seven, sometimes eight in the morning. And on Sundays even nine o'clock is too early for you. Is it normal to sleep like this? You should have been named Kumbhakarna. (*She continues to sweep around where He stands, treating his legs like any piece of furniture. He too does not move his legs.*) You're lucky it's me you have to put up with all this. Just wait till you get married. Then you'll be up at five. Not just that. It'll be 'Why do you get up, darling? I'll make your tea. Why don't you stay in bed, sweetheart. I'll fill the water.' I remember all of it. When my husband was alive, I never once had to make the tea or fill the water. He would even fetch the milk from the centre. It's three years now you've been here. And I've treated you like one of the family. But do you behave that way?

Sleeping till all hours as if this were a hotel. (*Gathers the sweeping, straightens up and looks at him for the first time.*) Why don't you say something? Are you angry with me for scolding you? I scold you because you're one of the family. D'you see? DO YOU SEE? (*He opens his mouth to speak and realizes it's full of toothpaste. Pointing to it, He goes to the bathroom.*) I'm glad you brush your teeth before you have your tea. There are people who must have their tea first thing in the morning. Bed tea, they call it. What filthy habits! But you're okay that way. The tea must be stone cold now. Or is that the way you like it? Some people like to pour into the saucer and blow and blow on it and have it. (*He screams suddenly from the bathroom.*) What happened? (*Pause.*) Did you slip and fall? Shall I come in? Hope you're dressed? Or are you in your underwear? Doesn't wash them for days. Dirty fellow. Only his teeth are worth showing. Can you hear me?

(*He comes out terrified, and stands leaning against the doorjamb. He manages to stumble over to the dressing table, where He glances in the mirror and gives a frightened start. He picks up a small mirror from the table and looks at it, and gives another start. Her chatter continues.*)

WOMAN: Cleanliness is all important after all. A person must be clean inside and out, his heart, his clothes, his habits.

HE (*shouts suddenly in a broken voice*): Will you shut up, woman?

(*For a moment she is dumbfounded. Then she is angry.*)

WOMAN: What was that you said?

HE: How you go on and on, and don't let me think even. (Drops into a chair.) Terrible.

WOMAN (*concerned*): What's the matter?

HE: Tell me. Are the mirrors in the house all okay?

WOMAN: What do you mean?

HE: Are they really okay?

WOMAN: What's okay supposed to mean? Don't I wipe them every day? Even mirrors ought to be spotless. It's no use your being clean. If the mirror is dirty, you will look dirty. Don't you agree?

HE: That's not what I meant. (*Pause.*) Will you come and have a look at the mirror in the bathroom please?

WOMAN: What for?

HE: Please.

WOMAN: I must know why.

HE: I say, please.

WOMAN: I refuse to enter a man's bathroom.

HE: Please. The mirror.

WOMAN: Oh, all right. What do I do with the mirror?

HE: Tell me what you see there.

WOMAN: You're nuts. What do people see in mirrors?

HE: Look at that one, just once, please.

WOMAN: All right. (*On her way to the bathroom.*) Now don't you follow me into the bathroom.

(*She goes in. Silence.*)

HE: Are you looking at the mirror?

WOMAN: Yes.

HE: Are you really?

WOMAN: I said yes.

HE: What do you see?

WOMAN: What am I supposed to see?

HE: You can't see anything either.

WOMAN: What do you mean anything? Should I see a ghost?

(*She comes out.*)

HE (*impatient, eager*): What did you see in the mirror?

WOMAN: Now you're being childish. What should I see in the mirror? I saw my reflection. That's all.

HE: You did?

WOMAN: Didn't I just? Such a lovely, elegant, graceful jar of ghee.

HE: Did you really see your reflection?

WOMAN: For God's sake. Would I see yours then? Really! The things you say.

HE: Will you come and have a look in this mirror?

WOMAN: Don't get fresh now.

HE: Please.

WOMAN: There's such a difference in age between us—think of that.

HE: Please look—

WOMAN: I have the purest feeling for you—

HE: Please! Please!

WOMAN: Well. I will if I must. (*Looks at herself lingeringly in the mirror, pleased with what she is seeing. Lost in herself she begins to hum.*) *Premnagar mein banaungi ghar mai, karke sab singar!*

WOMAN: This mirror was a wedding gift, you know. It used to be in our bedroom. (*Blushing.*) The things we two have seen in this mirror. He was so-o-o romantic. Do you think a little girth, just a bit more, would give me just that bit more grace?

HE: Can you see your reflection in that mirror?

WOMAN: Not again. What are mirrors meant for? What do *you* see in them?

HE: Nothing.

WOMAN: What?

HE: I cannot see a thing in the mirror.

WOMAN: Nothing? Not a thing?

HE: Nothing. I don't see a reflection or anything of the kind. I washed my face and looked in the mirror. Found it blank. Then I thought may be it's dirty. So I cleaned and looked. Still it was blank. I

screamed. Then I thought may be the mercury has come off. So
I took a look at these two mirrors out here. And it was the same,
Bai. I've lost my reflection. It has disappeared. It has gone away.
Left me and gone.

WOMAN: Where was the binge last night?

HE: Nowhere.

WOMAN: Of course there was a binge. You're still drunk.

HE: I've not drunk in a week.

WOMAN: Don't lie.

HE: It's the truth.

WOMAN: Come here. (*Walks up to him herself.*) Open your mouth. (*Forces
his mouth open and smells it.*) Smells of toothpaste. Are they making
tooth-paste-flavoured liquor these days?

HE: Stop joking.

WOMAN: It's no joke. You're crazy. How can you lose your reflection? It
must be hallucination. Or your mind is not there. Go and take
another look in the mirror. Get up. I'd just like to see how you
lose your reflection. Utter rot. You're a paying guest here. I'm
responsible if you lose something. I don't want to be accused of
strange things out of the blue. That's why I'm yelling at you all
the time, take care of your things, lock them up. Don't just sit
around. Get up and take a good look in the mirror again. (*He half
rises, but sits down again, scared.*) What are you scared of? Get
up. Go on. (*He shakes his head gloomily.*) What's the use of losing
your nerve? Get up. Get up. Come on, up.

(*She is all set to hoist him up. He gets up. Looks at the mirror decisively.
A stifled sound escapes him. She hurries across and looks in the mirror.*)

WOMAN: Really. Your image is not there in the mirror. This is the limit.
How funny!

HE: You think it's funny?

WOMAN: We should put it in the papers.

HE (*shouts*): No!

WOMAN: Do you have a recent photograph?

HE: It's not going to be in the papers.

WOMAN: Why not?

HE: No. I won't tell journalists. I won't tell anybody.

WOMAN: Imagine how famous you'll be.

HE: To hell with fame...

WOMAN: You'll be world famous in an instant.

HE: Don't want that kind of fame.

WOMAN: That kind and this kind. Fame is fame after all. Or else who knows whom in this city of Bombay? Does anyone know anyone else? Eh? Tell me. Does anyone? (*He shakes his head.*) So? Now is your chance. You have been staying with me for the last three years. But I do not know your name. Everyone calls you Blockhead. So I also call you Blockhead. Besides, it's easy to remember. Who'd remember a name? What odd names people have. Blockhead is fine for me. So the point is as soon as this news appears in the press, people will get to know you. People will throng the doors, windows, both sides of the road, the rooftops, and the branches of trees, just to catch a glimpse of you. People will make room for you in buses and local trains, cabbies won't diddle you, clerks, even in government offices, will be polite without provocation. Why! Even if thieves accost you, they will recognize you and let you go, saying 'What's he got after all?' See? That's fame. Once you're famous, doors will open automatically for you. The whole world will know you as 'The Man without a Reflection'! The wonder of wonders! Travel all over the world. Stand in front of a mirror and hold one man shows of the Man without a Reflection. Earn lakhs of rupees. Evade all taxes. Stay in Five Star hotels. Drink champagne. Get photographed with starlets from Hollywood. But, mind, that's about all. Nothing more. And when you're dead, I'll put up a plaque on this door. 'Here lived the famous Mr Blockhead who didn't make a reflection.' You silly fellow, why do you sit as if you are in mourning? Who has had such luck coming his way?

HE: You won't tell anybody. Will you?

WOMAN: Nobody?

HE: Not a soul. Not the neighbours. Not the family. No friends and associates, no police officers, rationing officers, the RTO men or my boss. They'll cancel my ration card. Take away my driving license. I'll lose my job.

WOMAN: Do you think all this'll happen?

HE: Yes.

WOMAN: Rot!

HE: Bai, it will.

WOMAN: Nonsense!

HE: People do not care for anything unexpected, unusual, or unnatural they get terrified. And in sheer panic they go on ridiculing the unnatural thing till it drops dead.

WOMAN: Go on. You're imagining things.

HE: I'm telling you. There was this boy in my class at school. He had this lump on his forehead. We teased him. Bumpy, Bumpy, till he threw himself into the pond.

WOMAN: Oh dear! I hope you're not going to kill yourself.

HE: I'd like to.

WOMAN: Not in my house, you won't. I don't mind if you fall ill and die. That's not a suspicious event. But if you kill yourself, I'll never get another paying guest. I'll get a mesh put on that window first thing today. We're on the fifth floor.

HE: Do you think ...?

WOMAN: What?

HE: That my reflection doesn't exist because perhaps I don't exist? Can you see me?

WOMAN: What do you mean?

HE: Can you?

WOMAN: Of course.

HE: What do I look like?

WOMAN: For heaven's sake. Like a blockhead.

HE: You mean you can really see me?

WOMAN: I said so once.

HE: You can see my body?

WOMAN: Want me to touch it and see?

(*She's about to touch him. He squirms.*)

HE: No, no. Don't. What'll that prove?

WOMAN: Prove? It'll prove you have a body. That it's not lost like your reflection.

HE: How can it prove that?

WOMAN: Now listen. There are only two ways to prove that a body exists. One, by reflection. Two, by another body. One thing proves the existence of another. Or else an object has no meaning. Now look at this inkpot. It gets its meaning from this pen. This pack of cigarettes. It has a meaning because of this box of matches. He always used to say—that's my late husband—you are a jar of ghee full to the brim, and me? I'm a beanpole. Like a pretty little mouse sitting on a jar of ghee. That's why we looked so good together. So you see, if you want to be sure of your own body, then you have to depend on another body. Now I'm prepared to do anything that is necessary for my paying guest. It's my job to see that all his needs are taken care of, and he's comfortable. I take such care of you. I don't even play my LP of the *Geeta Ramayana* or my tapes of the popular writers lest they disturb you.

HE: But Bai, is a reflection just a body?

WOMAN: What else? What do you see in the mirror—your mind? Your heart? Your soul?

HE: I wonder. What does a mirror show? What do we see?

WOMAN: Besides, instead of saying we look in the mirror, wouldn't it be more correct to say that it's the reflection in the mirror that looks at us?

HE: That's also true.

WOMAN: There. So your reflection must have got a little bored of looking at you. Thirty years is a long time to be looking at the same thing. It must have got fed up and walked off. How many years of blockheadedness can the poor thing take? Blockheads come a dime a dozen.

HE: Could my own reflection be bored of me?

WOMAN: Why not? Bodies are a tiresome thing anyway. The mind— now that is something you don't tire of. Naturally. Because things are constantly happening in the mind. At least you can make things happen there. You can always think—this or that will happen or I'll do this or that. Dream away—colourful, spicy, resplendent dreams. To hell with reflection. You've a mind, don't you? An honest-to-goodness real-and-alive mind? Keep it busy. You won't miss your reflection one bit then.

HE: But now my mind is going to be full of thoughts about my reflection. So it amounts to the same thing.

WOMAN: Why do you go on and on about your reflection? Were you really so fond of it?

HE: Fond of it? I wouldn't know.

WOMAN: So then?

HE: I didn't give it a thought while it was around, though it did scare me a couple of times. That should have put me on my guard. What happened was—there I was looking in the mirror—looking really hard, you know, asking, who are you, man? Who are you? Are you the same as I? I kept on asking the question eye-to-eye, with great bravado—keeping my eyes fixed on the eyes in the reflection. And those eyes—they stared back at me, not batting an eyelid—and then those eyes seemed to turn to marbles. If I'd shoved a finger in them it would have gone straight through and left a dark hole. No blood, nothing. It knocked me right off. I moved away fast. After that I didn't dare go anywhere near it. I might look sideways once in a while—and it was there still staring hard at me. What's come over it now? It has vanished without a qualm, no permission asked for, as if we had never known each other before.

WOMAN: Forget it! It makes no difference.

HE: True. It doesn't. But I can't bear the idea of living without it. Even the loss of a limb is okay. One manages somehow. But how can you live without your reflection, even if it is useless?

WOMAN: Don't allow such thoughts to enter your mind. Allow only good thoughts to come in.

HE: What do you mean allow? Do you think thoughts are sheep or cattle to be brought in by their ears?

WOMAN: *Aayya.* Why should you think of cattle and sheep? You are the limit. You are young. Your mind should have thoughts befitting a young man. As our *Rigveda* says: *Aa no bhadrah ritawo yantu vishwtah.* Let noble thoughts come to me from all directions.

HE: Huh! Vedas in 1984! Did these Veda chaps ever face a problem like mine?

WOMAN: Well then, there's a modern song which runs:

The doors of two minds are open,
The spring breeze lashes around.

HE: Sorry. That won't do for me.

WOMAN: Why don't you try? The one who tries, succeeds ...

HE: Is my problem going to be solved by rattling off quotations?

WOMAN: It may, you know. It will, actually. One should be prepared for everything. You shouldn't reject anything. The window of the mind should be kept open—always.

HE: Great!

WOMAN: Really, why don't you do one thing? Let's try it out. You tell me, no thoughts enter your mind. Suppose, I enter your mind. What do you say to that? (*Coyly.*) And then let's watch what all happens. Now this window ... It's the window to your mind, right? If I come through there, I enter your mind. Then there is fun, and nothing but fun. Great jubilation. Joy, oh what joy! Just try, and you'll forget all that nonsense about your reflection. Agreed? Then it's agreed. Hunh? I am coming. Keep the window open.

(*She hurries out of the door. He stares numbly at the closed window. A little while later there are fumbling sounds at the window. Then thumping, pushing and a high-pitched voice calling, 'Blockhead', 'Blockhead'. He doesn't move. Then the Woman uses muscle and shoves the window open.*)

WOMAN: Whew! How tightly closed the window of your mind was! Don't you ever open it? The hinges have quite rusted away.

(*She climbs on to the window-stilt and tries to come in. The window is too narrow for her size. She has to wriggle and squeeze her way in. At last she is through. She falls on the bed near the window with a thud. She is panting.*)

WOMAN: Oh dear! The window of your mind is so narrow. How can splendid, magnificent thoughts ever enter it? I made it though. And fell gently on your bed itself. (*She blushes and laughs. She's wearing a flimsy nightie over her* sari. *She goes to him softly on tip-toe like one trying to stop her anklets from tinkling. She stamps her foot lightly to draw his attention. He is unmoved. Again she stamps her foot lightly. He's still unmoved. Now she leaps in the air and comes down with a thudding of both feet on the floor.*) Kis soch mein dube huwe ho? Kya mujhse koi galati ho gayi? Mujhse naraj to nahin? Chalo hum Kashmir jayenge.

HE: For God's sake, Woman ...

WOMAN: Woman no more ... I'm Hema Malini and you Dharmindar. I'm Suvarnamalinivasant and you're Sootshekhar, I'm a dose of Hemgarbha and you are ...

HE: Oh, Bai, will you please stop for a little while?

WOMAN: No, no, no. I'm not stopping. The stopper's the loser. What dreams I've brought to your mind! Now let's both get lost in them. (*Sings.*) O my dream-buds!

HE (*shouts*): Stop it, Bai.

WOMAN: Oh, how loud you shout! Don't you know that the walls of the mind are fragile?

HE: Stop this drama.

WOMAN: But in your mind ...

HE: It's my mind, isn't it?

WOMAN: Yes.

HE: And you've come into it.

WOMAN: Yes.

HE: Then how can you decide what should happen in my mind? Eh? It's you who are singing, you who are dancing, you who are deciding to go to Kashmir! As for me, I'm not even going to my office today. You can't take charge of my mind like that. Out. Get out from here. Out.Out.

WOMAN: But—but won't you listen to me?

HE: Out. Get out. *Chalo*. I said, out! (*She moves towards the door.*) Not that way. (*Points to the window.*) Go out the way you came in.

(*She somehow manages to squeeze herself out of the window. Soon after she enters through the door.*)

WOMAN (*cunning*): So, what happened in your mind?

HE: Oh, this and that.

WOMAN: Please tell me. What happened after I entered your mind?

HE: Why should I?

WOMAN: Was it something you can't talk about?

HE: Don't you know?

WOMAN: Really! How would I know what's in your mind?

HE: Come on.

WOMAN: Yes, how?

HE (*threatening*): Just let me enter your mind and I'll show you how.

WOMAN: Ooh! D'you really want to enter my mind? Really? Why ever didn't you tell me all these days?

HE: Because I didn't want to all these days. But I want to now.

WOMAN: Come then. Come. Come quickly. And do wear that red, polka-dotted tie when you come. You look great in it. (*Hands over the tie to him.*) Hmh. Wear it. Go on. Come in now.

HE. Look out!

WOMAN: Hurry up. I really can't bear to wait.

HE: Okay! I'll show you.

(*He goes out of the door. She waits, excited, eager like a sixteen-year-old.*)

WOMAN: Yoohoo. Have you come? Come quick. The window's open. Come in straight. Oh, I hope you've not slipped from the balcony. How long will you keep me waiting? Can you hear me?

(*He leaps in through the window roaring like a tiger. Looks around. Roars again.*)

WOMAN: Why do you roar? You look like the MGM Lion.

HE: Silence!

WOMAN: The play is in session!

HE: Will you stop interrupting?

WOMAN: And do what? Bah! What a face you're making! Even paper tigers are better than that.

HE (*roars*): I'll tear you apart and devour you.

WOMAN: Go, jump. Talking of devouring me. Go, take a look at yourself in a mirror.

(*He roars angrily.*)

WOMAN: Oh my god! He can't see his face in the mirror. How could I forget that? (*He roars.*) Oh, drop dead. You want to be a tiger? And do you think I'm any less? *Arrey,* if you're a tiger, I am a tigress myself. If you're an urban one, I'm a wild one. D'you follow? Hunh?

(*She roars. His legs begin to tremble. He musters courage again and roars again. She roars. He roars. This continues till He begins to cough.*)

WOMAN: Have a cough drop, Mr Tiger.

HE: Hey, you tigress! Just you wait. If you're a tigress, I'm the ringmaster now. Get back. Back, I say.

(*Mimes a whiplash in the air.*)

WOMAN: Oh, yeah. But the last item's still left, Mr Ringmaster. I'll open my jaws and you stick your head in. Come.

(*Roars. Opens her mouth and walks up to him. Terrified, He moves back.*)

WOMAN: Why do you walk backwards? I too brush my teeth with toothpaste. People wouldn't want to put their heads in otherwise, would they?

(*Roars.*)

(*He loses his balance. Continues walking backwards while she keeps roaring and advancing, till He jumps out of the window and runs away. A while later He comes in through the door.*)

HE (*shouting*): This isn't fair.

WOMAN: Now what's the matter?

HE: When *you* enter my mind you're the one to decide what happens in it. Then when *I* enter yours it's you again who decides. This is patently unfair. I seem to have no voice in the matter.

WOMAN: What can *I* do about it?

HE: It's absolutely immoral.

WOMAN: There's nothing unfair or immoral about it. My willpower just happens to be stronger than yours. What can I do about that? And what can you do about your will-power being so weak? Get beaten. Get pushed around. Get trampled upon.

HE: Yes. And go lose your reflection!

WOMAN: Quite. If you want to hold on to what you have, you've got to fight back in this world.

HE: Fight against whom?

WOMAN: I couldn't tell you that. Fight means fight. Fight even against the wind. I even fight with myself.

HE: Against yourself?

WOMAN: Why not? I not only fight myself, I sing to myself and talk to myself. Not that I can sing. But I still sing to myself. I go off tune

even when I'm singing to myself of course. And the lovely chats
I have with myself. You just enter your own mind, make yourself
comfortable and settle down to a good chat. Why don't you
try it?

HE: Try what?

WOMAN: Entering your own mind. You think I'm unfair to you. So
leave me out of it. Enter your own mind. Maybe you'll find your
reflection there.

HE: In my mind?

WOMAN: Sure. You'll be surprised at the things you can find in your
mind. All you need to do is look. Things you've lost, forgotten,
discarded, thrown away. Things you don't want and do want,
the modern, the ancient, the brand new, things turned to sawdust
with white ants,—try doing it, you must have this experience.
It's like Alladin's treasure.

HE: Really?

WOMAN: I'm telling you.

HE: Shall I try?

WOMAN: You must. Would you like me to go with you to keep you
company?

HE: No, certainly not.

WOMAN: Oh, I offer to go because it is your first time.

HE: No, no.

WOMAN: Well, then, what do I care?

HE: Will you go out now? I want to try.

WOMAN: Sure, sure. And—good luck.

(*She goes out by the door. He thinks for a few moments, then He also
leaves by the door. In a little while He comes in through the window. The
light dims. Only a hazy spot remains on him. The rest is totally dark, in
a heavy strained silence. All of a sudden the telephone starts to ring. Soon
the alarm joins in. Then the doorbell. His breathing becomes heavy. The
spot on him disappears. The stage is unbelievably dark. Suddenly all three*

bells stop ringing. A terrible, tense silence—followed by a terrified scream.
Sound of somebody stumbling on the stage. Then silence. A moment later
the lights come on. The stage is empty. He comes in through the door
followed by the Woman.)

WOMAN: I'd said, be careful, it's the first time ...

HE: There's nothing there.

WOMAN: How can it be?

HE: That's the truth.

WOMAN: Don't fib.

HE: Just darkness. And deep silence. Like in a graveyard. (*Silence.*) Please
switch something on—the radio, anything. I can't bear this silence.

(*The Woman switches on the radio and turns the band knobs. There is a*
lot of babble and crackle.)

WOMAN: Is that better? (*He nods.*) Do you want it louder?

(*Turns up the volume. In a moment the ads begin. The telephone, doorbell,*
and alarm clock begin at the same time. She continues blabbering, her
voice rising above the cackle, shrill and high.)

WOMAN: I can't understand why you don't like silence. Do you know
how noise pollution has increased lately? Mind you, pollution
has its advantages though. People never see them. Actually we
should let every pollutant enter through. You will want to know
how. I thought you would. So let me explain. With illustrations.
We used to have a car in the old days, see? When my husband
was alive, see? Bought it second-hand. It was so old you couldn't
buy spare parts for it in the market. That's the kind of car it was.
But my husband used to drive it around, not one bit bothered.
And the car used to run, quite happily. Never needing servicing
or repairing. It always puzzled me as to how it ran at all. So one
day I asked my husband, and he says—d'you know what he
says?—It's simple, he says. It's simple. When you don't clean the
car all the parts remain stuck together tight. But the minute you
clean it, the parts become loose, rattle, and fall off. So you see—
are you feeling a little better now?

(He nods. As her speech proceeds, the other noises have petered off and died down. Only her voice and the doorbell continue, till she suddenly stops talking, leaving only the doorbell ringing away.)

WOMAN: What bell is that? Someone at the door, I think. (*She opens the door. A man enters. Delighted.*) Come in, Mr Flags, you are right on time.

FLAGS: So you've not had your breakfast yet? I left home without breakfast too.

WOMAN: Stop talking about breakfasts. What a morning it's been for us! Mr Blockhead has ... .

FLAGS: So Blockhead's playing hooky from work, eh?

WOMAN: Mr Blockhead has ...

FLAGS: Bastards. The minute you become an officer, corruption gets into you. Our union is planning a front against work shirkers like you.

WOMAN: Mr Blockhead ...

FLAGS: And what are you doing wearing a tie at home? Sarong below, tie above? Hybrid officers like you should be pushed into the sea. A bit of money in hand and they're in a hurry to forget their roots.

WOMAN: Block ...

FLAGS: Why are you going blocks-block all the time? Can't you let us talk?

HE (*suddenly*): Flags, I've lost my reflection.

FLAGS: And so?

WOMAN (*in great excitement*): That's what I say. You see he realized it this morning. It was like this. I came into the room this morning with a broom and a cup of tea. And he wandered into the bathroom brushing his teeth. Actually I hate people wandering around when they are brushing their teeth—there's a way to brush the teeth, you have to bend carefully over the basin. Anyway he wandered around and then stood looking in the mirror, brushing his teeth—and then—the way he screamed, I can't describe it. As if somebody had taken his life's savings. I said to him, what's happened, and he comes out shaking like a leaf and says he couldn't see his reflection. What fun!

FLAGS (*yawns*): Get me a cup of tea, please. You make such excellent tea. Pure nectar.

WOMAN: Sure, why just tea ... I can get you some toast and eggs as well.

FLAGS: That's what I call a big heart. The right spirit. Not like this wet rag here, sitting with his head in his hands, all limp and nervous. Just because his reflection has disappeared.

(*She smirks and goes out.*)

HE: You too, Flags!

FLAGS: Me too what?

HE: Such a precious possession ...

FLAGS: I don't believe in private property.

HE: Don't you understand my sorrow?

FLAGS: If you are going to sorrow over all the wrong and trivial things who is going to sympathize with you?

HE. Is losing one's reflection a trivial thing according to you?

FLAGS: Blocks, do you know that in this city alone ninety-nine per cent of the people live below the reflection line? Who listens to their complaint? Only the petite bourgeois like you go whining about things like that. You're really terrible people—selfish and self-centred. Constantly thinking of yourselves and your reflections. Arrey, why the hell do you need this worthless reflection? You're not such an Adonis that you should have a pretty reflection. Blocks, don't get angry if I tell you the truth. But when you're not actually before me, I just can't remember what you look like. However hard I try, I just see a vague shape. With eyes and nose and ears. That's not surprising. You're like a million or ten million other people. What would there be that's worth remembering in you, dear Blockhead? So why bother with fancy things like reflections? One wouldn't find you in a crowd if one tried. A crowd—that's the thing—what is one puny individual unit? And what difference will it make to the world if you've lost your reflection? What? Speak!

HE: Okay! It won't make any difference. But...

FLAGS: Of course it won't. Stop worrying. Shave and go off to work in style.

HE: But Flags, suppose everybody loses his reflection? What would happen then?

FLAGS: What's going to happen?

HE: Wouldn't it cause an upheaval? People will be frightened, furious. They will riot.

FLAGS: Nothing of the kind!

HE: Won't they!

FLAGS. Never. It's very simple. How many people are really conscious that they have a reflection? People in this city sweat away at their work from morning to night. They don't have the time even to wipe their sweat in front of mirrors. How do you think it's going to affect them even if they did lose their reflection? Only you conceited highbrow types can afford that luxury. And just suppose that everyone, every single person loses his reflection— then it's perfect, I say. It'll be the realization of the dream we have struggled for night and day. Equality will be established. Inequality destroyed. Everyone reduced to a single class. Splendid! What more would one want?

WOMAN (*through the window*): We would want tea. Want toast. Want eggs.

(*Disappears.*)

FLAGS: Want, want, want ...

HE: What's happened to you, all on a sudden?

FLAGS: The breakfast. My mind's full of it.

HE: But weren't you sermonizing on thoughts just the opposite?

FLAGS: Thoughts from the soul, all of them. I speak them out even in my sleep.

HE: Parrot—like!

FLAGS: D'you mean to say that I talk like a parrot?

HE: Yes, you do. You'll know when you lose your reflection.

FLAGS: Rubbish.

HE: What is rubbish?

FLAGS: Why should I lose it?

HE: You can never tell.

FLAGS: Nonsense!

HE: For all you know, it's already lost.

FLAGS: What rot!

HE: These are bad days. You'd better make sure. Better take care of it.

FLAG (*uneasy*): If it's lost, it's lost! If others have lost theirs and I haven't I'll smash it up myself. You hear? Just remember we are committed to our ideology.

HE: Why don't you have a look any way?

FLAGS: What for?

HE: Just have a look.

FLAGS: Okay. I'll do it. Just to satisfy you ... (*Walks over to the mirror and peers at it, but turns away almost at once.*) It's there.

HE: What's there?

FLAGS: My reflection. It's actually there. (*A sigh of relief.*) That's that.

HE: Yes. Go on, fib.

FLAGS: Come and have a look for yourself. Come, you won't see yourself in any case. Come.

(*Both go to the mirror and stand before it. He roars with laughter.*)

FLAGS: What's so funny? Stop neighing.

HE: You call that a reflection?

FLAGS: It is a reflection.

HE: Haw-Haw-Haw, Hee-Hee-Hee ...

(*He rolls on the carpet. The woman comes in with tea and toast.*)

WOMAN: Oh! So you've found your reflection?

HE: Ho-Ho-Ho!

WOMAN: It's back in the mirror, is it? So the real celebration is on! Hadn't I told you ...

HE: Bai, *aho* Bai, it's really the limit, you know.

WOMAN: Why the limit? Didn't I tell you, it must have got bored, and gone out for some fresh air or to take a pee, and it would come back? Where could it go after all?

HE: No, no, no. You've got it all wrong. We're not talking about my reflection.

WOMAN: No?

HE: No, it still hasn't come back.

WOMAN: Oh!

HE: We're talking about his reflection. We just saw it. Ho-Ho-Ho.

FLAGS: Stop it, Blocks! Reflectionless slob!

WOMAN: Will you please tell me what's going on?

HE: No. No. You tell. Go and have a look, and tell.

WOMAN: Really?

HE: Yes. Go and have a look. Go. Go on, Flags. Go, stand in front of the mirror once more.

WOMAN: Come, come.

FLAGS: What childishness is this!

HE: Hey, coward! Scared, huh?

FLAGS: Why should I be scared? Eh? Why should I be scared?

HE: Then why don't you go to the mirror? Go. (*To the Woman.*) Bai, now you can come and have a look.

(*Flags and the Woman go to the mirror. The Woman instantly blushes to the roots of her hair. She covers her eyes.*)

WOMAN: Oooh! My!

HE: What did you see? What did you see?

WOMAN: You're really naughty.

HE: What's naughty about it?

WOMAN: Of course, it's naughty. Quite wicked. Both of you.

HE: Naughty? Wicked? Don't blush. What did you see in the mirror?
    What did you see?

WOMAN: I'm not going to tell. No. No, I won't.

HE: What did you see? Shall I tell you?

WOMAN (*puts her fingers in her ears*): Go ahead.

HE: I saw a cock. I saw him reflected as a cock.

WOMAN (*taking her fingers out of her ears*): Did you? You too?

HE: You mean you saw it too?

WOMAN: You really did see a co-co-co. (*Giggles.*) I didn't know you
    were one of that kind.

HE: That kind?

WOMAN: Those that like co-co-huhuhu ...

HE. No, no. Who told you I like cocks? So, this cock of ours is crowing
    his little bit over and over again ...

WOMAN: Crowing his little bit? What cock are you talking about?

HE: What cock?

WOMAN: But when you say 'cock', don't you mean that (*Rolls her eyes
    significantly.*) ... well ... I mean I saw what it stands for ... oh my!
    I'm making it worse.

HE: Of course I mean this cock, that cock, any cock when I say cock.
    Now all cocks strut around and crow, don't they?

WOMAN: Oh, that. That's not what I saw.

HE: No. What did you see then?

WOMAN: I didn't see the bird. Not the one you're talking of.

HE: What did you see then?

WOMAN: Now, how can I say that? I feel so very very shy. You know Dilip Chitre, and his play *Mithu Mithu Popat?* Don't you remember the symbolic bird in it? Well, that's what I saw in the mirror.

FLAGS: No, that's enough. Enough. Saw a cock now, didn't you? Okay, it was a cock after all. You saw something at least. Not the blank that someone here faces.

(*He crows like a cock.*)

FLAGS: Doesn't bother me one bit.

(*He crows again.*)

WOMAN: Please stop it. The cock must be quite hungry. Would you care to eat something? Here's your toast. And tea. And eggs.

(*He crows.*)

FLAGS: You unbeliever! I'll finish you off, just wait.

HE: How?

FLAGS: Kill you. Annihilate you. Purge, liquidate.

HE: How would that help, Mr Cock Flags?

FLAGS: It's people like you who are the enemies of revolution. Once you are eliminated the path of revolution will go smooth.

HE: It won't.

FLAGS: It will.

HE: Never. Because even if you destroy us we'll enter your minds. So what will you do then?

FLAGS: That's impossible.

HE: We'll enter your minds and torture you. Give you feelings of guilt. Guilt complex!

FLAGS: Pooh! You don't have the guts!

HE: Want to see? Okay, then, I'll show you, old Flagstaff!

(*He runs out of the door.*)

WOMAN: He's gone bonkers. Don't let him bother you. Come, start
  eating.

(*He peeps in through the window.*)

HE: May I come in?

FLAGS: No. No.

HE: I'm coming.

FLAGS: Not while I'm having my breakfast.

HE: Coming. Coming. Coming.

(*He comes in through the window.*)

WOMAN: Do eat. Would you like me to feed you? Here. Have some
  toast. (*HE sits down in front of Flags.*) Would you like me to feed
  you? Here, take some words.

WOMAN: Here's some toast.

(*Puts toast into Flags's mouth.*)

HE: Here's some commitment.

(*Mimes feeding action.*)

WOMAN: Egg.

(*Same action.*)

HE: Exploitation.

(*Same action.*)

WOMAN: Tea.

(*Same action.*)

HE: Capitalism.

(*Same action.*)

WOMAN: Toast.

(*Same action.*)

HE: Class Struggle.

(*Same action.*)

WOMAN: Egg.

(*Same action.*)

HE: Blood.

(*Same action.*)

WOMAN: Tea.

(*Same action.*)

HE: Revolution.

(*Same action.*)

WOMAN: Toast.

(*Same action.*)

HE: The masses.

(*Same action.*)

FLAGS: Enough, enough, enough. I'm full.

HE: Have some more.

FLAGS: No, I can't.

HE: How can you be full so soon? I've cooked for you our favourite
words. Eat some more.

FLAGS: I can't. I'll burst.

HE: Why should you burst? Store them all up in your stomach. Then
you can bring them up when you want. Like a camel. There.

FLAGS: You bloody reactionary! You enter my mind and dare provoke
me! If I entered your mind, I'd make it real bad for you, I
promise you.

HE: Balls.

FLAGS: I'll show you, just you wait.

HE: Yes, yes. Show me, show.

FLAGS: Okay then. Here goes.

(*Flags leaves by the door.*)

WOMAN: Dear me! This is going to be a real mess. Blockhead's in Flags's
mind and now Flags is trying to get into Blockhead's. So A enters
B which is already in A!

(*Flags is at the window.*)

HE: Don't you bite off more than you can chew. You'll get a fright at the end.

FLAGS: Pooh! Pooh!

(*Flags bangs his head on the window trying to come in. Finally manages it. Instant darkness. Flags screams. Sounds of someone stumbling around.*)

HE: Don't say I didn't warn you.

FLAGS: God! How dark it is in here.

HE: Yell now!

FLAGS: Hey, how do I get out of here?

HE: Sit and whine! I'm off.

(*The stage lights up. He comes in through the door.*)

FLAGS (*mimes groping in the dark*): Hey! You've got out of my mind, and I'm still stuck in yours. Help! Help!

HE: Bother! Now have you got your sense back?

FLAGS: Help! Help me get free.

HE: Hold on. Bloody nuisance.

(*He goes out by the door and comes in through the window. Darkness.*)

HE: Okay. Now off you go. Move your ass, will you? Easy, or you'll bump your head again.

(*Sounds of stumbling. Light. Flags enters through the door.*)

FLAGS: Whew, I'm out! That was a nasty one. Blocks, better leave my mind now.

HE: Say 'give up'.

FLAGS: Okay, I give up.

HE: Now, that's better.

(*He steps out of the window and comes in through the door.*)

FLAGS (*furious*): Your types are like snakes in the grass. I must work out some instant measures. (*Goes out of the door muttering.*) Those who indulge in the luxury of private joys and sorrows (*Looks in the window.*) have no right to be living in this world.

You are the enemies of the people. The enemies of revolution. You—

(*He gets up irritated and slams the window shut, probably catching Flags's nose because you hear Flags scream outside.*)

HE: Thank God, that's over. Now I can relax.

WOMAN: Aren't you going to shave first?

HE: What for?

WOMAN: To go to work. It's almost eight-thirty.

HE: I'm taking French leave today.

WOMAN: How can you take so many French leaves?

HE: For all you know, my reflection is already there.

WOMAN: Where?

HE: In the office. It must have been really keen to go. So it went off. And here I am, looking all over for it. I refuse to go now.

WOMAN: And if the boss calls?

HE: Why should he? With my reflection there nobody will even notice I'm not there. Don't forget it's a government office.

WOMAN: Even so, I wish you'd shave.

HE: All right. (*Goes to the mirror.*) Hey. You' re crazy. How do I shave?

WOMAN: Oh my! That's true.

HE: Great! Another bore I'm through with. Hurray!

WOMAN: You sound cheerful.

HE: Laugh, laugh, so that you don't cry.

WOMAN: Laugh, laugh. Life is meant to be filled with laughter.

HE: That's very true. Whatever happens, go on laughing. I've got my freedom now. Freedom. You know how a sack feels once it's relieved of all the grain? That's the kind of freedom I now have. It's my Independence Day today. I must sing my song of freedom.

(*He stands up looking extremely solemn.*)

HE (*sings*): *Tanamanadhana soduni gele, gele maja pratibimba.* (My
  reflection has left my body, my mind, my wealth.)

WOMAN (*screams*): Stop it. Stop it at once.

HE: What's wrong?

WOMAN: Not that tune.

HE: Why not?

WOMAN: It's an insult to the National Anthem, don't you know? You're
  not Raja Dhale to do that.

HE: You're right there.

WOMAN: Set it to a classical tune. It'll sound lovely.

HE: Okay. Classical it will be! Listen. It's the raga Kalavati. (*Sings.*)

> It has gone
> My reflection
> And so to hell
> With boss and fat woman
> Bosom pal and politician
> I'm through with them all
> No worry remains
> But to exist on and on.
> Ahaha! What bliss in this freedom! What a sense of liberation!
> How can I describe its grandeur, its glory?
> Let's distribute sweets. We're free.
> Let's take leave. We're free.
> Drink, gamble, take bribes, We're free.
> Go naked, go bare, eat, shit, We're free.
> Do just what you like, who is to stop you?
> Nobody to stare from the mirror in anger.
> Cry if you like, laugh if you like.
> Live if you like, die if you like.
> WE'RE FREE, WE'RE FREE, WE'RE FREE!

Aah! What a great feeling. Beautiful darkness around me.
Darkness without. Darkness within. This is that moment of
darkness. This is the knowledge of the self. The knowledge of
life. The ultimate revelation.
(*Sings.*) *Aji mi Brahma pahile.* (I've seen Brahma today.)
(*The organ accompanies the song as in the traditional Marathi musical
plays. He continues the song, till the doorbell rings.*)

HE: There it tolls. The bell tolls. That's the last bell tolling. Who could
it be? Bai, Bai, open the door.

WOMAN: Wait till I've powdered my nose.

HE: Bai, Bai, open the door.

WOMAN: Wait till I've pinned up my hair.

HE: Bai, Bai, open the door.

WOMAN: Wait till my heart stops pounding.

(*A woman's sweet voice singing outside.*)

Oh King of Clerks!
If the world becomes a furnace
A saint should become water happily.

(*The Woman opens the door to let a young girl enter.*)

HE: Who is this, Muktabai, come to us?

GIRL: Namaskar.

HE: Who are you?

GIRL: You don't know me.

HE: That's why, I ask you. Who are you?

GIRL: Do I have a name?

HE: What do you mean?

GIRL: Means I do not have a name. No name. But people at home, or
outside, at the office, they all call me Broomstick.

HE: Broomstick?

GIRL: Yes. They're all dying to use me. (*Pause.*) Only you are different.

HE: Where do I come in?

GIRL: Very much.

HE: Now, now don't you drag me into something stupid.

WOMAN: Quite right. You better be careful.

GIRL: How are you not concerned? Don't we work in the same office, in the same section, in the same corner?

HE: I wouldn't know.

GIRL: What's wrong with you?

HE: Fifty girls to a section. They all wear synthetic saris. They all wear perfume. They all use lipstick. How am I supposed to remember them all?

GIRL: You have a point.

HE: You look quite sensible. I guess you are yet to marry!

GIRL: You're right.

HE: All girls are tolerant, sensible, and humble before marriage. But the moment they have hooked a husband, they start pontificating on liberation. By the way, did you come in by the door or through the window?

GIRL: The door. Why?

HE: I was scared for a moment. That's all.

GIRL: But why?

HE: If you came in by the window, I want you to leave the same way, this moment ...

GIRL: I've not come today to go away.

HE: What?

WOMAN: Look, I'm not having girls staying here. Suppose something goes wrong?

GIRL: In that case I'll take him away.

HE: Where?

GIRL: Anywhere.

HE: And where's that?

GIRL: Just anywhere. Anywhere in this wide world. I could go to the end of the earth with you.

HE: Why should you?

GIRL (*very sentimentally*): Now how am I tell you this? I love you. It's a silent love. I've gazed at you in the office with such longing for so long. How handsome you look—the incoming files to your right, the outgoing files to your left, their dusty yellow colour, the old table, the inkpot, the penholder, the paperweight, the calendar on the wall with the picture of an *adivasi* girl dangling her feet in water, and Mrs Gandhi's photograph, the Godrej cupboard. The records tied in red cloth to the left, and beyond that the broken door of the toilet which does not bolt. In the midst of all this, you, the lord of my heart, looking so good, so right, like the sun shining at the centre of the nine planets, like candy among popcorn, like a shining boot in a heap of old *chappals*.

HE: Have you been reading a lot of stories written by Marathi women writers?

GIRL: Why?

HE: Or has the heroine of a story stepped out of it to make an appearance here?

GIRL: (*shakes her head*).

HE: Eh?

GIRL: (*shakes her head again*).

HE: If you're one of those heroines, let me tell you that the trend has changed now. Nowadays the husbands of heroines live in Tokyo, or Zurich, or Rome and earn fat pay packets. The heroines fall in love with Japanese, Swiss, or Italian men, depending on where the husbands are posted. There's a lot of romancing all over the place with the husbands knowing what's gong on. The husbands endure all like the traditional Arya *pativratas*. Then the 'phoren' Romeos get bored with the heroines and ditch them. The heroines return to their native husbands and sob their broken hearts out, while the husbands say, 'there, there,' and make them cups of coffee. So you see? The heroines of Marathi stories have started philandering. The moment they sight a lone man, they pounce on him. In short, I'd advise you to get married, to feel liberated. Then you won't need to talk sentimentally like this. You will be militant then and talk about women's lib.

GIRL: Please. Do you think I don't mean what I say?

HE: Tell me what you have come here for.

GIRL: Would you like to know the truth?

HE: Yes. Please.

GIRL: I found out you'd lost your reflection.

HE: What?

GIRL: Yes.

HE: How did you *find* out?

GIRL: I did. Don't you remember the day you were looking at the mirror above the wash-basin in the canteen? You were looking quite half-heartedly, so you didn't notice it. But there was no reflection in the mirror.

HE: How did you know?

GIRL: I was standing right behind you.

HE: Don't tell lies.

GIRL: Cross my heart, I was.

HE: Now uncross your heart.

GIRL: Okay. I will.

HE: Leave me out. If you were behind me why was your reflection not there in the mirror?

GIRL: How could there be?

HE: Why?

GIRL: I've lost my reflection too.

(*He looks stunned.*)

HE: You're lying.

GIRL: No, honest. I hadn't noticed first, till one day Mother got furious with me. I've been watching you for days, she says. Why can't you wear the *kumkum* in its proper place? Sometimes it is there, sometimes it is not. When it's there, it's on your cheek or your nose! What's got into you? We women have to guard our kumkum with our lives. Both before marriage and after marriage.

WOMAN: Very true. When my husband was alive I used to wear a teeny-weeny dot. Because he was such a beanpole. Now I don't have to bother.

GIRL: So I took the kumkum out of my handbag and went to the mirror. And guess what? I couldn't see a thing. I just put the kumkum approximately where I thought it should be. And the mirror showed just this dot. It really scared me, but I didn't say a thing. I didn't mind losing my reflection' as long as my kumkum was safe.

HE: Terrific! Shake hands.

WOMAN: Oh no, you won't. (*To the girl.*) Now scream.

HE: Don't say that. We're comrades in sorrow—or in joy. When a broom comes into the house Dusserah must follow.

WOMAN: She's taking you for a ride. Don't trust her.

HE: Why do you say that?

WOMAN: It's an old trick we women use. Tears. And if she is telling the truth then your tragedy is no longer unique. Your monopoly is gone.

HE: Yes! You're right!

GIRL: Don't you believe me?

HE: Whether I do or don't what difference will it make to me? (*Suspicious.*) Look here. Are you laying some kind of trap for me?

GIRL: Trap?

HE: Have you knowingly hidden your reflection somewhere? In a bank vault or a false ceiling in the bathroom?

GIRL: What? Do you think a reflection is like a film star's black money?

HE: Or have you gifted it to someone on an impulse or because you were fed up with it? And now you cry thief. Bai's right. It is a trick to win sympathy. Huh! I don't feel a bit sympathetic. You'd better go away. Go and look after your problem and I'll look after mine.

GIRL: How impersonal a man without reflection becomes! How hard-hearted! How amoral! A-moral, I said; not immoral.

HE: Don't show off your intellectualism with your fine moral judgements. I'm through with all labels now, thank God!

GIRL: How unresponsible! Not irresponsible, but unresponsible.

HE: Did you do your Masters in linguistics by any chance?

GIRL: Yes. With philosophy. How else could I have got into the Accounts Section? We could do our thing ...

HE: We?

GIRL: I'm a girl after all. What can I do alone? Help me. And I'll help you. We are both people who have lost their reflections. We could help each other find them.

HE: Oh—you find mine, I find yours.

GIRL: Yes.

HE: Or each find his own.

GIRL: But together.

HE: Sorry. Can't be done.

GIRL: Why not? Hasn't it been said that the two wheels of the carriage of life ...

HE: What carriages are you talking about? Talk of spaceships. Soyuz. Here we are, drifting alone in space, weightless, reflectionless.

GIRL: But the two of us ...

HE: Now not a thing more. This doing things together is yet another old trick. The two of us together will fight for freedom. The two of us together will abolish inequality. The two of us together will serve society. The two of us together will set up an ashram for celibates. Nothing doing, sorry. It all ends up eventually in breeding brats. Now look, both of us being what we are, what do we achieve by begetting children without reflections? And what about their future? Set them adrift in space? To go floating about, all by themselves, without a direction, a drift? To float in the ocean of joy, bursting into ripples of joy? No, thanks. We are lucky we have got free by chance. Why give birth to new prisoners? Eh?—

GIRL: I really can't fathom your mind.

HE: Why should you want to? Really, you women have some ambition!

GIRL: All I ask for is a little corner of your mind to rest my tired head in. To help me forget my grief over my lost reflection.

HE: Good lord! What a range this girl covers! She is the LCM of all heroines in Marathi fiction.

WOMAN: Range my foot! She's a leech. Really, how sticky can you get. Now. Hold your lovey dovey nonsense.

GIRL: Give me a chance. Only one, I beg you.

HE: I tell you, there is total darkness in my mind. I can't see a thing there myself. Why do you want to go stumbling through a strange place?

GIRL: I'll light the lamp of my love there and remove the darkness.

WOMAN: Light!

HE: But what do you get by lighting up that place? You won't see a thing there anyway. Besides, what's light and what's darkness for those who have lost their reflections? Everything remains just the same.

GIRL: But you too ... one who does not care either way ... why should you be so obstinate about your mind?

HE: You've a point! Okay. Go. Go into my mind since you're so keen.

GIRL: Go? You mean come.

(*Turns to the door.*)

WOMAN: Leave your chappals outside, do you hear?

(*The Girl goes out.*)

HE: What a female! How can a person without a reflection be so optimistic?

WOMAN: Optimism is just another word for leechiness. (*The Girl returns.*) Now what?

GIRL: I feel scared.

WOMAN: Naturally. It is ...

GIRL: It's not that. But suppose somebody closes the window while I'm inside?

WOMAN (*flares up*): Don't we have other things to do? And suppose it shuts, push it open. The hinges are all rusty anyway. (*The Girl begins to go.*) And come out fast. The mind is not a bathroom. Behave yourself while you're there. And don't scamper around there like a mouse in a trap.

(*The Girl goes out of the door.*)

HE: You people have turned my mind into a railway platform today— You and Flags and Broomsticks.

(*The Girl opens the window gently and comes in. Stands in the middle of the stage. The darkness is total. There is a long silence, broken by two sobs, followed by silence again. The stage lights up. The Girl comes in through the door.*)

HE: Happy?

GIRL (*angry*): Are you?

HE: I'd warned you.

GIRL: How I sobbed in your mind! You could have spoken a few words of sympathy at least.

HE: But I didn't hear you sob.

WOMAN: Nor did I!

GIRL: Brutal. Heartless. Cruel.

HE: Bloody hell! It's the limit. That's the trouble with these suffering souls. They want the whole world to blow on their upped arses. Pains!

GIRL: You've never suffered. That's why you talk like this. You haven't suffered because you don't know what you've lost.

HE: Oh yes, I do, dear woman! I certainly do. But I know it's useless searching for what's lost. You don't agree. So go search. You and I are different. So our paths lie in opposite directions. Since we have got this freedom to go our different ways, why don't we enjoy the freedom?

GIRL: But the mind ...

HE: The mind! Why don't you understand? Is there such a thing as the mind? And if there is, it's impossible to understand other people's minds. We read other people's minds in the context of our own. We see all kinds of meanings—desirable and undesirable—which have nothing to do with the other chap's mind. They are all in our minds. You understand?—I ask you because you are an MA in philosophy.

GIRL: What has it got to do with my being an MA in philosophy? I am also a broomstick. You came into my mind, and you can see for yourself what I'm saying.

HE: Your mind? I suppose you have the works of Hegel and Kant there, so ...

GIRL: Not at all. They weren't there even when I was doing my MA Why don't you come and see?

HE: And do what?

WOMAN: Do nothing. Just talk.

GIRL: Just make sure ...

WOMAN: There will be no hanky-panky. Not in my house.

GIRL: ... that you are not the only one with a mind. Other people may have a mind too ...

HE: I'm really tired. I've been in and out of minds so many times today.

GIRL: This is my last request. I won't bother you after this.

WOMAN: Some favour, that.

HE: Okay. But I'm not going to stand for any more nonsense after this. You'll have to release me.

GIRL: Yes.

(*He goes to the door.*)

WOMAN: Hey. Take off that tie. Why do you want to go all dolled up as if it was a wedding reception?

(*He takes off his tie and goes out of the door.*)

WOMAN (*to the girl*): Doesn't change his underwear for days.

(*He comes softly in through the window. Slowly makes his way to centre-stage. The two are far apart. The stage is totally dark except for a faint light on the two of them.*)

HE: My dear girl, why play games? Aren't you tired of all this? Haven't we played this game a little too often in life? You have played it with some people, I with others. And it always ends up the same way. What do we gain from it? Do we achieve anything? Love is stumbling around in each other's darkness. What's the use? What is wrong with our own darkness? You'll say, but there is the body. So there is. But the same darkness flows in the arteries of the body. If you cut yourself, a black sticky fluid oozes out now. There's no ache. No pain. So much time has passed. My body has forgotten the touch of rain. And the scent of flowers. The warm smell of fresh bread, the moonlight above the lake, the ring of children's laughter, moist lips meeting passionately in the dark. I have them all preserved like dead butterflies pinned in a notebook. Slowly they too will turn to dust. That's all right. All these things have vanished along with my reflection. I began losing them one by one long ago. But I didn't notice. So. Good. Now I don't have to worry about the future, the past, and the present. Because all time is dark in the same way. And there is no difference between optimism and pessimism. Let me tell you a story. About two lovers. Both were young, beautiful, and intelligent. They were passionately in love with each other. They swore they would be with each other in this and all future lives. But soon, they got separated. He went to the war and never returned. He was reported missing. Everybody said he must be dead. But she remained steadfast. She said he would return. For forty years she remained true to her word and faithfully waited for him to return. One day she receives a message from him, 'I've returned. Meet me in the temple at the end of the village.' She said, 'See. Didn't I say so?' She ran. She reached the temple. But she couldn't see her lover there. The only person there was an ancient man, toothless, bald, with rheumy eyes. She said, there's nobody here. Some young hoodlum has fooled me. She went back, bitterly disappointed. The lover too got tired of waiting for her in the temple. Not a single creature turned up, except an old woman, bent, with matted hair and cataracts in her eyes. She peeped in briefly and went away, muttering to herself. He was also disappointed. He said, 'She hasn't waited for me. She's made a new life for herself. Didn't even come to meet me.'

(*After this only his lips are seen to move. Not a word is audible. Darkness. Light. Only the Woman is on the stage now. The Girl has disappeared. He comes in through the door.*)

WOMAN: She's gone.

HE: (*only the lips move*).

WOMAN: She kept yawning and looking at her wrist watch every now and then.

HE: (*only the lips move*).

WOMAN: I just can't hear anything at all.

(*He stares at her. Then at the objects in the room. Then He calmly walks to the window. Climbs up. Jumps out. The Woman runs to the window. Stands looking out. Turns back.*)

WOMAN: Nothing wrong in killing yourself. But after falling five floors right into the middle of the road without so much as a sound, or a blood-stain or a traffic pile-up, something huge and black gushed out spread on the road like sticky oil. What kind of a death is that! Huh!

(*She closes the window. Turns the sheet on the bed. The doorbell rings and stops. She runs to the mirror smoothing down her hair, stands rooted there. Stares at the mirror. Then turns to the audience with terror-stricken eyes. Then a never-ending unbroken scream breaks from her lips. The doorbell goes on ringing along with the scream. Darkness. Silence. The audience leaves in the dark as the organ plays*—Aji me Brahma pahile.)

CURTAIN

Sonata

Translated by
Mahesh Elkunchwar

Characters:

Aruna

Dolon

Subhadra

Act One

A fine terrace flat in one of the finer suburbs of Mumbai. The drawing room is filled with fragile, delicate objects. Glass table-tops, porcelain objets d'art, crystal vases. It is obvious that only women live here. Three steps down the drawing room is the terrace. The apron should be used for the terrace. On the left is a door leading to Aruna's room. Two doors in the back, one leads to the kitchen and the other serves as an entrance to the flat. Between the doors is a wooden cabinet with intricate carving, against the wall. The area on stage left has a coffee table and a few low chairs. Upstage on the left is Aruna's working desk and chair, and a rocking chair. On the right, another door leading to Dolon's room. Upstage, on the right, a sofa, a centre-table, and a TV facing the cyclorama. Near the door leading to Dolon's room is a small carved table on which is an array of perfume bottles of all shapes and colours.

Beyond this we see the skyline of skyscrapers. It is evening when the play opens. The windows of the skyscrapers will gradually light up and then fade as the play progresses.

Aruna and Dolon on the stage. Aruna, fortyish, once beautiful but now fading, in a Bengal handloom sari, glasses, a tight bun on her nape, very professorial, is correcting papers at her desk. Dolon, same age as Aruna, in an old, much worn but obviously expensive dressing gown, plump, stylish boy-cut, shuffling around aimlessly. She is one of those people who wear expensive clothes carelessly. She is perhaps trying to put the room in order

but in her effort to do so, she brings more disorder in it. Aruna is making
great effort to ignore her friend's noisy activity, but finally cannot take
it anymore.

ARUNA (*without taking her eyes off the papers*): Dolon. (*Dolon is oblivious*
    to her call.) Will you please stop that?

(*Pause.*)

DOLON (*opening the drawers of the chest noisily*): My perfume! Just
    bought it the other day. Don't see it anywhere. (*Pause.*) Finished
    the papers?

ARUNA: Please!

DOLON: You haven't seen it by any chance?

ARUNA: How she ignores me, meli!

DOLON (*laughing*): *Shotti!*

ARUNA: And where do you think you are going at this hour of the night
    wearing that perfume?

DOLON: You give me *gaalis* and you get them back in ample measure.

ARUNA: Gaalis she can hear alright.

DOLON: It was quite expensive. French.

ARUNA: Do you mind making a little less noise?

DOLON: Sorry. (*Pause.*) Bengali is so full of *mishti* gaalis.

ARUNA: Perfumes, clothes, make-up!

DOLON: What about dinner, Miss Ranade?

ARUNA: And food!

DOLON: The top priority of any blue-blooded Bengali! Got it. (*Puts the*
    perfume bottle on the centre-table.) Know something Aruna? I
    may be hopelessly Maharashtrianized, but scratch me and you'll
    find a gluttonous Bengali beneath. *Aami* gourmet!

ARUNA: And the way she blows her money!

DOLON: Shotti.

ARUNA: Gourmand. Not gourmet.

DOLON: I lost my sun-glasses yesterday.

ARUNA: Buy new ones. Expensive ones. Blow money.

DOLON: Dinner, dinner. How about some dinner?

ARUNA: Rice.

DOLON: It is not even seven yet. (*Dolon rearranges the perfume bottles, then picks up a green one.*) What a beautiful shape!

ARUNA: I've got to finish correcting this stack today.

DOLON (*opening the bottle and inhales deeply*): Haaa! (*Pause.*) Emerald green. *Ki shundor!*

ARUNA (*putting an angry red cross on the paper*): What rot do they write! (*Pause.*) Now while away your time like this. And then it will be pizza as always.

DOLON: No way, Pishima. (*Pause.*) No junk food anymore.

ARUNA: Or go out for dinner!

DOLON (*giggles*): You are suggesting it.
(*Inhales deeply from the bottle again.*)

ARUNA: Italian food. Thai food. Chinese.

DOLON: I'll swoon.

ARUNA: Talk of food and she swoons.

DOLON (*showing the bottle to Aruna*): Perfume. Perfume makes me swoon. (*Pause.*) Food too, of course. (*Giggling.*) It is empty but how the scent lingers!

ARUNA: Junk.

DOLON: Beautiful junk.

ARUNA: Junk.

DOLON: All right. Let me check the papers.

ARUNA: Throw that junk out. What's this silly attachment to empty bottles?

DOLON: Come on. Let me do the papers. Haven't forgotten my Sanskrit yet.

ARUNA: Thank you, ma'am. (*Pause.*) Every single girl will get hundred out of hundred. One hell of a Diwali for them.

DOLON: Why do these empty bottles irritate you so much? They are so beautiful. Throw them out! And what do I keep in their place? Vicks Vaporub? Iodex? (*Pause.*) Come on. Let's cook something.

ARUNA: You can see I'm busy. All that you'll get is rice and curry.

DOLON (*pretending to faint*): Now I'm really beginning to swoon.

ARUNA: Go wash the rice.

DOLON (*in mock pain*): It's Sunday!

ARUNA: Rice. That's that.

DOLON (*sighs exaggeratedly*): Are you as harsh as this to your students? *Ma go! Ki koshto!* (*Pause.*) That famous Marathi delicacy. Cheap and tasty!

ARUNA: Oh yes, as if you are some Debi Choudhurani!

DOLON: Let me take the news first. (*Surfs the channels absentmindedly and then switches off.*) Let me check the papers, Oru.

ARUNA: It's going to be only *bhat*, I'm warning you.

DOLON: *Oruma, tomaar raanaar haath bado bhalo.* (*Goes to Aruna and pinches her cheek fondly. Aruna recoils.*) You're the world's greatest cook.

ARUNA: Will you please let me work? (*Pause.*) And you're the world's greatest eater. Gourmand!

DOLON (*faking hurt*): Don't. (*Picks up a bowl of popcorn and instals herself in front of the TV, begins channel-surfing while eating.*) Nothing interesting. (*Pause.*) *Mudi Khabe?* (*Pause.*) Talk to me. We get only Sundays together. Why waste time on those silly papers? (*Long pause.*) I am going on a diet now.

(*Pause.*)

ARUNA: Not so loudly.

DOLON: What?

ARUNA: Someone might hear.

DOLON: I really am serious this time.

ARUNA (*running a line across the paper*): God only knows how they get through their BA.

DOLON: And aerobics. Diet and aerobics. (*Pause.*) Only fruit juice for breakfast. And sprouts. For lunch, salad. Coffee may be. Black coffee. No sugar, no cream. And plain rice for dinner. Rice, dal, a vegetable. No maida, no bread, no desserts. (*Pause.*) Only three meals a day. (*Long pause. With a giggle.*) How obsessed I am by food!

ARUNA: Now listen to this.

DOLON: But this time I'm going to take it dead seriously. (*Walking up to the mirror.*) What did you say?

ARUNA (*reading from the answer paper*): *Subhaashitena geetena, yuvateenaancha leelaya—*

DOLON (*preening at herself in the mirror, responds absentmindedly*): I see.

ARUNA: *Yasya na dravate chittam, sa vai muktothava pashuhu ...*

DOLON: I like that!

ARUNA: You know how this idiot has translated it?

DOLON: Funny, no?

ARUNA: 'One whose heart does not melt by a good saying, a song, or a beautiful woman is nothing but a herd of free cattle.'

DOLON: Wonderful!

ARUNA: Mukta! Pashu! Thawe!

DOLON: Do you think I've put on a bit?

ARUNA (*crosses the paper angrily*): This is the limit!

DOLON: Weight, I mean. (*Still looking into the mirror.*) Not so bad. (*Tucks her tummy in, holding her breath.*) Hun? What do you think? (*Aruna pretends she hasn't heard her.*) Your silence is vocal enough. (*Aruna reads from a paper and laughs.*) That is heartless. (*Aruna continues laughing.*) Not everybody can fast like you, baba.

ARUNA: These girls!

DOLON: You were laughing at the paper?

ARUNA: They are samples, really, all of them. (*Pause.*) Do I dare laugh at you?

DOLON: C'mon. Tell me. Have I really put on ...

ARUNA: Don't ask me. You have the scales in the bathroom.

DOLON (*grinning*): Broken. Under sheer pressure. Just you wait, Ranade. Within a month ...

ARUNA: Time for the News.

DOLON (*annoyed*): Will you kindly allow me to finish? Within a month, I'll have ...

ARUNA: BBC?

DOLON: Please!

ARUNA: Let's watch BBC.

DOLON: You are some sadist, I must say. (*Walks up to the TV.*) I ask you something and you don't even .... We're not getting BBC. Lots of snow on the screen.

(*Pause.*)

ARUNA: Do you ever tell a tiger that he has foul breath?

(*Dolon watches the TV silently and then picks up a cushion next to her and without removing her eyes from the screen, throws it at Aruna. Aruna ducks. Dolon bursts out laughing and eats popcorn.*)

ARUNA: Why are you always fishing? She wants compliments all the time!

DOLON (*in disbelief*): Compliments! From *you*?

ARUNA: Take Star News.

DOLON: *Aami bisshash korte parchi na.* Compliments from Miss Aruna Ranade! Ha! (*Suddenly.*) Eeks! I don't like this horse-faced news reader.

ARUNA: Let's watch Sa-Re-Ga-Ma.

DOLON: Give me Pranab Mukherjee. Anyday. (*Surfing the channels.*) You *will* pay me compliments soon enough. (*Consciously emphasizing the elongated vowel sounds.*) And it is Sa Re Gaa Maa.

ARUNA: Gaa! Maa!

DOLON: That is how it said in Hindi.

ARUNA: How can Gandhar be Gaa?

DOLON: Gaandhaar. It's Gaandhaar.

ARUNA: Rubbish!

DOLON: Gaandhaari! She was from Gaandhaar.

ARUNA: And Maa?

DOLON: That also must mean something. Why should the Marathis be always correct?

ARUNA: Aren't only the Bengalis always artistic and cultured?

DOLON (*giggling*): Together we could give the entire country a complex.

ARUNA: Talk like that in front of Subhadra and you have had it.

DOLON (*suddenly watching the TV alertly*): My my my my my ! Look at this! (*Pause.*) Can Subhi speak even one language straight? It is always a horrid cocktail of English, Hindi, Marathi. Watch this. Not a stitch on her. (*Pause. Then screaming.*) Studs!

ARUNA: My goodness! I almost ...

DOLON: Three!

ARUNA: Turn it off.

DOLON: They are so edible.

ARUNA: Watch stuff like that when Subhadra comes.

DOLON (*sighing*): Who are the lucky ones who get to ...

ARUNA: Dolon!

DOLON: All right, all right.

ARUNA: Forgot to tell you there is a couriered letter on the dresser waiting for you.

(*Aruna stops checking the papers for a minute, reclines on her chair, then gets up, goes to the window, looks out.*)

DOLON: Send money. There is no end to demands.

ARUNA: I'm planning to go home next week.

DOLON: Sure.

ARUNA: Twenty-five years in Mumbai but I still think of home.

DOLON: Cal. Give me Cal. Always.

ARUNA: Come with me.

DOLON: Once a Calcuttan, always a Calcuttan.

ARUNA: Let's go for a few days.

DOLON: No ma'am, thank you.

ARUNA: Come on.

DOLON: Lots of things on the card. Meetings, decisions to be taken.
    Full agenda.

ARUNA: My nephews and nieces will dance around you with joy.
    Dolonmawshi, Dolonmawshi.

DOLON: Watch this.

(*Aruna comes to the side table, begins to play with the perfume bottles.*)

ARUNA: That will be a nice change. You will feel refreshed.

DOLON: God! What devastation in Asaam! It's a deluge.

(*Aruna sniffs a bottle.*)

DOLON (*without looking at her*): Nice?

ARUNA: What else do you get to see these days. Deluge, earthquakes,
    accidents. (*Pause.*) Too sharp.

DOLON: French! It's a French perfume!!

ARUNA: It gives me a headache.

DOLON: How old are your nephews and nieces?

ARUNA: So you are not coming. The youngest is five, I think. Or six,
    maybe.

DOLON: You don't even remember that. (*Pause.*) You always say you'll
    go. You never do.

ARUNA (*playing with the bottle*): We had a carved sandal-wood box at
    home. My father's. It had three cut glass attar bottles in it. Kewra,

Gulab, Heena. Yellow, red, green. (*Pause.*) My dear brother lost them all.

DOLON (*getting up and going to the window*): Why isn't our flat sea-facing? (*Pause. Looking out.*) Seven fifty-five. Now, exactly at eight, on the stroke, the light in the third floor flat of that building will ...

ARUNA: Voyeur!

DOLON: Remember *Rear Window?*

ARUNA: I'll gift you binoculars on your birthday.

DOLON: Perfume. Give me perfume. (*Pause.*) What is wrong with just seeing? It doesn't hurt anybody.

ARUNA: Might. It might hurt you.

DOLON (*with glee*): The light is on.

ARUNA: Eight!

DOLON: Now she will open the shutters. (*Pause.*) There it goes. (*Pause.*) She will throw her handbag on the bed. (*Pause.*) Right! (*Pause.*) Now the earrings on the dresser. (*Pause.*) Done. (*Pause.*) Now a drink of water. (*Pause.*) Great. Lovely. (*Pause.*) Now she will instal herself in front of the PC and won't move her ass till midnight. (*Aruna returns to her desk.*) Isn't that enough for the day?

ARUNA: You think I like it?

DOLON: We should have called Subhadra over today.

ARUNA: Every paper is a nightmare.

DOLON: The three of us ... we would've painted the town red ...

ARUNA: It's fine with you. You don't have to bring work at home ...

DOLON: Like the good old college days ...

ARUNA: *Te hi no diwasaa gataaha!* (*Dolon indicates inverted comas with her fingers.*)

DOLON (*goes to Aruna's desk, peeps over her shoulder at the papers*): What has she written, this one? (*Pause.*) I slog in the bank. Eight to six, five days a week. (*Goes to the window, looks out, and mimics typing.*) Tuptuptuptup! (*Pause.*) She must be terribly friendless. Looks so alone. (*Pause. Mimes.*) Tuptuptuptup!

ARUNA: Call Subhadra.

DOLON: You think she'll come?

ARUNA: Try her mobile.

DOLON (*looking out*): Tuptuptup! (*Pause.*) Subhi hasn't bothered to show her face in six months. Let her come now, the bitch.

ARUNA: Close the shutters. (*Pause.*)Call her. She might come.

DOLON (*closing the shutters*): Where's the time for that dear? What with her new boy friend and all that. (*Pause.*) Hunk. He is. I'll say that.

ARUNA: Don't gossip.

DOLON (*opening the shutters*): It is so muggy in here, shee! (*Looks out.*) How does she manage to live all alone?

ARUNA: Close the shutters. Turn on the fan.

DOLON: We moved in here seventeen years ago. I've been watching her since then then, growing old gradually, imperceptibly. Hey Miss Typo!

ARUNA: Why don't you put on some music? '*Moonlight*' Sonata? (*Dolon is looking out, humming to herself.*) I started listening to that kind of music because of you. Otherwise Naatyasangeet is the height of our good taste.

DOLON: And that other thing. *Ki jeno?* Ramayan—*Geet Ramayan.*

ARUNA: Marathi answer to Robindroshangeet.

(*Dolon inserts a CD in the music system.*)

DOLON: Ha! Marathi answer! Nobody can answer us Bongos. (*The slow first movement of 'Moonlight' Sonata—Adagio sostenuto.*) It is a work of a genius and ...

ARUNA: Shut up. Let me listen.

DOLON: *Aamader jeeboner madhur borodaan!*

ARUNA: Shh!

(*Music continues. Aruna has tucked her pen in her bun and is now sitting in the rocking chair. Her habitual tense, strained expression begins to disappear gradually, her face becoming serene and beautiful. Dolon turns and looks at Aruna. Gasps.*)

DOLON: God!

ARUNA (*as if talking to herself, her eyes half closed*): What's her name? Who knows? You seem to know.(*Pause.*) She used to wear skirts in the beginning, you remember? Then she started wearing salwar-kameez. But her age doesn't get concealed. (*Sighs.*) Who is she, where from? (*Silence. The music plays on.*) There doesn't seem to be anyone in her life. (*Pause.*) There is a story by Gorky. Maxim Gorky. There is this woman who never receives any letters. Everybody she knows—her friends, her neighbours—they all get letters. She never does. And then all of a sudden she starts getting them. Every day. Sometimes two, three letters a day. (*Pause.*) Then she dies. It is discovered that she used to write those letters to herself. (*Pause.*) I haven't even seen this woman talking on the phone. (*Pause.*) She must be having somebody, somewhere. An occasional letter, a casual postcard! (*Pause.*) 'The roof is leaking. Need money for repairs. Mother sinking rapidly. Losing her vision too. Wonder if you can take her in for a few days? Bal failed again. We want to send him to a computer class. But where is the money, with all these expenses? This year Ganesh festival will be a poor affair. You mustn't tire yourself and come here.'

(*A long pause.*)

DOLON: Aruna!

ARUNA: Beethoven is a friend now.

DOLON: Do you know you are still stunningly beautiful?

ARUNA: 'Moonlight' Sonata. 'Emperor'. How much has he given us! (*Pause.*) Dolon! (*Dolon is watching her in fascination.*) Dolon!

DOLON: *Hyan, Ma!*

ARUNA: Take me once *tomar badi*. Introduce me to your Mashima, your Meshomoshay. *Tomar Manosh-da, tomar Boudi.* Your rivers. We will sail on them and listen to the Majhis singing.

DOLON: And eat *machher jhaal*. You'll have to eat it. (*With a serene smile on her face Aruna begins rocking the chair.*) Shotti!

ARUNA: Shhh!

DOLON: Divine!

ARUNA: Yes. Divine music.

DOLON: I'm talking about you.

ARUNA: Shhh!

DOLON: When are you going to learn to take compliments graciously, woman?

(*Pause. Dolon comes forward, takes a few pens from the desk, sticks them in Aruna's hair in a circle; then takes a silk chunni from the sofa, drapes it over the 'coiffure' she has just arranged. Then she retreats and watches Aruna like an artist looking at his canvas.*)

DOLON: Queen! (*Aruna freezes. Pause. Then Aruna takes away the chunni, the pens, gets up, and puts off the music.*) But you wanted that music.

(*Pause.*)

ARUNA: Queen of Kelshi!

DOLON: Shotti!

ARUNA: Idiot!

(*Goes to the window and looks out.*)

DOLON: She's sure to be there. Miss Typo. The moment she gets up, be sure it's midnight. I often watch her, na? Many times we put off our lights at the same time.

ARUNA: She knows us? I mean, you?

DOLON: Who knows?

(*Dolon lights a cigarette.*)

ARUNA: *Nako ga bai*! (*Dolon puffs like a chimney.*) Sing something. Robindroshangeet.

DOLON: Tried once. I waved my hand from my balcony and smiled. She slammed down her shutters.

ARUNA: Sing.

DOLON (*suddenly weary, sits on the sofa*): Why do people dislike me? (*Pause.*) Speak something, woman!

(*Pause.*)

ARUNA: Watch out now! (*Pause.*) Dolon. (*Pause. Dolon crushes the cigarette stub.*) Now you will take out the wine, smoke, and get sentimental. (*Pause.*) Don't.

DOLON: You afraid?

ARUNA: Sing.

DOLON: You straight-laced middle-class Maharashtrian!

ARUNA: Sing '*Megher porey*'.

DOLON: Be afraid. Cigarettes are bad. Wine is bad. Meat bad.

(*Pause.*)

ARUNA: Nobody dislikes you.

DOLON: Friendship with men bad. Unthinkable. (*Pause.*) You dislike me. (*Aruna rises, returns to her desk, begins checking the answer scripts.*) Sorry.

ARUNA: Be quiet.

DOLON: Sorry.

ARUNA: We've been sharing this apartment all these years. We've made it our home. Is that nothing to you?

DOLON: Sorry sorry sorry.

ARUNA: Go make some rice.

DOLON (*going to the cabinet*): Habit. We stay together out of habit.

ARUNA: If you say so.

DOLON: And these squabbles. Another routine.

(*Takes out a bottle of wine.*)

ARUNA (*with slight disapproval*): It is not such a bad idea to give up some bad habits.

DOLON (*aggressively*): You mean it is always I who starts fights? (*Aruna is deeply engrossed in her papers.*) Na baba. Can't live like you. Control. Total self-control. Perennial. The way you walk, talk, sit. Controlled.

I like to speak. I like to express myself. Yes. I am demonstrative. And I *am* not a bit ashamed of it. (*Subtly cruel.*) I don't want those severe lines on my face. A morose face, wooden movements. (*Suddenly realizing what she has just said, laughs apologetically.*) *Aami Dolon!* (*Sings.*) *Aami akaatare parantaake proloy dolay dolate chai.* (*Giggles. Raises her glass.*) Drink life to the lees. (*Makes a gesture of inverted commas with her fingers.*) Dear old Tennyson. (*Sipping.*) *Aami Dolon. Aami dolate chai.* Cheers! (*Sips, goes to the window.*) Cheers Miss Typo! (*Sipping.*) Hah! Bordeaux.

ARUNA: Get drunk.

DOLON: What would you know about the pleasures of wine. (*Sipping with affected panache. Aruna looks at her with amusement and affection.*)

ARUNA: Now it calls for some Robindrohangeet.

DOLON (*apologetically*): Only this one.

ARUNA: Go ahead. Drink all you want to.

DOLON: Honestly. (*Pause.*) Want to try it?

ARUNA (*frostily*): Thank you.

DOLON: You ...

ARUNA: ... straight laced middle-class Maharashtrian. Add Chittapawan Brahmin to that. *Watse, gaali paripoorna bhavati, astu!*

DOLON: That is no cussing. Cussing one should hear from Subhadra. What range! What repertoire! How she flings them! With what gusto! Simply love her for that.

ARUNA: It's all right when all that comes from her.

DOLON: Why don't we live like her? To the hilt.

ARUNA: You think we could have? Not everybody can do that.

DOLON: Subhi is ageless. (*Pause.*) At least she pretends to be. (*Looks out of the window.*) I want to see this woman at least once in an expensive sari, with a proper make-up, smiling. (*Turning abruptly.*) Did I show you? I bought a new dress.

(*Comes to the TV and surfs channels.*)

ARUNA: And burnt one more hole in your pocket!

DOLON: You'll of course not like my choice. That's to be expected. But I'll show it to you all the same. You can appreciate it. Just for a change. (*Starts moving towards her room.*) Haven't spent much, for your information.

(*Dolon disappears into her room. Aruna gets up, goes to the TV and changes the channel. MTV appears. She hurriedly changes it to a boring, whining Marathi serial. She watches it intently.*)

DOLON (*shouting from her room*): Keep the MTV on. Just matches my mood. And my dress. (*Only her face appears from behind the door.*) MTV please. (*Her face disappears.*) That's better.

(*Rhythmic pop music. Dolon comes out from within and stands in the door frame dramatically, striking, according to her, a provocative pose. The dress is a bit too tight for her and not very kind to her body. Dolon keeps looking at Aruna, her tummy tucked in, hoping to be complimented. Aruna gives her a long stare and then returns her gaze at the TV, and changes the channel. Hindi news. Slightly crestfallen, Dolon wanders around aimlessly and then goes to the mirror.*)

DOLON: So? What do you say?

ARUNA: Let's eat.

DOLON: I know. It's a bit tight. So what? It's so comfortable.

ARUNA: Good.

DOLON: Slightly jazzy, yes, but so comfortable.

ARUNA: I'll order some pizza.

DOLON: At my age one dresses for comfort.

ARUNA: Change that.

DOLON: I am still beauti ... good looking ...

ARUNA: What kind of pizza do you want? (*Pause.*) Was.

DOLON: I bought this for a song.

ARUNA (*staring at the TV*): Was.

DOLON: And I am going to wear it only when home.

ARUNA: *Was* goodlooking.

DOLON: You can live in the past tense all you like. Not me. (*Picks up the perfume bottle and comes to Aruna.*) Why are you so intentionally cruel to me?

ARUNA: I am being matter of fact.

DOLON: Matter of fact my foot! Sometimes you are abominably cruel to me. (*Pause.*) Okay. Was. I *was* good looking. History. Ancient Indian History.

ARUNA: But why do you need to do all this?

DOLON (*defiantly*): I do.

ARUNA: You're an ass.

DOLON: Fine. But I do.

ARUNA: Now use that 'paarfume'. Silly. You have so much charm. So bubbly, so smiling, always so full of zest. What do you need such stupid clothes for?

DOLON: Really?

ARUNA: Really.

DOLON (*opening the perfume bottle*): Goodness. (*Shakes the bottle.*) See? Gone. Evaporated. (*Goes to the side table.*) One more addition to the collection. (*While going to her room, winks at Aruna.*) Someone gave it to me in Paris.

(*Disappears.*)

ARUNA: How I envy you! I wish I could be like you. Laughing, making others laugh. Spreading joy wherever you go.

DOLON (*off. From her room*): People call me frivolous.

ARUNA: People are idiots.

DOLON (*peeping out*): You don't?

ARUNA: Don't fish, *Bangalan*!

DOLON: C'mon, tell me.

ARUNA: Don't be silly. (*Dolon grins. Disappears.*) We like it. This silliness of yours. I like it, Subhadra loves it. (*Dolon reappears in her old dressing gown.*) Now, that's better.

DOLON (*pouring herself some wine*): That's better! But the other one wasn't bad either. Cheese? Want some cheese? (*Aruna shakes her head.*) Swiss cheese. Try it dear. Wine and cheese. (*She comes to the sofa with her wine and cheese and instals herself in front of the TV.*) I'm going to be a compulsive eater. No anorexia here. Or bulimia. Eat like a pig. Grow fat. Grow so enormously fat *ki* on that fat the entire city of Mumbai can be kept illuminated from fifteenth of August to twenty-sixth of January. Some use of this body. As it is, it has outlived its purpose. (*Pause.*) If it had any to begin with.

(*Long pause. Aruna gets up and starts walking towards the cabinet.*)

DOLON (*without looking at her*): Now you'll bring out your knitting. (*Aruna freezes.*) Go ahead. We are so bloody familiar with each other's habits.

ARUNA: You have had two, by the way.

DOLON: What are you knitting?

ARUNA: You'll have to sing '*Megher porey*' if you take a third one. (*Sits on the rocking chair and begins knitting.*)

DOLON: What a lovely sunny yellow. Make me a cardigan and I'll sing non-stop for a week.

ARUNA: It's therapeutic. Everything begins to come together in your brain. You begin to organize your ... thoughts?

DOLON (*singing softly*): *aandhar kore aashey ...*

ARUNA: Nothing like knitting to relax you. Things begin to fall in place slowly as you knit along.

DOLON (*singing*): *.... jodi naa tumi dekhaa pao ...*

ARUNA: The mind becomes quiet.

DOLON (*singing*): *koro amaay hela ...*

ARUNA: Without a single thought. Without a single cloud.

(*Silence.*)

DOLON (*sharply*): I thought you wanted me to sing.

(*Pause.*)

ARUNA: Sorry. Sing again.

DOLON: You think I'm your lackey?

ARUNA: You were just humming. Sing please. Sing full-throated.

DOLON: Full throated. (*Pause.*) There was this porno movie, you know. Deep Throat or something like that. (*Pause.*) Never seen any of these though.

ARUNA: I think you've had enough wine.

DOLON: (*Bursting into full throated song*).

> *megher porey megh jomechhe*
> *aandhar korey aashey*
> *amaay keno boshiye raakho*
> *eka dwarer paashey*
> *kajer dine nana kaje*
> *thaki nana loker majhe*
> *aaj aami je boshe aachhi*
> *tomari aasshwashe*
> *amaay keno boshiye raakho*
> *eka dwarer paashey*

(*Dolon's voice gradually trails into a silence, long and heavy. The evening becomes deeper and heavier. Aruna is staring vacantly at the heap of papers. Dolon is shaking her empty wine glass listlessly and looking at the TV that is not on. Suddenly, the rumble of the lift is heard. Lift doors are opened, then slammed shut. Then the doorbell begins to ring non-stop. Aruna and Dolon look at each other.*)

ARUNA: Subhadra!

(*Dolon jumps out of the sofa, rushes to the door, opens it. It is Subhadra standing there. Same age as the other two. She has long, untied hair, a big nose stud, her eyes kohled like a dancer. She is carrying a night bag. Dolon hugs her.*)

DOLON: Shubhodra!

SUBHADRA: *Ari ari! Kya kar rahi ho!*

DOLON: *Esho naa ma.*

SUBHADRA: What has come over her Aru? (*To Dolon.*) *Meri hathini. Sookh gayi hai.*

(*Aruna just glances at Dolon's wine glass, indicating her disapproval.*)

SUBHADRA: How many under the belt by now? *Mere liye bhi kuch chhoda hai ke nahin?* (*Aruna raises two fingers.*) *Arre mujhe bhi kuch pilayegi ya taakti hi rahegi?* (*Dolon comes to the sofa, sits down and whimpers like a child.*) Aru, you must have quarrelled with her, poor darling. (*Aruna wrinkles her nose.*) Stop bickering *yaar*. For once. No *rona-dhona* today. We shall have fun. (*Takes out wool from her bag, gives it to Aruna.*) Shimla *gayee thi*. Keep it. (*Dolon sees that and turns her face and sulks. Subhadra smiles. Takes out a small perfume bottle and sitting next to Dolon, takes her in her arms.*) *Hua kya aakhir? Bolo bhi Bambai ki naaznin.* Here. This is for someone sulking. (*Dolon sees the perfume, puts her arms around Subhadra and wails.*) *Ab bas bhi karo Maateswari.* I want to spend the night here. Let's have some peace. (*Dolon whimpers, blows her nose, opens the bottle, and sniffs. Then taking a few drops out of it on her finger, she tries to apply it to Subhadra, who pushes it away with her hand.*) No thank you. I don't like perfumes. I smell of my man. That's my perfume.

(*Dolon smells her, wrinkles her nose in mock disgust, then applies the perfume on her own wrists, behind the ears, and at the throat.*)

DOLON: Divine.

SUBHADRA: Shall get you another one next time.

(*Dolon goes to Aruna and tries to apply it to her. Aruna recoils.*)

ARUNA: Chee!

DOLON (*reacting angrily*): How dare you!

ARUNA: I am allergic to it, you know it too well.

DOLON: It's a gift from Subhi.

ARUNA: But you know ...

DOLON: How can you insult her?

ARUNA: Who? Subhadra?

SUBHADRA: *Ab bas bhi karo!*

DOLON: That was in bad taste. Just awful.

ARUNA (*close to tears*): I didn't mean it that way.

DOLON: Don't you play those tricks on me anymore!

ARUNA: You really think ...

DOLON: I know you only too well.

ARUNA: But will you listen—

DOLON: I know, I know.

SUBHADRA (*screaming*): Shut up, will you? Both of you. (*Both fall silent like schoolgirls.*) Bitches. Come here any time, *sala*. They are perpetually fighting. Not a moment's peace.(*Shouting again.*) *Arre, kuch khanawana milega ke nahin is gharme*? (*Lowering her voice.*) All right, give me some wine.

(*Dolon pours her a drink. Aruna has been watching Subhadra all this while.*)

ARUNA: Subhadra Parashar!

SUBHADRA: *Boliye* Aruna Ranade.

ARUNA: What is that mark under the eye?

SUBHADRA: He hit me. *Aur kya!*

DOLON (*gasps*): Again?

SUBHADRA: It's our routine, Sweeti Pie.

DOLON (*delicately touching her under the eye*): Ma go!

SUBHADRA: I too gave him back. *Noch noch kar khoon nikala oos harami ka.*

ARUNA: Excellent!

DOLON: But who started it to-day? Not you, Subhe. How dare he?

SUBHADRA: It's all right yaar. (*Pause.*) Dolon, don't you like my Sangram?

DOLON: From a distance. From a distance.

ARUNA: Ass! Don't go back now for a few days.

DOLON: From a distance he is all right. All men in fact.

ARUNA: Let him come here and get down on his knees before you.

DOLON: Here? That boor—unwashed, unkempt?

ARUNA: Subhe, I am glad you didn't marry him.

DOLON: I'm sure he smells of diesel and petrol.

SUBHADRA (*brings her hand under Dolon's nose*): Find out.

ARUNA: You can walk out on him any time.

SUBHADRA: I will.

DOLON (*sighs*): And get another one.

(*Subhadra goes into peels of laughter.*)

SUBHADRA: Let me finish with this one first. (*Pause.*) He is good. Very.

DOLON (*pretending greediness*): Gimme more!

ARUNA (*rising*): I'll cook some rice.

SUBHADRA: See how she runs away!

DOLON: Prude!

SUBHADRA: *Baitho bhi* yaar. *Nahi bataungi.*

DOLON: Prude. She is such a prude.

SUBHADRA: She must be taking me for a walking encyclopedia of pornography.

ARUNA: Nonsense. I am not as—this—as you think.

DOLON: Sit down then. Sit.

SUBHADRA: See how interested Dolon is?

ARUNA: What is this schoolgirl nonsense? It is so juvenile. And vulgar.

SUBHADRA: Hay ! What's vulgar about it?

DOLON: Prude. Prude.

SUBHADRA (*to Dolon*): *Ek sutta dena jara.* (*To Aruna.*) What I was going to do was just give a clinical account.

DOLON: She will sit here if she has any guts.

ARUNA: You think I am afraid? But I tell you. I find it so—so—frivolous. (*Sits down unwillingly.*) Why should I be afraid? Do what you want, behave any way you like. How am I concerned?

DOLON: Balls. It requires balls.

ARUNA: This is your fourth glass. Some garagewala. Drunkard. But that's what you want. Do we say anything?

DOLON: Balls, balls. It requires balls.

ARUNA: Our friendship has survived worse things.

DOLON: You will never know what it requires. Balls.

ARUNA: You don't fit into my concept of correct living. But have I given up on you ever Subhadra?

DOLON: Can we ever?

SUBHADRA (*tenderly*): No. You two never gave up on me. Thank you Aru. Thank you Dolon. (*Pause.*) Don't I need a corner to rest my head after that bashing?

DOLON: Transit lounge?

ARUNA: Shut up.

DOLON: So that's what we are! A transit lounge.

ARUNA: Forget morality. You've kicked the society in the ah ... (*Stumbles.*) back.

DOLON: Say it. Say ass.

ARUNA: You've thrown everything to winds.

DOLON: Give up that bloody self-control at least once. We're a transit lounge anyway.

SUBHADRA: Will you stop that, woman? Or do you need to be spanked? (*Dolon whimpers.*) Spoilt brat. Dolon, don't start that act. I've had a full day and to round it off, a fight with that harami killer. (*Silence.*)

ARUNA: We object to nothing you do. But are you happy, Subhe?

SUBHADRA: Now that is an existential question. And which existential question has ever been answered?

DOLON: Existential, and a rude one at that.

SUBHADRA: I don't know if it is rude. But it certainly is an existential one.

ARUNA: Will you stop smoking for God's sake? I am nearly asphyxiated.

SUBHADRA (*crushes her cigarette*): Sorry.

DOLON: Don't, Subhe.

SUBHADRA: Why bother someone.

DOLON: Don't get bullied.

SUBHADRA: Anyway, I am not much of a smoker.

(*Aruna fetches a bottle of medicine from the cabinet.*)

ARUNA: And suppose I did all that. Smoked, drank. I can do that. I'm forty now and who is to stop me. (*Goes to Subhadra.*) Turn around. (*Holds Subhadra's face in her hands and turns it towards herself, scrutinizes it.*) Don't move. (*Applies cream below her eyes.*) Is that all? Or is there some more? (*Subhadra smiles and rubs her face against Aruna's stomach. Aruna puts her hand on her head affectionately.*) Idiot! (*Dolon is watching all this, almost moved to tears.*)

DOLON (*singsong*): Aruna Aruna Aruna!

ARUNA: It will go in a few days. Don't wander all over with that.

DOLON: Aru should have been a nurse. Florence Nightingle.

SUBHADRA: What happened to your doctoral thesis, Aru? Still at it?

ARUNA (*in a Marathi accent*): *Chal raha hai.*

SUBHADRA (*wistfully*): I should have continued with my Sanskrit.

ARUNA: Am I not glad you didn't. You witch, you would never let me top in the exams.

SUBHADRA: Who wanted to sit in that buddha moron's class, yaar. The Englit-walla was such a sexy guy. What was his name, that Parsee chap?

DOLON: Battiwala.

SUBHADRA: That's the name. What lips! Who was interested in subjects, Arunadevi. I found out who the handsomest, sexiest teachers were and opted for their subjects. How could I have survived those four years in the college otherwise, darling.

ARUNA: Good you dropped out. You would have ended being a schoolmarm like me.

DOLON: And she earns a pile.

SUBHADRA: Who me? Are you mad? Who told you journalists make a pile?

ARUNA: What even if they do? (*Obliquely.*) They squander it on some good-for-nothing.

SUBHADRA: But I love doing it.

DOLON: Very true.

SUBHADRA: Aru, I want to interview you one of these days.

ARUNA: You've laid it thick enough. What do you want to eat?

SUBHADRA: Yes friend. How you have risen in life. Writer, scholar, respected professor, an authority on ancient scriptures. The fame, the respect you command.

DOLON (*icily*): You know Subhadra, she has won an award for ...

ARUNA (*hurriedly getting up*): ... C'mon. Let's go out eat ...

SUBHADRA: What award? When?

ARUNA: Give us a ride in your car, Subhe.

SUBHADRA: No body ever tells me anything. What award?

DOLON: For her short story. What's it called? Something called ...

SUBHADRA: You didn't even ring me, Dolon.

ARUNA: What's going on here? I pushed my pen and wrote some minor stuff. That doesn't make me Tagore.

DOLON: An award is an award.

SUBHADRA: Yep. It's important.

DOLON (*her voice is icier now and has a cutting edge to it*): Calls for a celebration.

(*Aruna gets up and starts walking towards her room. The two get up with alacrity, grab her and make her sit on the sofa. Then they sit wedging her in between. Aruna tolerates it for a minute and then tries to get up. They push her back.*)

SUBHADRA: Relax, woman! You're among friends.

(*Aruna smiles, relaxes a bit.*)

DOLON: That's the spirit!

(*Subhadra sighs contentedly. Dolon puts her foot with exaggerated aplomb on the centre-table.*)

DOLON: Ha!

(*All three begin to look at the audience steadily.*)

SUBHADRA: Aruna !

ARUNA: *Bolo Bhavani.*

SUBHADRA: You asked me something a minute ago.

ARUNA: I asked nothing. Shut your mouth.

SUBHADRA: You asked me if I am happy.

ARUNA (*slightly restless*): Yes, I did.

SUBHADRA: The answer is yes. (*Pause.*) See how happy we three are! Pure bliss!

DOLON: Don't.

SUBHADRA: Don't what?

DOLON: Don't.

SUBHADRA: Whaaat?

DOLON: Just don't. (*Pause.*) Just don't put it in words. *Nazar lag jaati hai.*

(*Subhadra makes a gesture with her hands around Dolon as if to ward off evil.*)

ARUNA: Get pampered Dolon. All that she needs is an excuse.

(*They sit huddled together contentedly, staring at the audience. Then Dolon suddenly giggles.*)

SUBHADRA (*controlling her own laughter*): Now don't start that. (*Dolon is incapable of controlling her laughter and bursts into loud laughter like a champagne bottle being opened.*) Now this *chudail* ... chudail ... (*Trying to control herself desperately.*) ... will laugh and ...
(*Dolon's and Subhadra's eyes meet and then it is a riot. The harder they try to stop, the harder they laugh. Like possessed beings. Aruna watches them with amused happiness. After some time, their laughter subsides.*)

DOLON (*wiping her eyes*): Good lord! I haven't laughed like this in ages.

SUBHADRA: Me too.

ARUNA: It was like good old college days, wasn't it?

DOLON: Ya!

ARUNA: How the two of you used to laugh like donkeys braying.

SUBHADRA: Particularly during the Eco lectures.

DOLON (*dreamily*): He had a beautiful profile.

ARUNA: Who?

SUBHADRA: She is talking about Savalya, silly.

ARUNA: Oh Sawalapurkar.

DOLON: Handsome. Devastating profile.

ARUNA: Wasn't a bad teacher either.

DOLON: Who knows? Didn't he have a wonderful profile Subhe?

SUBHADRA: Whoever looked at his profile? Such thighs! Thunder thighs. My eyes were—(*Aruna tries to get up*). Sorry sorry sorry. Won't talk like that. Promise. (*Pushes Aruna back in her place.*) *Nahi aaya* sala *pangeme.* (*Pause.*) He had eyes only for you Aru. Who were we compared to you?

(*Aruna puts her fingers in her ears.*)

DOLON: Don't torment the prude, Subhya.

SUBHADRA: All right. Now silence.

(*Long pause. They stare at the audience, steadily, impersonally. Then without taking their eyes off the audience, they keep talking.*)

DOLON: What awful women are we!

ARUNA: We are all right. We're self-sufficient. We earn. We spend.

DOLON: Self-centred. Do nothing for the society.

SUBHADRA: Without any commitment. Without any ideal.

DOLON: No ideology.

SUBHADRA: We're not even feminists.

DOLON: We blow money, smoke, drink.

SUBHADRA: And my affairs.

DOLON (*giggling*): Sheeeee! What kind of people are we!

SUBHADRA: Decadent. But happy. We're happy.

DOLON: Unabashedly happy.

SUBHADRA: Abominably happy.

DOLON: Obscenely.

ARUNA (*getting into it*): Nirlajjam sada sukhi.
(*Dolon indicates inverted commas.*)

SUBHADRA: And what's that supposed to be?

DOLON: The professor always speaks in quotes.

SUBHADRA (*mockingly sad*): Duniya kya kahati hogi hame?

DOLON: Fuck duniya.

SUBHADRA: True. Why one man? Fuck the whole world and happiness is yours. (*Pause.*) How come Aru hasn't made for her room yet?

DOLON: That means she is happy. No Aruna? (*Aruna grins.*) See! She actually smiles.

SUBHADRA: Get me some wine darling.
(*Dolon picks up their glasses and goes to the cabin. Subhadra joins her. As both of them are refilling their glasses, Aruna, front stage speaks.*)

ARUNA: I wonder if I should try some today.
(*Dolon and Subhadra freeze for a moment.*)

DOLON AND SUBHADRA: Whaaaaat?

SUBHADRA: Aruna?

ARUNA: Just today.

DOLON: At last! The revolution has come. Come come come. Pour it yourself. (*Dolon and Subhadra sit at the round coffee table.*) Come na!

ARUNA: Let it be.

DOLON: Aruna!

ARUNA: Forget it.

DOLON: We'll spank you now.

SUBHADRA: I've poured some for you, darling.

DOLON: Now don't be a wet blanket. Come on.

SUBHADRA: *Arre, uth bhi. Tashrif ka tokra le aa idhar.* (*They drag Aruna to the table, force her in a chair, give her a glass of wine.*) Drink now. (*Pause.*) Drink. (*Aruna sips nervously.*) Good? How is it?

ARUNA: Sweet, sour? (*Pause.*) But good.

DOLON: Now you know how much time you have wasted not drinking it.

(*The three sip their wine in silence. Suddenly Subhadra's mobile starts ringing.*)

SUBHADRA: Hello! *Han, bolo* Sandeep. (*Listens for some time intently and then suddenly erupts.*) How dare he? And who the hell is he to fire me? (*Long Pause.*) I knew it. I smelt it. I'm sure that bony-ass *randi* is behind all this. (*Listens.*) Why are they so fucking paranoid? The skies aren't going to fall down if they print my copy as it is. Let them edit one word and they have had it. I've slogged and researched for months, man. (*Pause.*) No way, no way. That's impossible. No compromises, please. (*Pause.*) *Arrey, mai chane chabaake jeeungi. Ye haramjade kya muze blackmail karane nikale hain?* (*Pause.*) Moral turpitude? Hahaha! Look who is talking! That gateway of India son of a bitch wants to remove me for moral turpitude! That's the joke of the century! Let his letter come and then see. *Sale, teri kyun phatatee hain? Kayar sala, buzdil.* (*Pause.*) *Nahi loongi tera naam baba.* Now go and sleep in your wife's arms, baby. Thanks. (*Pause.*) For telling me yaar. (*Drops the phone in her purse.*) I was expecting this. (*Dolon and Arun are watching her.*) And now what? Why are you looking at me like that?

(*Pause.*)

ARUNA: We were so happy just a minute ago. And now this ...

SUBHADRA: I was bored stiff there anyway. Now it's freedom. I'll freelance. At least there will be more money in it. I want to buy a new car, yaar.

DOLON: What do you need cars for? Don't you have your garagewala?

SUBHADRA: At least for now. (*Pause.*) You know why we fought today?

DOLON: Go ahead, give us all the gory details, honey.

SUBHADRA: Sangram, he gets so jealous. I can't even look at anybody. He begins to see red at the drop of a hat.

DOLON: Passion. Raw passion.

ARUNA: Does he ... does he beat you a lot?

SUBHADRA: Do you think I take it lying down? I broke a glass jar on his head today.

ARUNA: What is this supposed to be? Love?

DOLON: A variety of love.

ARUNA: Leave him.

SUBHADRA: And do what? Sit at home like a *jogan*?

ARUNA: Get beaten!

SUBHADRA (*smiling*): Yes, and give it back too! (*Making a gesture of inverted commas.*) *Bhunkte bhojayate wa.* Gets jealous, *nikamma.* (*Pause.*) There is this kid who lives in the opposite building. Any time of the day, he is there stationed in the balcony, looking at me. Started making passes at me a few days ago. *Bittebharaka launda. Mujhe kartab dikhata hai!*

DOLON: Cute?

SUBHADRA: Sangram got mad at me instead of him. (*Pause.*) I won't go now. I'll stay here.

ARUNA: You must. Really.

SUBHADRA: It will be a *jashna* every day.

ARUNA: Yes, you must stay here.

DOLON: Eat, drink, and be merry.

(*Subhadra takes a sip from her glass, gets up, comes centre-stage and swirls around, humming.*)

DOLON: Subhe, loudly please.

(*Subhadra giggles, then puts one hand on her head, another on her hip and dances and sings.*)

> *Saawan ki aayi bahaar re*
> *Raajaa saawan ki aayi bahaar re*
> *Belaa chamlike mandawe tale raja*
> *Phoolon ki aayi bauchaar re*
> *Bhanwaraa to goon goon pukar re*
> *Raja, bhanwaraa to goon goon pukar re*
> *Ambuwaa ki daali pe, ambuwaa ki daali pe raja*
> *Jhulanaa jhulaay pade*
> *Koyal to koo koo pukar re*
> *Raja koyal to koo koo pukar re*

(*Dolon claps and keeps time delightedly. Subhadra gradually slows down.*)

DOLON: Fabulous.

(*Subhadra stops and collapses on the sofa.*)

SUBHADRA: *Haay mai mar gayee.*

ARUNA (*going to the window*): What will people say?

DOLON: Let them. Don't you close the shutters?

SUBHADRA: I get tired so easily these days. Getting old, I guess.

DOLON: Don't. Don't even talk about it.

ARUNA (*whispers*): Dolon ...

SUBHADRA: You better start accepting the reality.

ARUNA (*gestures frantically*): Come here.

DOLON: Miss Typo? She brushes her teeth at quarter to midnight.

(*Aruna shakes her head violently, then beckons Dolon to the window. Subhadra, up stage, is busy caressing her feet. Dolon goes and looks out of the window. Gasps.*)

SUBHADRA: There was a time when one danced through the night. Gave up my thesis for that idiocy. Bolted from home, became notorious. *Kya nahi kiya?* No regrets.

DOLON: Subhadra!

ARUNA: Close the window.

DOLON: Look who is here.

(*Subhadra turns, gives them a long, hard stare, then goes to the window and looks out.*)

SUBHADRA: And when did HE come? (*Pause.*) *Kabse khada hoga bechara!*

ARUNA: Shut the window.

SUBHADRA: 'Tisn't necessary. He'll stand there for a while and then go away.

DOLON (*looking out, shouts at him*): Beast!

SUBHADRA (*smiling*): He isn't that bad!

DOLON (*looking out*): *Rakkhosh!*

SUBHADRA: He's really like a child.

DOLON (*wrinkling her nose*): I can smell the grease right here.

(*Subhadra looks around, picks up a vase and hurls it at him through the window. Sound of it crashing on the footpath below.*)

ARUNA: Looks drunk.

DOLON (*giggling*): Like us. Let's call him up. Let's have a party.

(*Aruna strides up and closes the shutters with a slam. We hear Sangram calling Subhadra.*)

DOLON: Your Brando is calling Blanche, sorry Subhe.

ARUNA: Nobody is budging from here. (*Sangram calls again.*) Let him holler. You won't move. (*Aruna pours herself a glass of wine. Dolon watches her fascinated. Subhadra looks resigned.*) We three will live together. The two of us have been together. Now it will be three. The more the merrier. We'll take turns cooking. (*Dolon is horrified at the suggestion and shakes her head violently.*) We'll go shopping, see movies. You can drink everyday if you want. It's decided. You are going to live here.

(*Long pause.*)

SUBHADRA: I don't think I can live like you.

DOLON: Just imagine! Subhi cooking! I like that.

SUBHADRA: And I'm jobless now. I'll be a burden. (*Smiling.*) Jobless and my moral turpitude.

ARUNA: You are staying here. (*Subhadra touches Aruna's cheek tenderly, begins to collect her things and puts them in her bag.*) Leaving?

DOLON: You can see that.

ARUNA: What is the need?

SUBHADRA: You won't understand.

ARUNA (*stung*): I don't need to.

DOLON: She didn't mean it that way, Aru.

(*Subhadra goes to the window, looks out, comes back, looks around, picks up an alarm clock and throws it at him.*)

DOLON (*pained*): That was an antique!

(*Subhadra is still looking around. She is about to grab a porcelain figurine when Dolon hurriedly offers her an empty wine bottle. Subhadra throws that out. Comes to the sofa, sits, and covers her face with her hands.*)

DOLON: You'd better go Subhadra.

SUBHADRA (*to Aruna*): Didn't mean to hurt you.

ARUNA (*coldly*): That's all right.

SUBHADRA: We are friends, aren't we?

DOLON: Of course, silly!

(*Subhadra picks her bag and begins to leave.*)

ARUNA: Come again. (*Pause.*) If need be.

SUBHADRA (*smiling*): To the transit lounge? Certainly, dear.

(*Subhadra leaves. Sound of the lift going down. Silence. Then a car starts. Silence. Dolon goes to the window and looks out at the opposite building.*)

DOLON: Gone to bed. (*Looking at her wristwatch.*) My God!

ARUNA: It's past midnight. And we are still awake like ghosts. (*Gestures inverted commas.*) Yaa nishaa sarva bhootaanaam tasyam jaagarti Maitreeneehi. Wrong grammar. But correct meaning. (*She goes to her desk and looks at the books.*) Knowledge. Learning. Teaching. The pursuit of Knowledge. A whole life spent doing this. (*Beads of perspiration have appeared on her forehead, her bindi askew.*) A sensitive, creative, artistic life. (*Begins to take out her hairpins.*) Build life brick by brick. Make it a thing of beauty. (*Pause.*) I've so many friends. Vyas, Kalidas, Bhavabhooti, Shakespeare, Shelley, Eliot, Beethoven, Mozart, Bach. (*Pause.*) Is there any wine left?

DOLON: Don't drink anymore.

ARUNA: I'm not high. Not in the least. I was unnecessarily scared. (*Pause.*) Subhi shouldn't have taunted me.

(*Dolon refills the glasses.*)

DOLON: Why is she so-so-so-promiscuous?

ARUNA: Don't be judgmental.

DOLON: Such an expensive perfume she gave me! That Chandi is a giver. (*Pause.*) Not judgmental. But it's like a malaise.

ARUNA: Not a malaise. Symptom. Just a symptom. Of a malaise. That is what we think.

DOLON: At least she lives an unusual life. Wanton, unsafe, but rich. She should write stories.

ARUNA: If she finds time from all this.

DOLON: Much better than stories people write sitting in their ten by ten cocoon.

(*Long pause.*)

ARUNA: You are angry.

DOLON: No.

ARUNA: With me.

DOLON: No.

ARUNA: That comment was most uncalled for. (*Pause.*) Yes. I write stories sitting in my ten by ten cocoon. So what's your objection?

DOLON (*ignores her*): Time for me to hit the sack.

ARUNA: They don't harm anyone.

DOLON: Go to bed. You'll know tomorrow what a hangover is. (*Pause.*) Don't harm anyone? I'm not so sure.

ARUNA: Good and bad, small and big experiences, one can imagine them and live a rich life.

DOLON: Living by proxy! (*Pause.*) And you get awards for that.

ARUNA: Look here Dolon, I have no illusions about my talent. I know I am a mediocre writer. And that award. That tupenny award!

(*Pause.*)

DOLON: I read that story.

ARUNA: I know.

DOLON: What's the title? 'Maitra' or something.

ARUNA: When did you take that magazine from my room?

DOLON: 'Betrayal' would have been a better title.

ARUNA: Why do you go to my room in my absence?

DOLON: Because you've hijacked my life. For that tupenny award.

ARUNA: Don't speak in riddles, Dolon.

DOLON (*begins to put the room in order*): Why do we live under the same roof?

ARUNA: Saves money. Security.

DOLON: I don't have to do that. I earn a lot. I earn and spend. And I don't need security. (*Pause.*) 'Maitra' my foot. (*Aruna tries to touch her.*) Don't touch me. (*Aruna freezes.*) I touch you a lot, don't I? And those touches are dirty.

ARUNA: You deserve a tight one.

DOLON: That story is based on me.

ARUNA (*looking straight at her eyes*): No.

DOLON: The heroine of your story—she uses frilly, jazzy clothes, smokes, drinks.

ARUNA: Hundreds of women do that.

DOLON: And her Marathi is laced with Punjabi.

ARUNA: A totally imaginary character—

DOLON: Punjabi instead of Bengali. Why didn't you make her Bengali? It would've been more authentic.

ARUNA: Will you listen to me?

DOLON (*in a broken voice*): You shouldn't have done that. Such an old friendship. Gone in a minute. Phut! Just like that.

ARUNA: Look here. That woman is not you. May be some similarities— only a few externalities—

DOLON: Don't give me that bullshit. Good night.

ARUNA: Wait a minute.

DOLON: I'll pack my things first thing in the morning.

ARUNA: Will you please listen to me? You hold a big post in a multinational. She is a clerk. You are multilingual, she is almost an uneducated ...

DOLON: This is my flat. You should leave.

ARUNA: I will. But not unless I've thrashed this out. Yes, it's true. She is bubbly like you ...

DOLON: And she touches. Like me. (*Pause.*) Yes. I touch. But I touch easily and everybody. Kiss even. You find something like *that* in my touches? Like that Surinder's? (*Aruna gives her a long, hard stare and then turns to go to her room. Dolon shouts at Aruna.*) Why don't you thrash it out now?

(*Aruna is almost in tears. Sits down on the sofa.*)

ARUNA: So much *tamasha* for a tenth rate story!

DOLON: I want to thrash out. Now. (*Pause.*) I loved you. *Aamar sakhi.* My friend, sister, my soul-mate ...

ARUNA: I'm not used to people touching me.

DOLON: So? You'll misinterpret me?

ARUNA: Sorry.

DOLON: And sell it. For that tupenny award and that froth of fame.

ARUNA: Aren't you over-reacting, Dolon?

DOLON: Perhaps. Go to bed. (*Aruna rises and is about to go to her room.*) Wait a minute. (*Aruna turns towards Dolon.*) Are you sure you are not like that?

ARUNA (*horrified*): This is crazy!

DOLON: Are you sure? I'm sure I'm not. Are you? (*Pause.*) Maybe you are. (*Aruna begins to clean up the room.*) I'll do that. It is my house. (*Aruna stops dead in her tracks.*) Aren't you always surrounded by all those young girls?

ARUNA (*angry*): They are my students. They like me and my teaching.

DOLON: Touch this one under the chin, that one on her hair, put a hand on this one's back for a fraction of a second longer than necessary ...

ARUNA: This is sick.

DOLON: I am only talking. Just between the two of us. You wrote. Thousands have read it. Let's part.

ARUNA: I'm afraid of you.

DOLON: You mean ...

ARUNA: No no. Don't misunderstand me please. You love with abandon, shower it on people. I can't. I keep distance. Hurting you is the last thing I'll ever do.

DOLON (*sadly*): You've done that all right.

ARUNA (*puts her hand on Dolon's hand*): Sorry.

DOLON (*taking her hand away*): And is this spontaneous?

ARUNA: Yes, Dolo.

DOLON: That only means I'm more spontaneous than you, Aruna. That's all.

ARUNA: Truce.

DOLON: I was called Dolo after ages.

ARUNA: That's what we used to call you in college.

DOLON: Dolo-Rolo-Polo. You'd composed a song. Like 'eena mina dika'. I was a fatso even then, wasn't I?

ARUNA: Plump. Pleasantly plump.

DOLON: Manosh-da is asking for more money. He has enough to waste on a courier.

ARUNA: Don't send it.

DOLON: He'll come here to stay.

ARUNA: I asked Subhi to come and stay with us. If she does, where will she sleep?

DOLON: She can share my room, Miss Privacy. (*Moves to the window.*) Miss Typo has gone to bed. Asleep. Dead to the world.

ARUNA: It is pointless to go to bed now. It's almost three now. Let's finish this.

(*Aruna pours Dolon a glass, pours one for herself, sits on the steps leading to the terrace. Silence. Dolon begins to sing in a soft voice.*)

DOLON: *Shakhi aandhaare, ekela ghare*
 Mono mane na
 Mono mane na
 Shakhi aandhare

(*Silence.*)

 Mono mane na

(*Silence. Dolon's voice trails into an almost inaudible whisper.*)

 Mono mane na
 Mono mane na ...

(*Her voice trails off into silence. Aruna is staring vacantly into the audience. Her bun is undone, her* pallu *askew.*)

ARUNA: Dolon!

DOLON: Balo ma.

ARUNA: I ran into Avinash the other day. (*Dolon freezes.*) After twenty years. Suddenly. (*Pause.*) Suddenly we were standing facing each other, right in the middle of the road.

(*Pause.*)

DOLON: Then? (*Aruna's face twists in agony for a second.*) How is he? (*Aruna shakes her head distractedly.*) Panther! Chitah!

ARUNA: Still the same.

DOLON: Forget him. It's history now.

ARUNA: His eyes still burn with fire. Now mixed with pain. (*Pause.*) Or maybe I tried to tell myself that.

DOLON: I too haven't seen him in a long long time. Subhi tells me she chances to meet him from time to time.

ARUNA: You never told me that.

DOLON: How could I?

ARUNA: You did the right thing.

DOLON: You'd closed that chapter with such finality. (*Pause.*) Did you speak?

ARUNA: No. Couldn't. Neither of us. (*Pause.*) Then I did the silliest thing. I showed him my palms and said, 'See, how I am perspiring!' He saw that and left.

(*Pause.*)

DOLON: Is it too late, Aru?

ARUNA: Very.

DOLON: You terminated it, Aruna.

ARUNA: Yes, I did.

DOLON: You shouldn't have.

ARUNA: I am not so sure of that.

DOLON: What ego, Aruna! *Ki Ohonkar!*

ARUNA: I did then what I thought was right.

DOLON: He loved you. You loved him.

ARUNA: Yes, I did. (*Pause.*) But love doesn't last all one's life. I thought so then and I think so now.

DOLON: *Aami shotti bolchi, shon.* You were dreaming of a magnificent career. You were ambitious. Indology. Germany. America. Conferences and seminars. Rubbing shoulders with the cream of the world.

ARUNA: What is so wrong about it?

DOLON: He didn't fit in that scheme. So don't complain now.

ARUNA: Scheme is an insulting word. And who is complaining?

DOLON: Forget him.

ARUNA: I used to like his wildness. To a limit. But he never wanted to do anything worthwhile. I did not understand this. He was a wastrel. He still is, I hear.

DOLON: He is a most celebrated artist. Internationally recognized.

ARUNA: And here I am, writing soppy stories for women's magazines. (*Pause.*) He is celebrated, yes. But still a wastrel.

DOLON: And you've made a success of your life, haven't you?

ARUNA: Perhaps I wouldn't have been able to cope with him. (*Pause.*) No. I know I'm not a success. But not a failure either. I am living a tepid, monotonous, secure life, am I not? (*Pause.*) Life has passed us by, Dolo.

DOLON: It will soon be over. What a blessing people die.

ARUNA (*smiling*): *Modhur borodaan.*

(*Silence.*)

DOLON (*in a very quiet tone*):

Because I could not stop for death
He kindly stopped for me

(*Pause.*)
>   The carriage held just ourselves
>   And immortality.

(*Pause.*)

ARUNA: Emily.

DOLON: Dickinson.

ARUNA: Who wants it? Immortality?

DOLON: At the end of the day, we're all cowards.

ARUNA: I did what I did knowing full well what I was doing.

DOLON: Why are you such an ice-block then? You are afraid of crying even.

ARUNA (*making a joke of it*): I cry when I watch Hindi movies, don't I?

DOLON: I've seen you crying only once.

ARUNA: Don't, Dolon.

DOLON: Only once.

ARUNA: Don't rake it up.

DOLON: I went to see Avi because *you* asked me to. When I came back to the hostel room you were lying on your bed in the dark ...

ARUNA: Please ...

DOLON: Your tears running into the pillow.

ARUNA: It was a difficult decision. (*Pause.*) You did something beautiful then. You held me close.

DOLON: Touched your wet eyes with my lips.

ARUNA: You drank all my pain.

(*Pause.*)

DOLON: It never happened again.

ARUNA: No.

(*Pause.*)

DOLON: Aruna.

ARUNA: Balo, ma.

DOLON: You ever thought I was giving you signals?

ARUNA: Never.

DOLON: But you changed so much after that evening. Became remote.

ARUNA: I'll always cherish that moment, *pagli*. For the first time in my life, I hadn't recoiled from human contact. (*Pause.*) But I can't always be that. I was so ashamed you saw me crying.

DOLON (*in a heavy voice*): We are friends!

ARUNA: Have I hurt you? I know I have. Sorry.

(*Dolon shakes her head violently.*)

DOLON: On the contrary. *I* have hurt you. And you don't even know it. I have been hurting you for years.

ARUNA: Haven't we had enough of this sentimentality, Dolon?

DOLON: I accused you of betraying me.

ARUNA (*smiling*): Wasn't the first time you said something like that to me.

DOLON: *I* have betrayed you. (*Aruna stiffens.*) You and Avi parted ways on that day. And you said to me, 'Go, be with him. I can manage myself. But he is being ripped apart.' (*Pause.*) When I came back from him, I was full of him. (*Aruna keeps staring in the audience.*) And I never told you. When I went to him, he was writhing in pain. As I tried to console him—(*Pause.*) I forgot everything at that moment. Your relationship with him. Our friendship. The happiness I got was so overpowering. When I saw you crying, I felt like covering you with that happiness. (*Pause.*) I never met Avi after that.

(*Long silence. Aruna stirs, pours her wine in a nearby gamla. Rises. Goes into the drawing room.*)

ARUNA: What a mess this room is in! When Subhi comes, it is like a tornado hitting full blast.

DOLON: Will you ever forgive me?

ARUNA: What right did I have over him?

DOLON: I betrayed your trust.

ARUNA: I have never thought that others should not get what I cannot. (*Pause.*) What's so new in what you did, friend? All the *dootis* and sakhis from Sanskrit poetry have been doing it for ages. (*Dolon sobs. Aruna takes her in her arms.*) Enough, my precious. It is the past. Leave it behind. You needn't have told me all this. You did. So its okay. Getup now and chin up, honey.

(*Dolon rises, trips against the centre-table. The perfume bottle on it falls down.*)

DOLON: Ma go!

ARUNA: Subhadra gave it.

DOLON: Not a drop left. God!

ARUNA: Give it to me. (*Takes it and puts it in the collection on the side table*). One more addition to the collection. (*She ties up her hair in a knot*). These papers. I'll have to do them tomorrow. I must try a little snooze.

DOLON: I think I will read for a while. (*Dolon starts the CD player. The second movement of the 'Moonlight' Sonata*—allegretto. *Aruna is standing near her desk. Dolon wanders to the window.*) The day will break soon. You will go to your college, I to my bank. The night is over.

(*Comes back to the sofa, and sits. Aruna is still standing. Slow fade out while the music spreads into the silence.*)

CURTAIN

An Actor Exits

Eka Natacha Mrityu

Translated by
Supantha Bhattacharya

Characters:

He

Director's Mask

Her Mask

Chorus

Act One

It is dark on the stage. After a moment or two, a shaft of light descends from the roof to the exact centre of the stage, lighting that area. There is an immobile, still heap of something covered with cobwebs, centre-stage, where the shaft actually hits. In the reflected light we also see broken pieces of mirrors, old, broken photo frames, a couple of skulls, an old clock without hands floating in the air. Silence till the audience gets accustomed to the whole scene. After a while, a very faint sound of whining begins to emerge out of the heap. Gradually the whining turns into a weak weeping. The heap begins to stir very slowly, then makes uncertain efforts to get up and sit. Light increases slightly. The heap turns out to be a man and he is covered with cobwebs from head to foot. He looks at himself, startled and a bit frightened. Disgust, fear, surprise, curiosity play about on his face. He stares at the cobwebs for a long while and then gingerly picks up a thread with his right hand. The thread sticks to his fingers. He tries to remove it with his left hand and now the strand clings to his fingers on the right. He keeps trying to remove it from one hand while it keeps sticking to the other. His efforts begin to get more and more desperate. In panic, he feverishly tries to pull the cobwebs away from his body without any success. Finally he gives up. Tired and defeated, he looks at himself in utter helplessness. He is about to burst into a sob, but instead, begins to hum to suppress it. His words begin to emerge out of this humming.

HE: We were heartbroken when we left our old home. Only Mother
stayed calm. What to say about Baba? He was never home. The
day we left, Mother cleaned the house thoroughly, washed the
floors, cleaned the earthen stove, drew lines of turmeric and
kumkum on the stove and the threshold. Placed fistfuls of grain
in the empty family shrine, lit a lamp, and did namaskar. Then,
leaving the front door ajar, began to walk away, ramrod straight,
never once looking back. We kept turning back, tears streaming
down our eyes. But she, without ever looking back, her eyes fixed
nowhere, was walking away resolutely. She kept walking just like
this, and all of a sudden, disappeared from our sight. Never saw
her again. She was gone. Gone forever.(*Pause.Fidgets with the
cobwebs.*) Whatever happened, was for good, she had said. How
long could we care for junk? She had said. *Karatala bhiksha,
tarutala vasah*—alms on the palm, dwell under a tree. How much
does a man need? She didn't even ask us to look after ourselves.
(*Pause. Tries to pull the cobwebs off, but they cling stubbornly to his body.*)
Dearies, please get off my body. Why do you behave like unwelcome
love? Always clinging, always clutching. (*Pause.*) Perhaps you nurse
some hopes. That I'll feel affection for you lot. Attachment. What
optimism! Hope is bad, okay? Chains you down. *Asha naam
manushyanam, Kachid ashcharyashrinkhala, Yaya badhdhaha
pradhavanti,muktah tishthanti panguvat*—hope is a surprising
chain, men flee when bound by it—isn't that the saying? Get off
me. No? Okay. Stay then. (*Pause.*) Mother would have laughed. What
junk you keep collecting, she used to say. Easy for her to say this.
Sunrays her sari, and the skies her shelter. That was enough for her.
But what all I kept collecting! It wasn't stuff that others collected.
Like houses, cars etc. Nothing like that. My collection was different.
I collected what actors do. Like how someone walks, speaks. Save.
Control+S. Click. How you smile curling your lips, when you want
to show contempt. How to make the vein on your forehead throb
like someone else, when you want to display anger. Like this. You

know, I even learnt how to wriggle my ears! *Aangik Abhinay.* What
fun! Every actor must collect such capital. Real fun, isn't it?

(*Out of the darkness comes a Man's voice*: Junk!)

Just when I thought this was enough, I had to run into this guy.
Mister Director. I just told him, laughingly, that this is our box
of tricks. 'Junk!' he spat out. Snobbish, but intelligent. I affirmed
that an actor has to earn this capital.

(*Out of the darkness the voice comes again:* Junk!)

So what do I do, man? I asked. Discard everything I have collected?
(*Tries to remove the cobwebs again.*) Hello, Junk! Are you getting
off me? No? I'm feeling filthy. No? Okay. (*Pause.*) 'This junk you've
collected, chuck it all away. Go deep within yourself,' he said.
Same guy. Snobbish. But intelligent. 'Read, why don't you? Enrich
yourself.' He said. So I read. Read this, read that. Read what I
understood, read what I didn't. Treasures! The treasures of trash!
This author. That poet. Rob them. Like this.

(*Begins to hum to himself, and gradually begins to recite.*)

This is the time of tension
Between dying and birth
The place of solitude.

(*A Woman's voice comes out of the dark*: Eliot.)

This suspended realm
Where there are no shadows of anything
Sound becomes silence
The snow of breath
Accumulates on infinity.

(*The Woman's voice questions*: Eliot?)

HE: We would recite together. We would dramatize poems together.
With what zest did we repay our cultural debts! That too by
visiting the British Council!

WOMAN'S VOICE: Of course! To top it, money. And fame. What
a bonus!

HE: Whether it was Eliot, or Shakespeare, or Shaw, or Beckett et al,
Vyasa, Kalidasa, Bhavabhuti! You name it! The beauty of words.
The glow of meaning. Dnyaneshwar, you know? We collected so
much, and doled out so much. O Dnyandev, such a junk heap of
words we collected!
This is that skeleton of meaning
Adorned with the junk of words
Celebrating our petty lives.
We idiots!
(*Immediately folds his palms and cries.*) Sorry! Sorry! Sorry! She
would blow a fuse when anybody spoke like this about saints and
stuff. 'Don't make fun of saints-waints,' she would say. She wouldn't
even light her first cigarette of the day, without reading at least
four *ovis* of the Dnyaneshwari first. 'If you read this way, mind-
peace follows,' she used to say. Pardon me, pardon me, sister!
Blessed Sister, Holy Mother
Forgive this sinner for his sins
Forgive him his boorish ignorance.
(*Imitates the sounds of singing litany. After a moment's pause.*)
Amen !
(*He crosses himself.*)
WOMAN'S VOICE: There! Asshole now begins his performance!
(*Now He starts performing seriously for the audience.*)
HE: All movement is immersed
Ultimately in the sea of Time. What lives, dies.
Sound becomes mute.
Words finally melt into
Silence.
(*Pause.*)
(*To the audience.*) A very meaningful pause here! Eloquent silence!
WOMAN'S VOICE: Awestruck silence! Sound of applause!
HE (*pleased with himself, exuberantly*): Never ever stopped!

WOMAN'S VOICE (*mocking*): I could hear it. Even inside the greenroom where I would be removing my make-up. I used to smile and say, 'Here comes the bastard's act.' You would get down on your knees, pay your respects to the audience. Look at them with hurt, helpless eyes. As if you have unconditionally surrendered to them. You'd touch the floor with your forehead again. Stay like that till the curtains came down. Accompanied by the background music of the applause. Even after curtains, you would remain like that till someone came and touched you lightly on the back.

(*All these gestures are enacted by him like a seasoned professional even as she speaks. Applause in the background.*)

WOMAN'S VOICE: All just a bloody act!

(*Even as he resumes his former position, a Woman's mask appears within a frame in the darkness. The rest of her body is covered in dark clothes and therefore invisible. The light is entirely on her mask, preferably a Chhau mask. Throughout the play, the mask's gaze would keep turning and following the protagonist, but he will never look directly at them. His eyes would constantly be towards the auditorium, as if the words are coming from there.*)

WOMAN'S MASK: Hoax!

HE: This too is so routine.

WOMAN'S MASK: Have I ever said this before?

HE: I could clearly see the word in your eyes, in your gestures as you'd ignore me and light a cigarette when I entered the greenroom. So many little things. That word would hang all around you. Like the deodorant you used.

WOMAN'S MASK: Are you sure? Maybe, you'd only see in my eyes what was in your own mind. Quite possible. What was that famous statement you'd frequently use in your interviews? In a deep baritone, eyes rooted to the ground: 'I exist only in the eyes of other people.'

HE: So?

WOMAN'S MASK: Balls.

HE: It is true.

WOMAN'S MASK: Balls. Whose words are these? Sartre? Or Genet?

HE: Mine.

WOMAN'S MASK: Bullshit. Which actor ever uses his own words? He's eternally borrowing.

HE: Personal experience?

WOMAN'S MASK: So? This is how things are on the stage. Borrowed words, borrowed emotions. Just remove them along with the make-up. So simple. (*In mock humility.*) But what of us mortals? Mediocres all! *You* are a born actor! Always immersed in your art-fart. What's that other famous statement of yours? 'How real life seamlessly fuses into stage life and vice versa blah ... blah ... blah ...' So corny! What surprised me were the people. They would actually get mesmerized by this conning!

HE: You're jealous.

WOMAN'S MASK: Nonsense! Why should I feel jealous? I would receive as much applause as you and just as much money! Don't talk rubbish! But I never pretended, did I? Play over. Make-up off. Mask of the character ripped.

HE: To put on yet another mask. This a party dress, this one for travelling, this a night dress. The same way. This mask for this occasion, that one for another.

WOMAN'S MASK: That's how it is. It was not like someone claiming: 'I've removed my mask and showing my true self.' Then, put on a mask of vulnerability, modesty, sensitivity. That's *your* style. What else!

HE: Really! Huh!

WOMAN'S MASK: Yeah!

HE: So we both wore masks. Two masks loved each other, slept with each other, made a home together, then separated. Which means that nothing happened in reality. Just like theatre. All make-believe. But did nothing really happen in such a long stretch of life? Two people came together and nothing happened? (*To himself.*) What did you do in your life, *yaar*? (*Plays with the cobwebs.*) Collected these. Acted. Who says acting is false?

(*Lights off from the Woman's mask.*)

Switch on, switch off. That's what she used to say. Click. (*Enacts switching on a light button.*) Click. (*Enacts switching it off.*) Is it ever like this? That theatre is just faking it? Remove the pretences and you are free to live. Is it ever like this? Oh no! It's a quest. Acting is. (*Hums and plays with the cobwebs.*) What is the quest all about? Is it really that way? A quest? Or is it just a cover-up process, using rags to hide the wretched emptiness within? Camouflaging? (*He hums and wanders around aimlessly. Finally, grabs a floating mirror fragment, sits down, and starts scrutinizing himself in it.*) Hey, no make-up today? Bravo. *Teri pyari pyari surat ko kisi ki nazar na lage hun ... hun ... hun ...*

(*Pause. Disgustingly coy.*)

Tell me, O mirror, how do I look?

How do I look? (*Displeased with himself.*) Unh-hunh. No.

(*Suddenly assuming the voice and gestures of a seasoned actor.*)

And moving through a mirror clear
That hangs before her all the year
Shadows of the world appear.

(*Pause. Satisfied.*) Ha! That's better. (*Again theatrically.*)

I am half sick of the shadows
Said the Lady of Shallott.

(*A man's voice from the darkness: Narcissus!*)

Shadows, what shadows? Are the things that we see in mirrors, false? If they are false, how do we see them? Isn't it said often, 'The stage is the mirror of life'? This implies the mirror is real. So? And if the mirror is false, then how can we see ourselves in it? If the mirror is false, then everything is false. That's how things are. If the mirror is false then it's only logical that we use words first, as a matter of formality. And only subsequently do we make ourselves feel the emotions they represent. Like fear, etc. Anger, love, trust, friendship etc. Who was that guy who said it? Jung? Or was it somebody else? That if you act angry, you feel angry. If you act loving ...

MAN'S VOICE (*from the darkness*): *You* feel love! *You!* Bloody Narcissus! *You* feel love?

(*The Man's Mask appears in another frame.*)

MAN'S MASK: I told you this, Mister Duffer. It's either by Jung or by Freud. It was I who told you this. Remember?

HE: All crap. Work up a hard-on first and then start feeling horny. Does it work that way? *Never!* (*Pause. Giggles to himself.*) What fun!

MAN'S MASK: Stimulation. If an actor is to reach his primaeval impulses hidden within, then he must first stimulate himself on a sensory level. What have you understood of Artaud? You bloody second-raters all. You lot will never understand me.

HE: Ask the bastard any inconvenient question and instantly I am a second-rater. Just don't ask anything. Keep agreeing to whatever he says. If possible, fix an expression of sublime reverence on your face. And the bugger's happy.

MAN'S MASK: Actors are born lazy. Absolutely no spirit of quest. Just illustrate whatever they have read, and that is acting for them! No quest. No spirit of internal inquiry.

HE: What shit did he understand about me? (*To the reflection in the mirror.*) All that I ever had was you.

MAN'S MASK: Just use the physique, that's enough! To begin with, he should have something within him, shouldn't he? What else can you do?

HE: Maybe, maybe you are right. Whatever you say. But tell me, what do *you* have within you?

MAN'S MASK: Don't be so bloody cheeky.

HE: All right, I am a Narcissus, but how are you different from me?

Always '*My* actor, *my* actor, *my* production.' So, basically we are all the same.

MAN'S MASK: Concern for you. That's what I had in mind. Concern for you all.

HE (*laughing*): Crap.

MAN'S MASK: You were my children, all my sons. (*A church organ strikes up.*) I am the Father. You're my children.

HE (*kneeling down, clasping his hands, bowing his head low, in a voice choked with false humility*): Our Father who art in Heaven ...

MAN'S MASK: My Lambs ...

HE: Shower me with Divine Love. (*Singing.*)

    Poorvi Davidacha ghari
    Gotha bala janmale
    Tevha aaine gavhani
    Preme bal thevale

MAN'S MASK: That's all you can bloody do. Ridicule.

HE (*acting serious all of a sudden*): O Father! Father, gone from us, lost to us. Grant unto us that we may sit, one on Thy right hand and the other on the left, in Thy Glory. (*Organ stops playing.*) Amen! (*He crosses himself.*)

MAN'S MASK: Always lampooning!

HE: But even as I was lampooning, all of a sudden, I got gooseflesh. Out of the lines I just recited, something real suddenly came alive. I still have it. See! (*Extends his hands.*) O shit. These cobwebs will get more tangled now.

MAN'S MASK: Is it possible to act just by borrowing? From here, there, everywhere? Acting is within ourselves. To go deep down the self and search for the self. Once that is found, it creates its own body language. This is what I had been drilling into you for ever, you dimwits. Gestures of others, picked up mannerisms, borrowed emotions; I taught you to forget all these and sink deep within yourselves. That is where I knew the key to true acting can be found.

HE: I see. (*Pause.*) Once, I was taken ill, and you stepped in as my replacement. The curtains had to be lowered in five minutes. Boos, wolf whistles. Why? Weren't *you* able to go deep within yourself? You can only ride high on your camel of theory, and provide directions to the herd.

MAN'S MASK: That is mean. I am a teacher. Guru.

HE: *Gururbrahma, Gururvishnu ...*

MAN'S MASK: I am telling you all this because I too have found something within myself.

HE: I would like to believe that.

MAN'S MASK: I gave you whatever I found. That's how it is. The relationship between a Director and an Actor.

HE: O yeah! Care, concern for the actor. Leading him by the fingers into deep waters. Being fulfilled by his development. What? Rich? Meaningful? (*Pause.*) When it came to taking the curtain calls, you took it all by yourself.

MAN'S MASK: That is mean.

HE: Even in the ads: 'So and so presents ...'

MAN'S MASK: That too had been a part of your training. The trap of fame is evil. Once you are caught in it, that's the end of your quest. Bye-bye.

HE: Friend, Philosopher, Guide (*Pause.*) Lover. (*Lights off from the Man's Mask.*) Did you ever have an affair with him? (*Now he turns and looks at the frame which had the Woman's Mask. The frame is empty. Addressing the empty frame.*) Did you sleep with each other? (*Pause.*) We did. Once. (*Pause.*) 'To explore a new territory of experience,' that's what he'd said. And me? Anything for a new experience. I was out for it. He was greedily trying to 'explore' this territory inside me. I found nothing. (*Pause.*) He was in pain. Great emotional pain. It left me cold. (*Pause.*) Does this ever

happen? Can you pre-decide an experience? If you can, then
doesn't it change the essential nature of the experience? (*Looking
at the empty frame.*) We risked it. Ultimately that is what matters.
(*Begins to hum, picks up the mirror fragment and looks at his reflection
for long and addresses it.*)

Who are you, brother? Why am I living inside you? And who
was it that'd decided that I should live inside you? (*Pause.*) Funny,
isn't it? We are such strangers to each other, and yet we are forced
to live together. If you are such a stranger, then how strange must
the others be to me? Yet we have love and all that jazz. (*Pause.*)
Are all these strangers deceiving each other nonstop in the name
of love, or what? (*Pause.*) Shouldn't deceive. Right? Have mutual
faith, trust. Right? Only then may love survive. This is a theory.
Hypothesis. But this perhaps can happen between two people.
(*In the darkness behind, two masked figures come close and begin to
make love.*)

I didn't feel any anger or sorrow. It didn't matter to me that they
had slept together. But I kept wondering if they had found
something unusual while fucking? Something precious,
something rare? Something which I might not have found when
I had sex with her. (*To the reflection.*) Why me? Wretched body,
even you didn't find it.

(*Light on both the masks that are now separated.*)

WOMAN'S MASK: He isn't normal.

MAN'S MASK: Who is?

WOMAN'S MASK: What does he always look at in the mirror?

MAN'S MASK: They are all like that. Narcissus.

WOMAN'S MASK: Does he arouse himself by watching himself in the
mirror? What am I here for?

MAN'S MASK: Leave him be.

WOMAN'S MASK: He is so good. Simple, loving, a little dumb. But he
loves me so much. A little too much for comfort perhaps. Rather

unnerving. Not really proper. He looks into my eyes in such a
way, I tell you! Scary!

MAN'S MASK: We must help him. Save him.

WOMAN'S MASK: No way man! Who wants to leap into a dark hell-
hole? He thinks we sleep together. Fucking Paranoid! (*Pause.*)
What is he always looking for in me?

(*Light disappears from them. He is busy fingering his cobwebs.*)

HE: When did these gather on my body?
How come I am able to see them only now?
They keep multiplying by the day. I hadn't even realized it.
Keep growing. Keep growing.
No pause no rest no peace.
On and on.
This must stop.

(*Singsong.*)

Concludeconcludeconclude it will all conclude.

(*In an actor's voice.*)

All things have rest and ripen toward the grave
In silence.
Ripen, fall and cease.

(*Looking into the mirror*).

You will cease.
Will end.
Was that my true fear?
Were the words just a cover for this?
Roles I played, my loves, my apparently meaningful but
    ultimately meaningless interactions.
A new mask for every occasion.
What a repertoire of masks!
Ya buddy! So many new masks! Have fun!

If I only knew why I live inside you-u-u-u! Why would I have
put on the masks? So simple. Had I known that why would I

have needed you, in the first place? What do you say? (*Staring fixedly at the reflection.*) See how the bastard's staring at me! You're on a high! A victor's high! A high because you knew I couldn't do without you. She would ask me: 'What makes you act so high and mighty?' I'd reply: 'It's merely a mask, honey! I wear it so as not to reveal my inner terror. I can easily remove it. But first, just love me a little. In an honest way.' At this, she would stare at me as if I were an idiot! (*Pause. To his reflection.*) Or was it you she was staring at? (*Pause.*) I mean we never really know, do we, what is it that we really love when we talk about this 'love' business! Therefore, masks!

'How do I love thee? Let me count the ways!'

Two masks loving each other.

A-ha A-ha!

(*Sings.*)

A-ha aai milan ki bela hun-hun-hun ...

Promise the whole sky but deliver a meagre droplet. But it's love after all!

(*Sings.*)

Char bundonwalla hanh hanh!

Even we felt we were infinitely in love with each other. Now, had the masks slipped even a teeny-weeny bit, then what?

Answer: We would have seen our true selves. Question: Friend, It's fine with you. You are concrete. With a nose, eyes and all. But do tell me what is meant by 'true self'? And if we start peeling off these masks, do we really discover our true selves? Or is it like peeling onions?

(*The Woman's face reappears within the frame.*)

Masks are false, and therefore illusory. In the same way, our true selves are also illusions. So it is proved that masks loving masks is equally illusory. Answer. What is fundamentally important is that illusions create a world of illusions so that the illusion of existence remains intact. (*Pause.*) Wasted all my life just in this fucking business!

WOMAN'S MASK: How you swear!

HE: Consider them illusions. *Vyaghropi mithya, palayanapi mithya*—the tiger is an illusion, and so is running away from it. Hasn't man found this one and the only truth? We imagine there is something beyond these illusions and so mess up our lives utterly. All sheer stupidity.

(*To his reflection.*)

You are the truth. Only you are the truth. You are the only truth. You are real. You are the actuality. You are the final truth.

(*Starts slapping himself.*)

I should have forgotten myself by becoming one with you. That's what I didn't do. (*Holds his ears.*) My mistake.

(*Begins to move gently, rhythmically, as if sexually aroused.*)

My body. Her body.

The only hard, ringing truth.

The moment eyes meet, an electric current passes through the spine. Just a whiff of the body's scent, and serpents begin to uncoil in the loins. Even a fleeting touch makes one's ears steam. (*Moves to the rhythm of the sexual act.*) Body on body. Body into body. Bodies together. Only bodies. Within within, creating havoc, wrecking devastation, sweat, blood, semen. Fuck her—fuck her—O my God! (*Stops suddenly as if utterly spent. Then chuckles aloud.*) So many times I had unpeeled this particular onion as well! Onions! The only truth in life. New editions of it every day. (*Pause.*) When our bodies were twisted together, we would look deep into each others' eyes. When we couldn't find anything in there, we would proudly proclaim, 'We haven't concealed anything from each other. How we love each other!'

WOMAN'S MASK: It was you who would spout this kind of poetry!

HE: How useful it was on such occasions, being an actor.

WOMAN'S MASK: You think an actress didn't realize this? (*Laughs.*) What fun! We played games, dear! The game of Prem.

HE: That talk was never intended for you. I would speak it only for myself. To reassure myself that I really loved you.

WOMAN'S MASK: I think you took it a bit too seriously. (*Pause.*) I would be so amused playing this game. When you spoke with such wistful eyes, I too would pretend to almost faint with ecstasy. I did it so well, didn't I? All this just to please you, Sweetie Pie!

HE: You think I didn't see through it too? I'd wonder who were you thinking of at that moment?

WOMAN'S MASK: Sprouts to be cooked for breakfast. Something on those lines.

(*Woman's Mask vanishes.*)

HE: Masks. Masks upon masks.

Life is equal to a cover-up job,
And being terrified of death.
So love someone as much as you can.
Or a career of a social worker,
Talk shop about art et cetera,
Believing that you have lived fully.
Some calculated friendships, a few insipid enmities.
Done. Lived.
Born. Breathed. Died.
Some people say this.
'We must have such a reason for existence
That would connect us to others. 'Raison d'etre.'
And where the hell is this reason? Outside? Inside?
O my God! My God!
Why am I like this?
Why?
That is the question.
Why is the question.

Puppet men, and their puppet concerns
Perform onstage for an instant,
And return to their boxes, dismantled.
I did this and I did that.
He did this and he did that.
Rama ruled over a Ramrajya, naturally.
Alexander conquered the world.
Brutus' knife in the guts, and Ram's arrow
In Vali's back.
Draupadi was stripped, and Medea
Killed her children and became Ganga's sister.
Yami made forbidden love to Yama
And Oedipus was rapt in coitus with his mother.
I lived all this. I lived all these lives.
Yet. Even then. Even then.
Mandhata nriparaj jo kaliyugalankara jhala mruta
Jene Ravana Kumbhakarna vadhile to Ram jhala mruta.

MAN'S MASK: Lucky guy! You lived a hundred lives.

HE: Borrowed ones!

MAN'S MASK: You lived off them. Lived *through* them.

HE: And *you* lived off me. Lived through me. Every evening, even if it
was only for three hours, even if it was illusory, *I lived!* You would
just watch me from the wings like a voyeur watching others making
love. (*Pause.*) Even at the rehearsals. Do this. Do that. Try this. Try
that. Was it necessary to do all that? I think you made me do all
that for which you yourself didn't have the guts.

MAN'S MASK: It was my duty to show you the path to self-quest.

HE: And it was you who would walk on those paths. You charted the
ways for me. (*Pause.*) There were times when, while performing,
those paths would slip into oblivion. Utterly new ones, never
seen before, would spring up under my feet. I would sense that
these are surely *my* paths. And at that moment, the abated breath
of the audience, their spellbound stares would tell me that they

too have seen this path for the first time. My soul and theirs would fuse into each other during this unforeseen adventure. (*Pause.*) This is true theatre. (*Pause.*) Who told you I like applause? It is this charged moment I would thirst for.

MAN'S MASK: Cut that crap!

HE: *You* used to junk it out calling it indulgence.

MAN'S MASK: Cut it.

HE: I think you used to be scared shitless. The very idea that this guy had found something absolutely unattainable for you, scared you to death. 'Creative togetherness!' Where was it? Mutual exploitation, wasn't that the true meaning of our relationship? You'd call it 'Creative togetherness', she'd call it 'Love'. That's all. Celebration of junk words.

(*He wanders around, comes near a frame and peeps out of it.*)

Arrey! Darkness!

(*Looks out through the other frame.*)

Darkness again!

(*Looks through the third frame.*)

Yoo-hoo! Anybody home? (*Pause.*) N-o-o-o!

(*Sings.*) There's no one here, absolutely no one to look at us!

(*Comes back and looks into the mirror fragment again.*)

No one! Now it's only I for you and you for me. Hey man. Give me company man. Company Sarkar! B-u-g-g-e-r! Never really liked you! That nose of yours, that bald pate, that complexion. And what a height. I hated it all, shorty! Why do I live inside you? Why not inside a tall, handsome body? People would comment, 'the bald patch is growing.' Mine? What did I have to do with it?

(*Desperately tries to remove the cobwebs from his body.*)

Hating you all the while, scornful of you all the time, I kept using you. I showed anger, displayed affection, hatred, love. All via you. And you too gave me excruciating pleasure at times, and infernal pain at others. Fair enough. We hated and loved each other, and lived like Siamese twins.

(*Pause.*)
> People would say admiringly, what beautiful eyes, what a voice, what a gait! People are crazy. They wouldn't understand that those eyes didn't belong to me or you, but to Othello. The voice was Othello's. The gait Othello's. All gestures, all movements, everything was his. Othello's.
>   You and me together would create a third entity. Third Reality! Shankaracharya would be stunned hearing this. Hey, this guy is one step ahead of me, he would say, I have only two realities, but this fellow has found three!

(*Bolo Shri Shankaracharya ki jai!*)
> This is terrific! One shadow reality creates yet another shadow reality and the two together illuminate some fundamental truth of existence, the third reality!

(*Pause.*)
> Do you know what this Director bugger once said to me? That I should do a certain scene in the nude. Arrey *wah re* wah! I said to him, when I act with this body, the eyes are Othello's, the limbs and eyes and nose are of Othello too. But how can the penis be Othello's? That belongs to this body. Mine. So I refuse to show it, I said. Does the dick ever play-act? This suggestion is completely unwarranted artistically, I said. What nonsense! Otherwise I have no problems with obscenity. If ever the censor boardwallahs turn up for a show, I might even exhibit it. What fun! And show me an actor who doesn't enjoy displaying his body! But won't do anything that is artistically unwarranted! (*Looks into the mirror.*) That's how I saved your reputation, you dumbo! The only organ you have which doesn't know how to play-act! (*Tries to remove cobwebs.*) And even then. Even then why was I so panic-stricken when the first molar was extracted, as if I'd lost something permanent? It wasn't *my* molar anyway, or was it? This was the beginning, Company Sarkar! The beginning. The beginning of an end. Molars were removed. Hair lost. Deaf in one ear. Vision impaired.

All things come to an end. Cease and fall. Slowly but surely everything burns out,

Bharya grihadwari mitrashmashane dehaschitayam. A wife is with you up to the threshold of your home, a friend till the crematorium, your body till the pyre.

(*To a hanging skull.*)

Hi!

That skull had a tongue in it

And could sing once.

(*Bringing two skulls together.*) Make love. (*To his reflection.*) I panic even if I see you lose a single bloody hair. What'll happen to me once I see you in flames on the funeral pyre? They have given you a name and all that . The *Shraddha* will be performed in your name. Rituals and all that shit. You'll be so mollycoddled.

Amukapretasya pretatyavimokshartham addyehani shradhdham karishye. A *pinda* right in the centre, in your name. Centre-stage here too, hunh? Always! Bastard! It is because of *me* that you are called an actor, don't you forget it Mister! Hanh! And I'll be able to see that the *darbha* has been placed to the left by mistake. The flowers have wilted. And the pinda is drying up. But won't be able to do a thing! (*Grips the mirror.*) Please don't leave me! My only hope, my only saviour. I won't let you go. Won't. (*The glass of the mirror digs into his trembling palms.*) I'll hold you tight in a death grip.

(*A second Woman's mask appears within the frame.*)

2ND WOMAN'S MASK: I swept the house, removed the cobwebs before I abandoned it. Wiped it clean, applied rangoli, and once I stepped out, never ever looked back.

(*The mask disappears. He drops the mirror fragment only to see it shatter into smaller bits. Looks at them terrified.*)

The mirror cracked from side to side.

The curse is upon me-e-e cried ...

(*He frantically begins to collect the pieces of the mirror, like a beggar scrambling for leftover food.*)

This has one of your eyes. This has your lips. Your left ear is in this one. This one, your chin. Where is the whole you?

(*He tries to rearrange those fragments into a complete mirror. Looks into it and cries out.*)

Curse! Curse! Who is this utter stranger in this? The eyes are under the nose. This can't be you! (*Rearranges the pieces once again.*) No no. This too isn't you. (*Rearranges them again.*) O my god, O my god! Where are you?

(*Drops the pieces, wanders around aimlessly, crying. Keens heartbreakingly as if someone has died. Stops abruptly. Collapses in a heap as if paralysed, centre-stage. We hear a very faint, weak whine coming out of the heap. Figures wearing black gowns and masks come out from various direction, surround him in a semi-circle, and stare at him fixedly.*)

HE: Let me go.

MASK 1: *You* let us go.

HE: I do not want your thoughts, your words, your shadows upon me.

MASK 2: You collected us. Now you are rejecting us. A moment of reckoning.

MASK 3: Look at us just once.

MASK 4: I am sure you'll recognize me. The girl next door. With buck teeth. And you always called her Miss Toothsie! Mean!

MASK 5: Kept promising you'll return a friend's money. Finally, pretending you'd forgotten. You never did.

MASK 6: You stole a role from a colleague by sending him away on a false pretext just before the auditions.

MASK 7: When your mother came visiting for a few days, you behaved in such a way that she wondered if she ought to leave.

MASK 8: 'I never asked you to give birth to me' is what you said to your father.

(*All the masks begin to talk simultaneously. We can only hear their mutterings. After a while it fades out. All speak together in a chorus.*)

Coming close and drawing away.
To sin and to forgive
Darkness and Light
Light and Death
Two faces of the same coin.

You clinked this coin long enough. Drop it here. This currency
is invalid in the new territory.

(*He raises his head in a gesture of surrender and trust. Those masks
disappear into the darkness. He looks at the cobwebs on his body with tender
affection. Even touches them tenderly. Silence for a while.*

*Figures emerge from both the wings, five on each side, carrying candles,
humming in unison [Gregorian chant may be used on the soundtrack.]
They form a semicircle. An eleventh figure comes from the back and joins
them, standing at the centre of the semicircle. She doesn't have a candle.
The semicircle begins to move very slowly towards him, and stands close
to him. He looks up at the figure in the centre, his face illuminated in the
candlelight. This figure raises him to its lap like the Madonna holding
the corpse of the Crucified Jesus, creating a vision of Michelangelo's Pieta.
Very gently, the figure brushes its fingers over his body, and the cobwebs
come off easily. He looks like a newborn; naked, pure. There is a smile on
his face. The figure lightly kisses his forehead. Slowly lowers him to the
ground. The semicircle of figures disappears in the dark. Music stops.
Silence. He looks at himself in great joy and wonder as if he has seen
something so beautiful for the first time.*)

HE: Mother brought me thus far.

Gave me all this.

Once she bathed me, combed and parted my hair, put new
clothes on me, and said, 'You know, your father is coming today.'

You didn't come then, Baba.

You'll come today, won't you?

You never took me anywhere,

Never showed me anything,

Never gave me anything.

That was deliberate, wasn't it? Just for this day?

I know it.

You'll not let go of my hand now.

(*A visual of Michelangelo's* The Creation of Man *is created. He raises his hand upwards. A shaft of light comes down, and touches his fingers. Religious music begins.*)

How light I feel!

Where have you brought me, father!

My word! How fast we are moving, how vast the space! The blue earth is receding at such tremendous speed. Baba, Baba I want this. I'll make a ring of this blue stone. And this Jupiter. I'll make a locket out of this. How fast are these planets receding. And this ... and this ... so many planetary systems, they are all falling back so fast. And now even this galaxy is left behind. Now a second one. And now a third! How many such are there? The garlands of galaxies around my neck. And infinity is not enough to cover me.

(*Music increases. In a profound tone.*)

Everywhere it is only you and I

You are me and I am you

And the two of us together is me.

Music.

When I had everything I wasn't there

When there is nothing, I am everywhere

Only me.

I am all. Within me. From me. Back to me.

(*The music gradually begins to merge with the chanting of the incantations.*)

Om Poornamadah poornamidam poornat poornamudachyate

Poornasya poornamaday poornamevavashishyate

Om shantih shantih shantih!

CURTAIN

Production Histories
A Note

Garbo

Garbo was first performed in the original Marathi version at Bhulabhai Desai Auditorium, Mumbai, in a production by Roopvedh on 25 August 1973 at 4 pm with the following cast and credits:

Cast:
Intuc: Shreeram Lagoo
Shrimant: Datta Bhat
Pansy: Amol Palekar
Garbo: Deepa Shreeram

Credits:
Set design: Bapu Limaye
Lighting design: Bal Moghe
Sound: Pradeep Deshpande
Make-up: Murlalidhar Acharekar
Stage manager: Dileep Jadhav, Shashi Bane
Director: Shreeram Lagoo

Desire in the Rocks (*Vasanakand*)

STAGE HISTORY AND CENSORSHIP

Mahesh Elkunchwar wrote *Vasanakand* in 1973 and the first reading was given at the historic playwrights' workshop conceptualized and organized by Satyadev Dubey (who was working on a Homi Bhabha Fellowship at that time) in Pune in May 1973. A young theatre group, Aniket, founded by Amol and Chitra (Anuya) Palekar in 1970, which already had a couple of important experimental plays in its repertoire, decided to stage this play. The problem arose when the play, in routine course, was sent to the Stage Performance Scrutiny Board, Government of Maharashtra, for a mandatory permission required for any play to be produced and staged in Maharashtra (a practice that continues even today). The Board came down heavily on the play which deals with the incestuous relationship between a brother and sister, finding it 'grossly immoral', 'obscene', 'without any indication of remorse on the part of the two', and with 'no predominant artistic and social purpose'. A letter banning the play was sent to Aniket on 18 June 1974.

Vijay Tendulkar, President, and Girish Karnad, Vice-President of Aniket, taking a strong stand against the ban and deciding to fight it out, issued a joint statement to the press:

There is no need to underline the point that the creative realization of a play remains incomplete unless and until it is staged. The last two years have witnessed the emergence of various tendencies which threaten the freedom of expression. Aniket has decided to wage a fight against this threat because it is not merely a question of the performance of this particular play, but one which amounts to handing over all decisions in matters of art to the government machinery and/or allowing them to be resolved on mere technical grounds. We believe the time has come for us to adopt a determined stand on this question of freedom of expression. We have written to a number of cultural organizations requesting their support in the fight.

Amol Palekar, Founder-Secretary, Aniket, registered an appeal in the Bombay High Court against the Board's decision. The applicants of this appeal were invited by Pratibha Patil, then Minister for Cultural Affairs, Government of Maharashtra (now President of India) for a round table. The discussions did not lead to any decision in favour of lifting the ban. A stay order was, however, passed. A private performance was held on 17 August 1974, followed by one more, for a group of invitees. Around this time, a shuffle in the portfolios resulted in the appointment of a new Minister for Culture, Sundar Rao Salunke, who requested another performance of the play. After watching it, he declared quite unequivocally, that there was nothing obscene or immoral whatsoever in the play. The ban was immediately lifted, and the court case dismissed. But the expenses incurred during this gruelling battle against the censors and the government completely exhausted Aniket's funds and rendered it impossible to put up even one more show of the play after the ban was lifted.

Artistes and intellectuals rendered unstinted support to the cause, buttressed by the print media—*The Times of India, Maharashtra Times, Indian Express, Loksatta*—which followed the case very closely, coming down heavily on the ban, and carried articles and editorials on the issue, supporting the play.

The original Marathi production of *Vasanakand* (*Desire in the Rocks*) by Aniket, Mumbai opened as a private performance before invitees at Ravindra Natya Mandir, Prabhadevi, Mumbai on 17 August 1974 at 7 pm with the following cast and credits:

Lalita: Chitra (Anuya) Palekar
Hemakant: Amol Palekar

Set design: D.R. Patil
Lighting design: Bal Moghe
Sound: Sanjay Damle
Sound recording: S.L. Recording Studio
Make-up: Muralidhar Acharekar
Backstage: Satish Namniak, Nalen Bhiwandkar, Pramod Guruji, Shakuntala Murdeshwar, Arundhati Murdeshwar, Anant Bhave
Assistant Director: Dilip Kulkarni
Director: Amol Palekar

In all, the production had three performances even under the ban, on the condition that there would be no sale of tickets and no press publicity, and that the audience would be restricted to less than one hundred at a time. This play has never been performed again in the original Marathi.

Sai Paranjape produced it at the All India Arts Theatre, New Delhi in 1974, in Hindi, with Kusum Haider as Lalita and Nigam Prakash as Hemakant.

Vasanakand was translated by Shanta Gokhale and was published in *Enact*, 1974, under the title *A Breath of Scandal*. While reworking the text for this edition, the translator herself was unhappy with the title because it 'trivializes' the import of the play. The playwright suggested that it be rechristened *Desire in the Rocks*.

❦

Old Stone Mansion (Wada Chirebandi)

1. Of all Mahesh Elkunchwar's plays, *Wada Chirebandi* is the only one which was produced on the commercial circuit by a professional theatre company. The production required a large amount of money and Mohan Tondwalkar, the owner of Kalavaibhav, was prepared to produce the play, giving a free rein to the playwright and the director to work according to their ideas, unhampered by commercial considerations.

Later on two more plays, *Magna Talyakathi* and *Yugant*—sequels to *Wada Chirebandi*—were written in 1992, making it a trilogy. The trilogy (which had a playing time of eight hours, and was played at a stretch and performed all over Maharashtra), was produced in 1994 by Awishkar, Mumbai, a non-commercial theatre group, under the able stewardship of Arun Kakde and directed by Chandrakant Kulkarni. Awishkar folded the show after forty stagings, incurring heavy losses.

2. Elkunchwar received the Sahitya Akademi Award (2002) and the Saraswati Samman (2003), for his *Wada trilogy*. He had received the Sangeet Natak Akademi Award in 1989 after his path-breaking

Wada Chirebandi. The first part of the trilogy has been translated and performed in Hindi, Kannada, Bengali, and Garhwali. It is also available in unpublished French (translated by Dr Gerdi Gerschhaimer) and German translations, but has not been performed in English or any other European language.

3. The terms of address in the play are familial terms in a Maharashtrian household. 'Aai' means mother.' 'Aaji' is an honorific appellate for grandmother. 'Tatyaji' is a general term of respect for any elderly person and also one of the formal forms of address for father. Prabha and her siblings call their father 'Tatyaji', but Parag calls his father 'Baba', a more commonly used term. Younger brothers-in-law address their sisters-in-laws as 'Vahini'. 'Bhauji' and 'Vansa' are brother-in-law and sister-in-law, respectively. Prabha is 'Vansa' to both her sisters-in-law as she calls them 'Vahini'. Chandu and Sudhir are 'Bhauji' to Vahini, while Bhaskar and Chandu are 'Bhauji' to Anjali (Vahini). Mothers-in-law call their daughters-in-law 'Soonbai'. 'Kaka' means father's brother.

4. Deshpandes are Deshastha Brahmins while Anjali is a Konknastha Brahmin. Brahmins are sub-divided into about three major Brahmin categories, each considering itself superior to the others.

5. Vahini is prone to misusing English words to a rather comic effect; for example, she says 'nonsenseness' and 'mechanicals' when she means nonsense and 'mechanics' respectively, 'shot' instead of shock. 'handicraft' instead of handicap, 'septum' instead of septic.

6. *Bhaitad* means idiot. It is a very popular cuss word used freely in Vidarbha that indicates all shades of stupidity, depending on the nature of stupidity.

*

Wada Chirebandi (Old Stone Mansion) was first performed in the original Marathi by Kalavaibhav, Mumbai at Shivaji Mandir, Dadar, Mumbai on 1 May 1985 at 10 am with the following cast and credits:
Cast:
Dadi: Sulabha Korrane
Aai: Vijaya Mehta

Bhaskar: Achyut Potdar
Sudhir: Uday Mhaiskar
Prabha: Aruna Joglekar
Chandu: Pramod Pawar
Vahini: Girija Katdare
Anjali: Swaroop Khopkar
Parag: Shirish Joshi
Ranju: Suparna Sawarkar

Credits:
Direction: Vijaya Mehta
Production: Mohan Tondwalkar
Music: Raja Desai, Atul Bhagat
Design: Raghuveer Talashilkar
Lighting: Dileep Kolhatkar
Assistant: Pratima Kulkarni

*

A shorter version of this production in Hindi was telecast under the name *Haveli Buland Thi*.

*

Virasat, a Hindi translation of the play by Vasant Dev, was produced for the first time by the National School of Drama (NSD), New Delhi, at Shri Ram Centre Auditorium on 13 December 1985, with the following cast:

Dadi: Neelam Prasad
Aai: Nutan Surya
Bhaskar: Shrivallbh Vyas
Sudhir: Anang Desai
Prabha: Aruna Karamkar
Chandu: Om Prakash
Vahini: Uttara Baokar
Anjali: Dolly Ahluwalia

Parag: Shirish Joshi
Ranju's teacher: Govind Namdev

Credits:
Direction: Satyadev Dubey
Assistant Director: Uttara Baokar
Stage Design: Vasant Josalkar
Lighting: G.S. Marathe
Sound: Suresh Shetty, S.N. Dasgupta

In the NSD production, Satyadev Dubey had used a fantasy scene between Ranju and his teacher, which was part of the first draft, and deleted subsequently. It has never been used in any other production, nor has it been incorporated in any of the printed editions of the play.

＊

Uttaradhikar, an adaptation in Bengali by Subrata Nandi, was produced for the first time by Ensemble at Gyan Manch, Calcutta, on 24 February 1989 with the following cast and credits:

Cast:
Dai: Buddhadeb Samaddar
Aai: Swapna Mitra
Bhaskar: Ati Das
Sudhir: Tapas Thakur
Prabha: Swaroopa Das
Chandu: Rajat Sengupta
Vahini: Alaknanda Datta
Anjali: Madhuchhanda Ghosh
Parag: Ashis Naskar
Ranju: Sangeeta Chakravarti

Credits:
Direction: Sohag Sen
Stage design: Khaled Chowdhury
Lighting design: Naveen Kishore

Sound: Partha Chatterjee
Costume: Jayoti Bose

ᘛ⚬᙮

Reflection (Pratibimb)

Pratibimb (*Reflection*) was first performed in the original Marathi in a production by Theatre Unit at the Karnatak Sangh Hall, Mumbai, on 24 February 1987, and directed by Satyadev Dubey, with the following cast:

He: Kishore Kadam
Woman: Suneela Pradhan
Flags: Ganesh Yadav
Girl: Rahashri Sawant

*

Satyadev Dubey directed a production in Hindi for Padatik, Calcutta, which opened on 23 February 1987, with the following cast at Padatik Open Air Theatre, Kolkata.

He: Pradeep Roy
Woman: Deepti Bhat
Flags: Balmukund Hada
Girl: Isha Uppal

*

A second production in Hindi, this time for Theatre Unit, Mumbai, opened at the Karnatak Sangh Hall, Mumbai, on 17 March 1987 with the following cast:

He: Naseeruddin Shah
Woman: Suhas Joshi

Flags: Satyadev Dubey
Girl: Ratna Pathak-Shah

❧✦❧

Sonata

The title of the play takes its name from one of the most important forms in Western classical music, the sonata. It might be useful for the reader to know a little about the form, as the plot and the characters draw interesting structural and tonal qualities from it. The structure and the pace of the play conforms perfectly to the three movements— *adagio, allegretto*, and *rondo* of 'Moonlight sonata' that forms the musical matrix of the narrative, even the behavioural patterns of the three movements in that form. There are also a number of Sanskrit shlokas/adages in the course of the play. The explanations/meanings are listed with the original shlokas.

SONATA

Originally from the Italian *sonare*, meaning 'to play' (French *sonate*; German *sonate*). Commonly used to mean a work usually in three or four contrasting movements, either for piano alone (piano sonata), or for piano with one other instrument, for instance, violin sonata for piano and violin, clarinet sonata for piano and clarinet, and with one or more movements structured in sonata form. In a treatise written in 1793, *Introductory Essay on Composition: The Mechanical Rules of Melody*, Heinrich Christoph Koch first defined the form of the first movement, now known as *sonata form* or *first-movement form*. More recent opinion divides the movement into the following three sections:

   i) an EXPOSITION (usually repeated), incorporating a first theme or a group of themes in the tonic; a second (often more lyrical) theme or group in the dominant or the relative major (if the movement is in a minor key); and a closing (frequently cadential) theme also in the dominant or relative major—with the different themes connected by appropriate transitions or bridge passages;

ii) a DEVELOPMENT in which the motifs or themes from the EXPOSITION are presented in new aspects or combinations, in the course of which modulations may be made to relatively remote keys;

iii) a RECAPITULATION, in which the material of the EXPOSITION is restated in the original order, but with all the themes in the tonic; a *coda* might sometimes follow the recapitulation.

This is the most important type of instrumental music from the Baroque period to the present times. The title 'sonata' has been used by composers since the end of the sixteenth century. Although it has changed in meaning over the years, it has almost invariably been used to describe an instrumental work for a soloist or a small group of players. The outline of the sonata form is obviously an abstraction, with particular emphasis on the key scheme and the melodic-thematic ideas. Thus defined and understood, it fits into the majority of sonata movements of the latter half of the Classical period (1750–1810)— which followed the Baroque period and preceded nineteenth century Romanticism—and the nineteenth century, but there are many which are distinguished by significant creative departures.

'MOONLIGHT' SONATA

Nickname of Ludwig van Beethoven (1770–1827)'s Piano Sonata No. 14 in C sharp minor, Op. 27 No. 2 (1801) sub-titled 'quasi una fantasia'. It took on this nickname when the poet Heinrich Rellstab wrote that the slow first movement, *Adagio sostenuto*, reminded him of Lake Lucerne by moonlight. The second movement *Allegretto*, is in minuet and trio form, and the third movement *Presto agitato* is in sonata form.

*

SANSKRIT SHLOKAS/ADAGES USED IN THE PLAY

1. *Subhashiten geeten ... yasya na dravate chittam*
   Sa vai muktothawa pashuhu ...

Anyone who does not get moved by a good axiom, a song, and a young girl's coy gestures must either be a yogi or an animal.

The girl whose paper Aruna is checking has mistranslated it

2. *Te hi no diwasa gatah* ...: Gone are those days forever. A quote from Bhavabhooti's *Uttar Ramcharitam.*

3. *Nirlajjam sada sukhi*: A shameless person is perpetually happy.

4. *Watse, gaali paripoorna bhavati Astu!*: Child, the cuss word becomes complete, that's that!

5. *Bhunkte bhojayate* ...: gives and takes a meal.

The shloka in its full form:

Dadati pratigrinhati, guhyamakhyati pruchhati

Bunkte bhojayate chai va shadwidham snehalakshanam

Six indications of affection and friendship—between friends, we give gifts and take them, we tell secrets and listen to them, we give a meal and take it from a friend.

6. *Ya nisha sarvabhootanam tasyam jagarti maitrinihi*: When it is night for the whole world, friends keep awake.

Aruna has deliberately distorted the original shloka, replacing 'yogis' with 'friends'—*Ya nisha sarvabhootanam tasyam jagarti sanyami*: When the whole world is asleep, yogis keep awake.

*

A NOTE ON THE DRAMATIS PERSONAE

In the first draft of the play, Aruna's character was called Shubhada. It was changed because of the phonetic similarity between the names Shubhada and Subhadra, and to avoid any confusion that the audience might have with the names. Amal Allana, the director of the English version of *Sonata*, decided to change 'Subhadra' to 'Aruna' while retaining Shubhada. In the Marathi version, Shubhada [renamed Aruna in this translation] becomes Maneesha. In this translation, thoroughly revised by the playwright, the characters are Aruna, Subhadra, and Dolon.

Stage History

The play was originally written in Marathi, but first produced in English, with the Marathi production being staged four years after the English production.

Sonata was first performed in its English version by Theatre and Television Associates on 4 April 2002 at Abhimanch Auditorium, National School of Drama (NSD), New Delhi, at 7 pm with the following cast and crew:

Shubhada Ranade: Saleema Raza
Dolon: Mona Chawla
Aruna Parashar: Kusum Haider

Sets and lights: Nissar Allana
Music: Kabir Singh
Costume: Urvashi Bhargava
Slides processed and operated by: Rahaab Allana
Set Assistants: Asaavari Capoor, Rakesh Pandey, Ramesh Sonik
Direction: Amal Allana

This production used a number of slides from the works of the following important contemporary Indian painters:

Arpita Singh, *Durga* 1992; *Two Figures Lying on a Bed* 1987
Gieve Patel, *Drowned Woman* 1984
Jogen Chowdhury, *Life II* 1976
Nalini Malani, *Woman Series* 1974
Bikash Bhattacharya, *An Imported Mask* 1983; *Portrait of Das* 1980
Rameshwar Broota, *Man 22* 1988
Rekha Rodwittiya, *Sharing Secrets* 1996
Vasundhara Tiwari, *Subterranean* 1991
Tyeb Mehta, *Diagonal Series* 1972
Paramjeet Singh, *Stone on the Wall* 1970

Sonata was first performed in the original Marathi version by Samanvay, Pune, on 6 July 2007 at Sudarshan Rangamanch, Pune, at 7 pm with the following cast and crew:

Dolon: Gargi Phule
Aruna: Ashwini Giri
Subhadra: Rajeshree Savane Vaad

Sets: Kiran Yadnopavit
Lights: Ashutosh Parandkar
Lights execution: Sameer Vidvans, Ashutosh Parandkar
Costume: Kalyani Kulkarni
Music design: Nipun Dharmadhikari, Rochan Ganu
Backstage: Sanket Kulkarni, Sanket Deshpande, Shruti Dhavale, Mayur
Wadkar, Hemant Dhome, Hrishikesh Lokapure
Production Controller: Hrishikesh Lokapure
Production in-charge: Hemant Dhome
Direction: Sandesh Kulkarni

❧❀☙

An Actor Exits (Eka Natacha Mrityu)

1. *Karatala bhiksha tarutala wasah:* alms on the palm of a hand and
abode under a tree. From Aaddya Shankaracharya's *Charpatpanjarika*
2. *Asha naam manushyanam kachid ashcharya shrinkhala*
    Yaya baddhah pradhavanti muktah tishthanti panguvat
    Hope is a strange fetter. People chained by it run fast while people
freed from its shackles are rendered immobile like invalids.
3. *Poorvi davidachya ghari*
    Gotha bal janmale
    Tenvha aaine gavhani
    Preme bal thevile
    A Christian song in Marathi describing the birth of Jesus. It says:
Once upon a time, a child was born in the barn of David. The mother
of the child put him lovingly in the haystack.
4. *Vyaghropi mitthya palayanapi mitthya:* The tiger is an illusion; running
away from it is also an illusion.
    A teacher, explaining the illusory nature of life to his pupil, started
running when he saw a tiger. The puzzled pupil asked him why he should

run when the tiger was an illusion. And this is what the teacher said while running for his life.

5. *Gururbrhama gururvishnu....*
Guru is Brahma, Guru is Vishnu ...

6. *Bharya grihadwari mitrasmshane dehaschitayam ...*
(After a man's death, his) wife comes up to the door (with him), his friend up to the crematorium, and his body up to the funeral pyre (after that he is alone).

7. *Mandhata nriparaj jo kaliyugalankara jhala mruta*
Jene Ravana Kumbhakarna vadhile to Ram jhala mruta.
Mandhata, king of the kings, who bejewelled Kaliyuga, died
And Rama who killed Ravana and Kumbhakarna, also had to die

8. *Amukapretasya pretayavimokshartham addyehani shraddham karishye*
This is a corpse of so and so, and for the moksha of this corpse, shraddha (funerary rite) is being performed.

This is a Vidhi mantra. It is chanted when the actual funerary rites are being performed.

9. *Om Poornamadah poornamidam poornat poornamudachyate*
Poornasya poornamadaya poornamevavashishyate
Om shantih shantih shantih
That is full, and so is this. Fullness comes out of the Full. Even if the Full is taken from the Full, what remains is Full itself. AUM, Peace, Peace, Peace.

An elaborate translation of this Invocation from the *Ishopanishad* would be:

That (Supreme Brahman) is Infinite and this (Conditioned Brahman) is Infinite. The Infinite (Conditioned Brahman) proceeds from the Infinite (Supreme Brahman). Then through knowledge, taking the Infinite of the Infinite (Conditioned Brahman), it remains as the Infinite (Unconditioned Brahman) alone.

—from the translation by Swami Gambhirananda

English quotations:
1. This is the time of tension
   Between dying and birth
   The place of solitude.

—*Ash Wednesday* IV: TS Eliot

2. (a) And moving through a mirror clear
   That hangs before her all the year
   Shadows of the world appear.
   (b) I am half sick of the shadows
   Said the Lady of Shallott.
   (c) The mirror cracked from side to side
   'The curse is upon me-e-e' cried ...

—*Lady of Shallott*, Lord Alfred Tennyson

3. All things have rest, and ripen toward the grave
   In silence.
   Ripen, fall and cease.

—Choric song, *The Lotus Eaters*, Lord Alfred Tennyson

4. O Father, Father, gone from us, lost to us. Grant unto us that we may sit, one on thy right side and the other on the left, in Thy glory.

—Mark 10.37, Chapter 10, Holy Bible

Notes on Theatre

by Mahesh Elkunchwar

After all these years, I have realized that the division 'literature' and 'performative text' is basically flawed. The truth is that if the text is performance-worthy, then it inevitably becomes literature and if it is not performance-worthy, then no matter how beautiful or 'literary' a language it is written in, forget being dramatic, it is not even literature and is full of tedious superfluities. (There are numerous such texts in Hindi.) Dramatic grammar is different from the grammar of fiction and an informed reader keeps this in mind while studying drama; therefore, he can read (only) those texts as literature which reveal their performance-worthiness to them. One basic rule in drama is that whatever appears irrelevant and unnecessary vis-à-vis the dramatic intention onstage, automatically becomes redundant, 'unbeautiful,' and parasitic. A scene, a character, a dialogue, even a single line of dialogue, each of them has to deliver at least one if not all the following functions in a text: it must propel the dramatic action further, it must illuminate the scene and consequently the entire text, it must reveal a new aspect of a character/characters, and it must create and add to the ambience. Therefore, if a playscript is full of unnecessary and unwarranted embellishments, used only to decorate the text due to wrong notions of 'beauty in drama', the reader refuses to acknowledge such plays as literature. As opposed to this, there are texts which may not qualify to be called literature in the conventional sense of the word, but still observe the grammar of drama and thus they inevitably acquire literary value, and that text is studied as literature. Today we read *Waiting* for *Godot* or *Chairs* as modern classics of literature as well as theatre. The first and last condition for a playscript to acquire literary value is the performance-worthiness of that text. These are not two separate issues. One is internalized within the other. They are thus one and the same.

In those days (in the late 1960s, when I started writing), the equation that basically, experimentation in theatre means (only) rebellion had become so prevalent that anybody who wrote in the conventional modes already available to him was automatically dismissed with a sneer and the label of 'regressive' was promptly slapped on him, as though the very existence of experimentation is impossible without rebellion. All right, rebellion against what? 'Against tradition', pat came an ambiguous answer. Now if we must rebel thus, then it is necessary to understand what tradition we are rebelling against. Here, I use the word 'tradition' not just in the limited sense of dramatic tradition, but in the all-encompassing sense as tradition in every aspect of life, the tradition of a complete way of life, the tradition that encompasses the lives of a particular milieu. Tradition must not be confused with custom or norms. Customs die and norms become obsolete. But traditions constitute a dynamic vital force that keep the 'riverness' of a people flowing. If we limit ourselves to only a rebellion against dramatic tradition, then it has to be against some now-disowned tradition within life itself; because dramatic tradition is, after all, connected to that way of life, and probably blossomed from within that very life. Therefore, before rebelling in this way, one must understand all these traditions, and study them well with an unbiased, acute perception. Nowhere does a tradition or a rebellion against it flourish in a sterile vacuum. There have to be some theoretical positions behind a rebellion, which is often born out of the fundamental questions about life itself. If there is no conscious effort fortified by a relentless intellectual rigour to understand what we are rebelling against, then not only is such a rebellion shallow and short-lived, but it just ends in a whimper, yielding nothing substantial. When I analyse the Indian theatre scene, it does not appear as if the rebellion in it was created out of any unquenchable metaphysical quest or conscious theoretical analyses of life. Our rebellions are merely against existing styles and they just keep roaring momentarily within a vacuous space. It is true that such rebellions and experiments can dazzle us momentarily, but the most they can do is ignite for a while and burn themselves out in no time. They have no past nor future. Hence, they leave no impression on our artistic traditions.

When I say tradition, I do not mean what it was a few hundred years ago. We never accept a tradition in its entirety because traditions keep changing, acquiring newer forms in accordance with the changing times. This happens because those who are perceptive reject whatever is outdated within a tradition and only embrace its essence. If ever the essence of tradition and the force of modernity can be united, then experimentation can acquire a focused and definite direction, otherwise only impermanence and limitation are its destiny.

Is it my intention to state that awareness of tradition is the same as being indigenous? I do not think so. It may be possible only if we extend the meaning of the word 'indigenous'. Indian culture and tradition are constantly proved by, broken by, and renewed by so many assorted and varied influences, that it is difficult to decide what is indigenous. If we carefully observe the history of India, we realize that India has an uncanny genius to absorb, assimilate, and digest external influences whenever it suits us. And now in the rush for globalization, it is impossible to quarantine oneself. Now, instead of merely deliberating over Indian traditions, if only we could display the openness and the nobility required to reach the forefront of international traditions, can our creative body get more and more nourishment. Do we resist international influences and traditions because of a lack of confidence? I myself am not worried about Western influences because I am too confident of my Indianness to let it bother me. I shall lift and digest as much of that influence as I want. Knowledge, art, and the treasury of various cultures are not the monopoly of any one country or one human community. This treasury is open to all. I feel that it is dangerous to limit the meaning of 'indigenous' and restrict our own growth. And if we have to speak about our indigenous tradition, then its very beginning was from '*Aa no bhadrah kratavo yantu vishwatah*' (Let noble thoughts come to us from all over the universe).

I often feel that it is our practice of seeking definite meanings in works of art that creates the problems in experiencing them. We need to understand the 'meaning' of every work of art through our 'intellect' followed by its analysis and classification (which is again an intellectual activity), otherwise we do not feel that we have had a proper artistic experience. We cannot rest until and unless we understand everything intellectually, catalogue it, and put it in a slot. In the process, the meaning of a work may become occasionally accessible, but the 'joy of experiencing' a play is perhaps lost forever. The meaning is found, but in the process of finding it, the experience slips out of the hand. How can we explain the meaning of Grace's poetry? (It has been done in a textbook they say. My best wishes to that teacher!) There are many more things there that are beyond words. If we are to experience and relish them, then we have to sheath the weapon of the intellect and surrender ourselves to the poetry. M.V. Dhond has used certain tools to explain the implications of Mardhekar's poetry; I do not think the same implements can be used to comprehend Grace's poetry. Some plays fall in this category. If we do not get involved in attributing intellectual implications to Beckett's plays, then a vast universe of indefinable angst that transcends time, opens up.

This can happen in connection with drama too. Unfortunately, the playwright himself ensures that his text remains unidimensional. By predeciding the meaning at the very start, he himself blocks the routes to go beyond his immediate experience. One such way of predeciding uni-dimensionality is the generous usage of words. The meaning is oft-repeated, clarified in words, and underlined, and in this pandemonium of words, the voice of experience gradually grows faint and dies. Once a play is made so determinedly uni-dimensional, the question of it containing one or more sub-texts does not arise.

In the attempt to keep the play uni-dimensional by making its intellectual comprehension easier, we sacrifice a very important matter, and that is free space within the text. This space is filled by the multiple possibilities of experience, the possibilities that an actor has to seek out and fill them up that space with his acting. There are one or many sub-texts hiding within that space and to bring them to the surface is the true calling of an actor. In the finest of plays, there is a constant resonance of multiple meanings between these sub-texts. Whoever is able to create that is a first-rate playwright.

I was once very critical of our actors for their inability to internalize their roles. I found them just illustrating the written lines with their usual box of tricks and superfluous gesture language. But it began to dawn on me that I was responsible for it, at least partially. Actors are actors and would like to act. If a playwright does not offer them open spaces in the text and the opportunity to decode them because of an overwritten text, the actor is hardly to be blamed. A playwright has to learn to have faith in his actors, place responsibility on his shoulders, and leave him with ample room to explore and delve into the unsaid. Great acting is possible only if the playwright can create these creative possibilities for his actors. After all, he is the king in theatre.

When it comes to ideology in theatre, I am perhaps the most unsuitable person to say anything about it. I am not an ideological animal; and for years, I was ridiculed by my friends for this vital character flaw in me. I was called a decadent hedonist, a self-indulgent Narcissus, a reactionary of the deepest dye, and a whole list of other adjectives was used to instil a feeling of guilt in me, just because I decided to write about the private aches and pains of individuals. I dutifully tried to feel guilty, did not, and felt the worse for it. At a time when the whole atmosphere was charged with idealism and full of people wedded to some cause or the other, I found myself belonging to a minority of 'self-centered bourgeoisie'. But the chasm it created between me and my friends was painful. I had friends whose credentials were impeccable, whose integrity was unquestionable, and whom I respected deeply for their convictions, and envied for their unshakeable belief that they could change the world. I admired and respected them but sorrowfully found myself having reservations about the kind of theatre they were doing and vice-versa. There seemed to be no common ground wherein our respective theatres could meet. At the same time, I did not understand why we were taking such polarized positions. There was little or no attempt among us to understand each other or the functions of each others' theatres. If I was living in my ivory tower, they were living in their impregnable forts. Derision and almost a fanatic rejection of each other emerged simply from a lack of any empathy. There was not even an attempt at empathy.

It was much later that it began to dawn on me that we had become too judgmental and narrow to allow the other the freedom to express himself in the way he wanted to. My friends and I did not realize that we were taking two different positions because we were different people seeking different objectives in life and in theatre. I wanted to first understand myself and the likes of me in relation to the society I lived in before I could take on 'larger socio-political issues'; and they wanted to change this very society 'radically', hoping to create a better one. Our concerns were different, we were hearing different drums, which found reflection in two different kinds of theatre. But why one kind of concern/position/theatre should be more correct/moral/valid than the other was and is beyond my comprehension even today. I wonder if a hierarchy of theatres is necessary at all. Those who use theatre as an instrument or a weapon to bring about socio-political change are at perfect liberty to do so: it is a perfectly legitimate exercise. But when they do it, one hopes that they are aware that theatre is many things to many people, its functions are multiple, and that it can rightfully fulfil the aspirations of a wide spectrum of the society.

I have fortunately seen some excellent theatre of ideology where art and ideology were not only balanced but harmonized, thereby creating a memorable experience. Kanhailal is one good example of this. But I have also seen theatre where art was not only at loggerheads with ideology but was completely disregarded, with disastrous results. It is about this kind of theatre that I propose to make a few observations and to draw your attention to its pitfalls.

This theatre often rejects the probe of human experience to itself and to other theatres, unless it comes in a codified political language. Emotion is taboo. Emotion gets sanctity and legitimacy only if it comes in relation to the cause that this theatre is championing. Unfocused passion and blind anger often diffuse the issue instead of highlighting it. A focused attention to the given issue is replaced by angry jargon. In the process, art gets sacrificed because it has become a dirty word. If we disregard the basic principles of art and aesthetics (regardless of charges of 'elitism'), we are merely exchanging one form of mediocrity for another. The weapon becomes ineffectual because its user is either incompetent and does not know how to use it or is too indifferent to the results. The whole exercise can be self-defeating.

A monotonous, artless, self-righteous tirade against 'the unseen, invisible Enemy' ultimately results in a politically ineffective theatrical statement. Meaningful political action/analysis is often replaced by radical clichéd explosions and hackneyed compositions. In place of cool perception and thought, we are given verbiage, used so indiscriminately that the play begins to lose its power and meaning. The honest desire to dramatize for the sake of curing a malaise peters down to a sentimental, melodramatic theatre, in effect, rendering itself negative. The multi-layeredness of drama and the unfathomable depths of life are sacrificed in favour of monolithic thinking.

These are some of the traps that this theatre can walk into if creative vision is allowed to be blurred by ideas that are extraneous and irrelevant to theatre. A pursuit of ideology must not close doors to deep human experience. The personal, private, metaphysical side of human life must not be eclipsed by the public and political imperatives of the day.

I have already mentioned Kanhailal's theatre as a sterling example of this kind of theatre where art is blended with ideology with great concern, understanding, and respect for the former. Ideological theatre has a decided destination and once it reaches there, it has nothing much to offer which would keep resonating in one's mind. It makes no further demands on a writer once the destination is set. All that remains is to invent convenient routes to safely reach there. I, as a writer, however, would not be able to do it. These are my reasons.

When I write, I expect a personal response from my reader/viewer and not a conditioned reflex which is always a result of the preconceived codification of life. Although I have felt close to certain ideologies at various stages in my life, I have always been convinced that no ideology is greater than LIFE itself. If I am not using theatre as a weapon, if it is a means of self-expression for me, my writing will concern itself with life as I experience it, and not with doctrine. As Ionesco says, 'Any work of art which is ideological and nothing less, would be pointless, tautological, inferior to the doctrine it claims to demonstrate.' An honest writer writes from a very private core of his being, which is beyond the control of intellect and so a major part of his perception is often subjective. It is to this that the reader/viewer has to respond in the same spirit.

In my everyday life, I go on making choices that are ultimately political. It is inevitable as every moment of our existence is dominated by politics. Whether I do my shopping in America or India is very much a political decision. But these decisions change as situations change. However, when one writes, one leaves all this behind and tries to reach the unchanging fundamentals of human life. Ideologies are fine, they do offer a little bit of relief and change the societies from time to time. But there is no religion, no ideology, no political programme that has ever brought complete happiness or relief to humanity. No ideology can liberate us 'from the pain of living and fear of death or our thirst for the Absolute'. Art tries to transcend tangible reality and aspires to journey into an unnamable, indefinable reality that is constantly pulsating beneath the topical. It cannot limit itself only to concrete ideological thinking. When a writer writes, he writes about the subjective man who is the epicentre of his experience. That is why an individual's private pain is as important as the pain of a mass of humanity, and can also be easily shared as a universal experience.

I notice a strange rejection of poetry in theatre from a certain section of the audience, at least in Maharashtra. The moment the audience senses it, it hurriedly labels it as 'literary,' a much-maligned term in theatre, meaning that it is verbose and non-dramatic, melodramatic, pseudo. It is because people do not really have a definite idea of what poetry in theatre is and they confuse it with poetic narrative. Poetry in theatre is a different proposition altogether; it is never literary and never ornamental if that is what is being suggested by people who object to it, and it can be created with the help of very banal, ordinary, and sparse dialogue, silences, and the use of visual space. I take the liberty to quote instances from my own work. The scene from *Raktapushp* where Raja dissects a flower and gives a clinical account of what constitutes a flower is a very poetic moment. In *Old Stone Mansion*, Vahini donning her ornaments silently while she hears the monotonous drone of her husband is another one. Dolon in *Sonata* putting a 'chunni' on Aruna's head is still another one. There is no use of literary language here, neither are too many words wasted to achieve the poetic. Poetry in theatre is often a consequence of how the visual and acoustic spaces are used. The actors can either heighten it with their sensitive understanding of it or ruin it by allowing to degenerate in melodrama. A play written in excellent 'literary' verse may fail to be poetic while a text unadorned by any literary flourishes may have situations that impart a poetic glow to the play. *Waiting for Godot* is a wonderful example. I also wonder if an entire text can be poetic. It is only a few moments or scenes in any text that are poetic but they lend a poetic charge and luminescence to the whole text by their evocative power.

The rejection of this kind of poetry often comes from a refusal to confront raw emotion, deep feelings, and naked display of passions. People squirm in their seats and dismiss it on 'aesthetic grounds' while the real reason lies in their incapability to meet the depiction in the eye. It is always embarrassing to see someone baring his soul in all its nakedness. So 'poetic' is confused with 'literary' and dismissed.

Often certain images are employed by a dramatist to achieve this effect. These images recur in his work and lend a deep sense of poetry to it. I am tempted to quote T.S Eliot: 'This imagery comes from the whole of his (author's) sensitive life since early childhood. The song of one bird, the leap of one fish ... such memories may have symbolic value, but of what we cannot tell, for they come to represent *the depths of feelings into which we cannot peer.*' (italics mine)

It is this depth of feeling which Eliot talks about that gives drama a poetic quality. An audience that fails to attune to it might fail to experience its import.

A playwright may employ many techniques to infuse his work with poetry. One of the ways is to dissolve the narrative technique of fiction in the dramatic (Chekhov has always done it), thereby expanding it, and taking the dramatic action to the inner landscape of the characters rather than keeping it external.

The main problem is that all agencies—the writer, the actor, and the audience—somehow seem to have lost their ability to rejoice in words in theatre. Word is taboo, it is not modern, it is inferior art. I wonder if this attitude is a fallout of the gestural, body language theatre. 'The joy of the writer writing them, the radiant eloquence of its composition' as Miller puts it is almost banished from theatre by the new advocates of 'visual theatre', much to their loss, in particular, and to that of drama, in general. What do they do with Williams, Lorca, and Strindberg? Recently, I watched Girish Karnad's *Flowers*, and though many moderns turned their noses up at it, I enjoyed it immensely for the sheer beauty of its language, so well-written and so well-spoken. And the most important thing is that it had not impressed me when I had read the text in the privacy of my study. But (despite its predictability), it suddenly got illuminated in the theatre space, conclusively proving that it *is* theatre, in fact, nothing else. It is considered passé to say that a well-written and well-spoken text can also be a valid theatrical experience. An important genre is being junked out. I wonder if some people walk into an auditorium with predetermined ideas of what is good theatre and what is bad, what is modern and what is not, creating slots and shutting themselves to everything that does not fit into these slots.

The most glorious moments in theatre are those when the play goes on the rehearsal floor. That is when those involved in the play are trapped in a closed, almost claustrophobic space, emotional and otherwise, this is where we are compelled to drop our masks, lay bare our vulnerabilities, unite in an excruciatingly joyous journey of exploring the text, ourselves, each other. This is the real togetherness that we are all hungry for, a creative togetherness. This is when we hate, love, and despair together with all our defences dropped. This is when real human contact is established which is otherwise so rare, almost shunned, in our fiercely individuated, independent lives. But the magic disappears the moment the play opens. Standing ovations, rave notices, adulation, and fame may follow but they are fringe benefits. They mean little or nothing to an artist who is undertaking a voyage into the interior and in search of genuine human contact.

I have been reading theatre criticism for nearly three decades and it has helped me concretize my ideas to a great extent. I may have borrowed a few phrases from a variety of critics here and there but having now forgotten the sources that enriched my thinking, I am unable to mention all of them here. I acknowledge my debt to all of them.

Notes on Translators

SHANTA GOKHALE is a noted novelist, translator, playwright, and theatre critic.

MAHESH ELKUNCHWAR is an acclaimed playwright, screenwriter, and essayist.

SUPANTHA BHATTACHARYA is Professor, Department of English, Hislop College, Nagpur.